Published by Chroma Mystic, LLC
30 South 15th Street, Suite 1550
PMB 285213 Philadelphia, Pennsylvania 19102
www.ChromaMystic.com

Book Cover by Bernard Charles

First edition 2024

TABLE OF CONTENTS

Memorable Mystics

To past, present, and future mystics.

I want to acknowledge (in no particular order) those I've met to make this book possible: Mila R. Manley, for your Archmage Emeritus contribution during the summer book launch party; Stephanie Haynes, for your travel agent skills and open heart, which inspired me to get out of the house; Alexis Rupert, for your couch and direction during a dark period of homelessness; Serenity Wallace, for your love of fashion and a zesty reminder to dance through life; Quelcy Kogel, for the cookies and conversations that make life worth tasting and Matthew, my husband, for the serendipity to meet during a global pandemic to love and be loved in return. A mystic never walks alone.

INTRODUCTION

The Boy & The Orange Scarf

Before you can understand *The Color Mage Oracle* and how it will change your life and work, you must first look at the origins of its creation and get to know me as a human being. I am Bernard. I was born and raised in a small rural town in Northeast Pennsylvania. Memories of pinecones and fire halls litter my mind when I look back to the 1990s. Life wasn't handed to me on a silver platter. I recall trips to the store using food stamps, never having money for the schoolbook fairs, and countless nights sobbing whenever I heard my parents arguing downstairs and throwing things at each other, like the Christmas tree and shoes. My father pushed my mom into the cabinet once, and the shattered glass cut her hand. That moment, seeing my mom wounded, bleeding, and abused, was the day I made an everlasting vow to cut any mental and emotional cords I had with my father. I felt responsible for the drama because I was an empath. I soak in energetic vibrations like a sponge and subconsciously lean into intense emotional experiences. It's human to feel. But that day, it was clear to me that his abuse toward us was not worthy of my energy. I don't owe him, and he does not own my feelings. My father always had a short fuse. I remember when he flung me off my bed in our trailer. My head hit the metallic closet door, and I instantly thought he didn't love me. I felt shell-shocked and ran to my mom. Her own Aries nature often headbutted my Virgo father's tumultuous bipolar personality swings constantly. She was young when she had me. Forced to grow up not having the luxurious space to feel safe in the world, she weathered so many storms as a teenage parent. She also felt her hands were tied when I was a teenager dealing with bullying at school and the antagonism at home from her ex and his family. It wasn't easy growing up, navigating people's mood swings and understanding their place in the world.

Through the outbursts, scoldings, and spankings, I accepted that my father loved the idea of me. Like most parents, he feels a sense of entitlement that views their children as property. I made you, so you must obey my ideologies and practice my religion, and if you live under my roof, then follow my rules. This image of having children makes them look good on paper, but when it comes to caregiving and providing stability, it holds no value because there's no accountability. The motivation is solely for optics. Because of the performative parenting and abuse, I believed that I was just another meaningless object he could toss around the house and break because he owned the house, thus owning the family. My parents divorced shortly after the cabinet broke.

I always felt different. I have a keen sense of intuition, critical thinking, and a passion for color. I'm reserved and use this to observe my surroundings, but primarily because of my disability, I'm hard of hearing. It's unclear why I'm partially deaf, but my brain gets tired from over-processing information daily, and I've always used color-like subtitles. The way I see the world is heightened because of my disability. My sensory experience of the world is different from yours. I intend to inspire people to use color more consciously in their lives and work to reprogram their realities and create paradigm shifts for the greater good.

The highs and lows in your life and work are there to uncover the essence of who you are as a person. Through color, I would explore all areas of my life, even during dark days. Whenever I was bored as a child, my mom insisted I pull out the container of crayons and color. In school, I found a refuge in the art room and library. Later, while being bullied, I sought shelter in the guidance counselor's office. Like a whirling dervish in a sea of chaos and adversity, you must make your own momentum to find balance. On top of being a child of divorce, below the poverty line, and disabled, I had to come to terms with being gay. This was the most challenging realization because the entire association I had with being gay was through bullying and harassment. Being gay was terrible. Not to mention, it was commonly whispered among the adults behind closed doors as a "sin" and viewed as a rebellious phase that I would outgrow. These adults are wrong. I wasn't only bullied in school but also at home. My mom's ex-boyfriend was a cop and used his power to scare me into respecting authority by taking me out on a night watch task to hunt homeless people in the back alleys of Scranton.

He was weaponizing homelessness to prove a very shallow and misguided point of respect. He then tried to enroll me in a junior police academy to teach me to toughen up and be a man. His family was so stuck on making sure my gender was defined according to their beliefs and standards that I rebelled more so by building an emotional wall and keeping my distance. We refused to acknowledge each other's presence in the room, so I retreated to my room most days and escaped some weekends to visit my grandmother. Any inquisitive and independent child would, but I was forced to grow up fast and saw many inequalities displacing me because of my differences. In astrology, I'm an Aries sun sign with a Capricorn moon; I don't back off from speaking my mind when an injustice is in play. I push boundaries. I was born to be different and to confront society's backward logic and socioeconomic propaganda. Bernard means "bold as a bear," and it shows when I find others oppressing self-expression, gender identity, and spirituality to sustain an archaic heteronormative worldview.

I didn't end up going to that summer boot camp for junior police cadets because I was kicked out of the house and forced to live with my grandmother, and towards the end of the summer, my mom and siblings moved out of that toxic house. And I was accepted to attend Milton Hershey School later that fall. MHS is a private boarding school for low-income children, and it would be the call in my hero's journey that would help me pursue the power of color and share it with you. While attending this school, I joined an art museum investigator club that invited students to visit museums and learn about art. I loved everything about this off-campus experience. We dined at fancy restaurants and were given a small stipend of cash to buy something at the gift shop. At a small found object museum outside of Philadelphia, I found an orange scarf (get the full story in my book, *Rainbow Revolution: Unblock Resistance, Create Change, and Be Happy with Yourself*).

The TL: DR version of the story is that back in 2007, I was in the gift shop and asked the universe to show me a sign for what to buy. My eyes found an orange scarf, and since the school enforced a dress code, I found a loophole in wearing a scarf to express myself. At the same time as finding this scarf, I came out to myself. I accepted that I am physically and romantically attracted to men. Big whoop. I used this scarf to walk the halls with my head held high. I felt unashamed to take up more space in my life. I joined more clubs and explored new-age spirituality through music and documentaries I would find at the library. It wasn't all perfect, and I still felt worthless and struggled with anyone telling me who I should be. However, I leaned into my spiritual practice and any interesting subjects. I adamantly refused to pick classes based on an overgeneralized matrix that didn't light me up. I was on a quest to learn according to my passion and happiness. My orange scarf helped me to feel creative in all aspects of my coming of age, but more so, it gave me the confidence to confront what was being handed to me and the power to choose another possibility.

The Man & The Technicolor Coat

After graduating, I went to college in Pittsburgh using my free Hershey chocolate scholarship to pursue a path in multimedia communications and art. This was the early days when having a social media manager was unheard of, and the concept of influencers/content creators didn't exist the same way it does today. I had dreams of becoming a television talk show host. Watching *Ellen* was my inspiration, and I knew if she could improve my mindset, I wanted to do the same for others but in my way. I started a blog and focused on video production. In between classes, I walked to the local New Age bookstore and got lost in the books, crystals, and spiritual tools. I became certified in crystal healing and bought my first tarot deck. The internet made connections with spiritual people and witchy folk fun, and I found a home online. Going to college was the most important thing my mom insisted I do with my life. Everything else was up to me, but I had to attend college. Education was this magic bullet answer to getting out of the projects and over the poverty line. I did what I was told. I followed the book. I got an internship. I aced the classes. I graduated Cum Laude a semester earlier than my peers in 2012. Since I have a college degree and years of recalling adults telling me higher education is the answer, I looked for a job. I felt entitled to one because I did what the system told me. But no luck.

Hundreds of applications, I had nothing to show for it. Even local grocery stores refused to hire me because of my degree, seeing me as overqualified. My family would mock my education and use that against me, projecting the idea that I see myself as better than them because I went to college. The reality is that I don't see myself as better; I know the system is wrong. I came to this planet with standards. This might be my Venus placement in my astrological birth chart or my stubborn worldview that every single adult is entitled to a baseline amount of money to survive as a consumer in modern society. However, that ultimate altruism ruffles feathers because it's rooted in democratic socialism. No one wanted to give me the chance to work. I was forced to set clear boundaries and defend myself and my mood daily. Nothing is worse than being called an "entitled freeloader" after you graduate from college by a narcissist who's bumming off your family's phone plan and offended by your unwillingness to encourage and validate their ego, parking itself in conversations to take up as much space as possible. The first six months after graduating college were a pressurizing period for me. That same person who called me a freeloader made it their mission to be petty and toxic toward me instead of being mature and actualized. The gritty details are exhausting, but in the summer of 2013, I was bound to move in with my father after a debacle involving boarding up an entryway and having to retrieve my toiletries from the bathroom. The lesson is that I hate narcissists. I had nowhere else to go, but I did have color as a tool to guide me during the turbulence.

My father welcomed me warmly and my suitcase of crystals, books, and tarot cards. I packed all the clothes that made me feel safe and complete. Including a multicolored robe, I got from my first boyfriend. It was part of a theater production of *Joseph and the Amazing Technicolor Dreamcoat*. This souvenir was a uniform I wore to connect with the Universe. While in the upstairs kitchenette overlooking the trees, meditating and reading about my destiny, I realized I could create a card deck of my own. Incense of cinnamon swirled around me while Native American music played in the background, so I began researching ways to self-publish and make my kind of magic in the world using color.

The Color Mage

On September 17, 2014, I published a blog post out of anger called *The Rise of a Color Warmage*. The post is no longer available online, but I have a copy of all my posts tenderly tucked away for a rainy day. This was the first time I uncensored my dreams and stopped feeling anxious, worried, and unsure about creating something of my own. I had many thoughts that held me back, and I needed to unlearn feeling unworthy and, at the same time, rewrite vows I made against my father and, ultimately, against myself. The post was raw and honest and carried an overarching theme of overcoming poverty consciousness. Here's a snippet:

"I wish I could give the people what they want, but sadly, I must find it myself, which leads me to the point in writing all this to you. I have been working with color energy profusely for over seven years. The past two years have been more in tune with card readings and some fundamental scientific education about the power of light and color. The practical bits. Well, it has come to a point through my color journey as a soulful, spirited young mage to announce something I have been holding back from you. This resistance of riding with the flow is another factor in my frustration, and at this moment, I am starting to feel uplifted. A calm. I want to tell you that I have created a 108-color card deck of my own."

I kept this project hidden. I felt ashamed because there were other color decks out in the world. I had to relinquish my limited manhood to embrace the magic of becoming a mage. I realized that this is the only person who has the exact life experience and intuitive style like me to deliver this project. I'm hands-on and prefer practical experience over intellectual theories and educated guesses. It's why this book has taken ten years to make since I wrote that blog post, thrusting me out of the shadows and into the light of my destiny. I know intuition and spirit in all forms don't need a book to communicate a lesson, but it's only one format and medium to contextualize divine intelligence. It's like that scene from *Practical Magic* about how you can't practice your craft by simply looking your nose down at it. True magic is as tangible as it is imaginative. You are a co-creative being in this Universe. Like color therapy, magic is an active living energy constantly expanding and contracting the vibrational frequencies of our Universe—the choices you make and do not make influence the moment. I hoped you could use color to influence your life and work like I must make something good.

From Mage to Mystic

What I have now that I didn't have then was life experience, my first Saturn return, and equally so, the world wasn't ready like it is now post-pandemic to understand the tangible connections these colors have in the social, political, spiritual, and emotional spheres of our human experience. The 2020 pandemic was a wake-up call in more ways than one: I had to delete social media and go offline. At that time, I recalibrated my academic field and luckily found a job nine months before the social distancing and remote work hit in March 2020. By allowing myself to camouflage in the menagerie of corporate politics, I used my color cards to connect with co-workers and practice what I've preached online. I must tell you that a 9 to 5 job versus working for yourself as a solopreneur are vastly different experiences, and both have taught me a lot about my strengths and blind spots in bureaucracy.

Being your boss has perks, but seeing yourself win and make mistakes in a team environment while having health benefits is a reprieve from reinventing the wheel and struggling financially. I see the investments in both, so I am comfortable juggling a corporate day job and passion projects at night. I acquired a project management certificate and rebranded my color therapy work under Chroma Mystic. It's a larger vision of what I am here to provide the world through the power of color. I want to demystify Corporate Chaos. In my mystic era, I'm focused on helping others experience mysticism and build an Elysian future using color. *The Color Mage Oracle* has always been a tool used in coaching, training, and part of personal collections worldwide. Still, this guidebook is a conduit of culture and insight that challenges you to look at your situation differently. And be comfortable knowing that no matter your race, religion, or region in which you live, you are born of love, light, and color.

What is a Color Therapy

Color therapy, also known as chromotherapy, is a practical and effective holistic healing modality that uses the vibrational frequencies of colors to restore balance and harmony within the body and mind. Each color emits a specific frequency and energy that can influence our physical health, emotions, and mental state. Incorporating colors into our environment and daily practices can promote healing, enhance mood, and achieve greater well-being. This knowledge empowers us to take control of our health and well-being.

What Can Color Do

Colors can profoundly affect various aspects of your life and work, which most artists, designers, and creative crafters understand naturally. Here are some ways color can influence you:

- **Emotional Healing:** Different colors can evoke specific emotions and feelings, helping to uplift your mood or calm your mind.
- **Physical Well-being:** Colors can influence physiological responses, such as improving circulation or reducing stress.
- **Creativity and Productivity:** Certain colors can stimulate creativity and enhance focus, increasing productivity.
- **Personal Growth:** Colors can support your spiritual journey, providing insight and guidance.

Why Do Color Readings Matter

Color readings can provide valuable insights into your current state of being and guide personal growth, such as tarot cards and other oracle cards. Tuning into the energies of different colors can help you better understand your emotions, challenges, and opportunities. Color readings also help you connect with your intuition and inner wisdom, empowering you to make informed and inspired choices. Adding color to your readings creates a unique color scheme that might not readily be seen if you just used tarot or other oracle cards. People often love it when the colors match other cards in a reading, and it's a tremendous affirmation of the messages coming through when you're randomly shuffling the deck, thinking about your frustrations, and inquiring about decisions.

Where to Apply Color

You can integrate the power of color in many areas of your life:

- **Home and Workspace:** Use color in your interior design to create environments that support your goals and well-being.
- **Clothing and Accessories:** Wear colors that align with your intentions for the day, whether to feel confident, relaxed, or energized.
- **Art and Creativity:** Incorporate color into your creative projects to express emotions and ideas.
- **Personal Rituals:** Use colored candles, crystals, or other tools in your spiritual practices.

When to Use The Color Mage Oracle

The Color Mage Oracle can be used in various situations to provide insight and guidance like tarot and other oracle cards:

- **Daily Draws:** Pull a card each morning to set an intention or receive guidance.
- **Meditation:** Use the cards to focus your meditation practice on specific colors and their energies.
- **Decision Making:** Consult the Oracle for clarity and perspective when making important decisions.
- **Healing Sessions:** Incorporate the cards into healing practices, such as Reiki or crystal healing.

How to Use The Guidebook

The Color Mage Oracle guidebook is designed to be an accessible and powerful resource for anyone looking to explore the world of color therapy and get to know *The Color Mage Oracle*. This guidebook provides instructions on how to use the Oracle, including:

- **Card Layouts and Spreads:** Different ways to lay out the cards for various readings.
- **Card Interpretations:** Detailed explanations of each card's meaning and how it applies to your life.
- **Practical Tips:** Advice on integrating color therapy into your daily routine and work environment.

This guidebook is your key to unlocking the transformative power of color magic. It will be your companion on a journey of self-discovery and personal growth as you learn to harness the power of color in all aspects of your life. The color cards are grouped into their respective chakra families: root, sacral, solar plexus, heart, throat, third eye, crown, earth star, and universal chakras. The remaining combination of color cards is referenced under The Kaleidoscope section for narrative layers, cultural patterns, and themes related to the five elements, mythology and our galaxy. This is a guidebook of anecdotes and connections, but it's not intended to replace your intuition by any stretch of the imagination. Use this guidebook for inspiration and reference it when you're feeling stuck. But please refrain from using it as a crutch or as an end-all-be-all bible because it's not intended to replace your own mysticism and unique human experiences. These pages are handrails in your saga as you cross between worlds, dimensions, and timelines.

The Chroma Mystic***ka*** Project

Everyone has a unique relationship with the reality they experience. So, although color is a great way to communicate ideas, emotions, and messages, at the end of the day, color is subjective. And my green might be different than your green. That's perfectly okay! Not everyone will receive color in the same way, and the application of color can vary from person to person. If you require additional insight or want a peer review of your reading, please get in touch with *The Chroma Mystic****ka*** *Project*. This is a dedicated space for mystics and mages like yourself to explore color and connect with the cards in a new way.

Card Layouts

There is no right or wrong way to lay your cards out to read. Sometimes, colors will jump out while you're shuffling, and that's okay. You need to ask yourself whether or not those cards are meant for the spread. It's entirely up to you how you want to lay your cards out for a reading. Here are a few examples of card layouts. I use three-card spreads mostly when working with *The Color Mage Oracle*.

One Card Spread—This method is usually the quickest way to find your color of the day mood. If you're looking for a fast, intuitive reading to jumpstart your journaling or want to flash in some color inspiration for a project, you can pull one card and scope the situation in one large, broad stroke.

Three Card Draw—The power of three will set you free. This is my favorite spread for examining the mood of the universe. It can represent the past, present, and future. This is usually the spread I use throughout the week to understand how energy moves around the world. This layout lets you feel the beginning, middle, and end of your day or situation in a trio of feelings. You can also look at it as a way of seeing what's coming in, what's staying, and what's leaving while you read your situation.

Celtic Cross – The most traditional card spread for divination is the Celtic Cross. It tells a unique story of energy, and the colors in this layout will touch on all the themes you would find in traditional tarot. This layout is the most complimentary for infusing your tarot readings with more color to give your reading more practical ways to tap into the benefits and strengths of the situation.

A Note About Upright and Upside Down

Although tarot and other oracle cards may emphasize the positioning of the card, working with color is a little different. You may need to interpret the colors as positive or negative in your readings should they appear upside down. But it's not always conclusive or productive to the situation. Flittering back and forth in your mind's eye can get quite disheveled when you teeter between right and wrong—at the same time, struggling to keep your ego and generational trauma in check while doing so. No obvious line is drawn between the positive and negative inherent to the color's message. The cards will tell a story, but they might need more context from other cards, and you need to see the color as a whole instead of breaking it apart to serve a particular angle.

The more you work with the cards, the easier it will be to identify the stranger things about color showing up in a reading upside down, leaving you equipped to recognize patterns in your chakra system and mood swings and know when the energy is expanding in your favor or contracting out of protection. Consider the card position if you genuinely feel it's right to do so. Don't be afraid to turn the card right-side up if it simplifies the message and makes it more accessible to see your situation with clarity instead of scarcity.

In times of great sorrow and deep darkness, may you feel the power of love, light, and color.

Root Chakra

Burgundy - Passions & Sex

Burgundy, a rich and alluring color, is known by many names worldwide. Midnight Pomegranate, Maroon, Blood - each name evokes a different image and feeling. But to me, Burgundy represents something much more profound. The color reveals our animated consciousness, reminding us that we are alive and connected to something greater than ourselves. Burgundy is defined as the first card in *The Color Mage Oracle* deck because, without passion or desire in our lives, we wouldn't exist. Just as the slow throbbing burn of magma keeps the earth moving, the blood of passionate ideology continues to drive human existence forward.

Burgundy is the color of survival, and it wants us to embrace life with fervor and purpose in our personal and professional endeavors. What is fueling your passions right now? This vibrant hue resides in the root chakra, igniting our kundalini energy and energizing our aura. As someone who works with clients and friends on harnessing their inner power and drive, I recommend tapping into Burgundy energy when feeling disconnected from oneself or society's restrictive beliefs about sex, career choices, and individualism.

This color can elevate emotions over a prolonged period. I remember wearing a Burgundy garnet bracelet while going on my first dates as a gay man, using its healing properties to overcome past sexual trauma. I also wear Burgundy when facing criticism or doubts about my entrepreneurship journey - it serves as a reminder to protect my self-worth and passion for chasing my dreams. Burgundy is not just a color; it's a symbol of strength, resilience, and unwavering determination.

Burgundy entices you to embrace a life full of passion and vitality instead of merely surviving on a passive existence. Do you feel the weight of external expectations pushing you towards a path devoid of raw, unadulterated passion? Which aspect of your current situation feels desolate and lacking in fulfillment? Seeing this color card serves as a reminder that you hold the power to create miracles. What will you truly pour your blood, sweat, and tears into? Be truthful to yourself. Burgundy has allowed me to fully inhabit my body before, during, and after moments of intimacy. It has given me the energy to transcend emotional and mental barriers that previously made me question my will to survive due to past experiences with bullying, domestic violence, and sexual trauma. However, be cautious not to overindulge in Burgundy's shadowy aspects if you struggle with addiction to sex, abuse, narcissistic narratives, false information, or have trouble acknowledging your anger. To balance its intensity, use Burgundy with colors such as Gold, Sapphire, and Brown to avoid being consumed by rage and enslaved by predatory desires. Your body is designed for desire; now is the time to utilize Burgundy's potent energy to shatter passivity and create a more fulfilling existence for yourself. Use it to heal the wounds inflicted upon you and reclaim your rightful place in the world.

Red Merlot - Relationships

On the porch, bathed in the warm glow of a sunset, Red Merlot sits leisurely sipping on a glass of deep red wine. Its presence exudes confidence and sensuality, inviting you to embrace those qualities within yourself. Originating from the rich wine region of Burgundy, this color represents your desire for connections and relationships - both romantic and platonic. Take a step back and reflect on how you see yourself with others and this current situation. What roles do you typically fall into when it comes to people? Do you reach for specific identities out of habit or routine? We all have patterns when it comes to our interactions with others. Maybe you always turn to one friend for juicy gossip or call another because they make you feel infallible. Red Merlot is here to unveil these layers you put on yourself and others, driven by your ego's need for control and attractiveness. This color also symbolizes socialization and standing within society - the power color often seen in magazines and referenced by image consultants. It may hint at your tendency to compare yourself and your status to that of others. It's like drinking a "Comparison Cosmo" - constantly seeking validation and approval from others. It also highlights how we build networks to thrive in our environment. Take a moment to think about the last ten people you contacted - why are they in your life? What do you gain or lose from their presence and opinions? Like fine wines, our histories with different individuals age within our minds, blending personalities and reaffirming our reasons for choosing specific people to play particular roles in our lives. But sometimes, we can become stubborn about relating our social experiences to our social identity, romanticizing motives, and ignoring warning signs. Red Merlot wants us to be mindful of these tendencies and control who we allow into our inner circle. We inherently want to be liked and accepted, often going to great mental lengths to see only what we want to see, even if it requires giving up who we are for love or a job.

Red Merlot's deep, rich hue shimmers and swirls in the glass, reflecting the dim light of a cozy evening. The full-bodied flavor dances across your taste buds as you sip, awakening your senses to the complex layers of grape and earthy notes. But beyond its physical presence, Red Merlot has a message for you - that you are naturally attractive but may need more clarity on who influences your identity and relationships.

We often have distorted expectations of others because we fail to see and accept their full spectrum upon first meeting them. Or perhaps we never delve deeper into ourselves or those closest to us, afraid of what we might discover about how little they genuinely add to our lives. But Red Merlot's appearance in a reading strongly indicates that it's time to review our relationships and question any conformity holding us back.

Now, Red Merlot wants you to reflect on what makes relationships desirable and meaningful. After all, as humans, we need each other. Are there ways you may be hindering others from evolving within your mind? And though we may wish for people to fit perfectly into our expectations, sometimes the best relationships are the ones that allow us to grow and sip from our cup.

So let Red Merlot's bold flavor awaken within you a desire for genuine connections that reflect who you truly desire to be.

Scarlet - Success & Fortune

The vibrant hue of scarlet stretches across the bustling boulevard of Hollywood, drawing the eye and commanding attention. This is the color of elite events, red carpets, and galas, radiating a deep materialistic energy that symbolizes the need for significance, recognition, and success. But underneath this glamorous surface lies a hidden darkness - a trail of crumbs left by ignorance, manipulation, and even murder. Like all shades of red, Scarlet reveals the extreme lengths we will go to in pursuit of fortune and fame.

But when this color appears in a reading, it serves as a reminder of the milestones and sacrifices that have led us to where we are now. It invites us to examine our privilege and acknowledge the systemic rewards that exist in our world. Because when it comes down to it, is it simply surviving or getting by all we can hope for? Shouldn't our quest for prosperity be more elegant, luxurious, and fulfilling without sacrificing our values?

As you consider your current situation, Scarlet urges you to envision success in all its forms - how it looks, tastes, and sounds in your life and work. While it may be tempting to dwell on missed opportunities or feel rejected by societal norms or expectations from figures like God or Hollywood elites, know that blessings often come disguised as boundaries. Embrace this vivid color and use its powerful energy to attract synchronicity and good fortune. Remember that even in rejection and hardship lies the potential for growth and transformation.

Many socio-economic practices and campaigns in our society mold individuals into what best suits those in power. Scarlet is the formidable outlier who questions the integrity of this situation. Don't be afraid to demand more information; scarcity is merely an illusion - a parlor trick to manipulate your self-worth. The ego revels in creating competition and sensationalizing success. Remember that struggle is unnecessary in achieving greatness. Each person's effort comes in different flavors, and no two paths to fortune look alike. The media and entertainment industry play a significant role in shaping our desires and ideals. Are you too harsh on yourself or others, striving for an unattainable dream? Are you trapped in the mindset of "Mommy Dearest," constantly comparing yourself to others and believing life is a Lifetime drama? Remember, success looks different for everyone, and chasing perfection often blinds us to the unique factors that led to someone else's success. Don't believe the glorified stories of self-made millionaires - they are just another tool used to keep those without wealth feeling inferior and hopeless. Savor some saffron in your tea or smoothie as a reminder that simply existing makes you a star in your own right.

Ruby Rose - Loving Your Soul Path

Every human on this planet walks their unique soul path, a journey of personal growth and self-development. But there are moments when we merge onto the bustling highway of humanity, joining others in a common purpose. During these times, Ruby Rose, the color of ruby slippers, ripe strawberries, and the bold red lip look of Alexandria Ocasio-Cortez (also known as AOC), can be seen shining bright. This vibrant hue shields our hearts and souls, protecting us from the lies and false promises often spread by political action committees and those romanticizing corruption through social compliments or convenient sympathy. If you find yourself drawn to this color now, it begs the question: how are you loving and nurturing your soul amidst the distractions that litter your path? As I delved deeper into helping people through color psychology, I noticed that Ruby Rose often arises because it forces us to confront what our heart truly desires. And if you've been paying attention, you'll know that *The Color Mage Oracle* is a no-nonsense tool designed to help deprogram deceit from our lives. So, when Ruby Rose appears, it's like finding ourselves in a Little Red Riding Hood fairy tale - one where we may stray off the path due to tempting distractions such as smelling the roses. But then comes the wolf, representing toxic masculinity, fear, or racism - reminding us that our soul path may lead us into dire circumstances, but we are not ill-equipped to handle them. Ruby Rose commands us to take off those rose-colored glasses and instead equip ourselves with the brain, heart, and courage needed to face the wickedness of our current reality. It serves as a potent reminder that we are not separated from more significant conversations that affect all of humanity. We are deeply connected to revolution, protest, and social justice matters. Ruby Rose is here to fasten us tighter into the fabric of the Universe, reminding us of our place and purpose in this world. This is your story to rivet the soul and revolt against a stark society that suppresses love.

The color of Ruby Rose is a rich, vibrant hue that beckons the soul to explore beyond its familiar boundaries. It is a compilation of world religions, Gods, Goddesses, and spiritual teachings, all intertwined in a tapestry of divine curiosity. When this color appears in your reading, it signifies a time when you must consciously step off your pre-made path and test the mettle of your heart and soul. The Universe may make it happen without your permission, but it is a call to adventure that cannot be ignored. As you embark on this journey, be aware of distractions and deceptions and embrace the opportunity to delve into practices, systems, and ideas outside your comfort zone and culture. Your soul is craving something new that will better the greater good and allow you to express love in deeper ways. With ruby red lips, believe that you are exactly where you are meant to be now. You can choose whether to continue your current path or veer off in a new direction; be flexible and allow your heart to lead the way. Your soul will thank you for following its yearnings.

Grapefruit - Generous Energy

With a tangy scent and vibrant color, grapefruit bursts into your consciousness. Its presence is a reminder to give more than you think you are receiving, to align with a more significant collective movement, and to engage in deeper conversations. This fruit encourages you to invest more energy, time, and money into gathering evidence and experiences. It often appears when the spirit wants you to know that you may not have all the information necessary to make an informed decision - take your time and be open to receiving guidance from the universe. However, this does not mean giving endlessly without discernment. Grapefruit urges you to only give to those people, places, and things that align with your values and purpose in life. Say no to racism, classism, and blood money. Generosity should not come at the cost of your well-being or financial stability. At its core, giving should not be motivated by expectations of receiving something in return. What conditions are attached to what you're giving? While it's natural to desire some form of reciprocation, expecting others to owe you indefinitely is unrealistic. Kindness is often not repaid in the same way it is given. Right now, focusing on acts of service rather than a scarcity mentality is essential. There is enough abundance in the world for everyone, but you may have been blocking yourself from receiving blessings because you are too focused on what others have that you do not. Spirit shows us what others have (like babies, pay raises, and viral social media moments) as a reflection of our inherent desires. Embrace the joy and nourishment of philanthropy like juicy grapefruit. The thief of grapefruit's joy in your life right now may be the inability to differentiate between what you give and receive. Stay mindful of this balance as you navigate your generosity with others.

Imagine yourself as the center of a Grapefruit flow chart, with lines reaching out to all the people, places, and things in your life. Write down what you give and receive from each entity. Then, switch perspectives and imagine yourself in their shoes. Create parallel lines coming back to you, detailing what they offer and receive in return. You will have four channels - a freeway of energetic exchanges. Some repetition is expected, but it's your task to focus on the most significant aspects of these interactions. Once you have completed this flow chart, mark any channel that feels like "service" or "support" with a star. Circle any channel that feels like "sacrifice" or "debt." This exercise is a way to measure how clear you are on the energetic exchanges in your life and work. Red ink is recommended for this exercise, as we are actively proofreading your philanthropy. As you go through this process, you may feel a pull toward letting go of certain things or redesigning others. Feel free to ask for help in making these adjustments. Remember, grapefruit is about giving permission - letting go of what no longer serves you and embracing new opportunities for growth and fulfillment.

Coral - Mercy & Forgiveness

The vibrant hue of coral is like a flaming reminder of the past, burning on your skin as a warning that you don't have to repeat the same mistakes. It's a color that wants to free you from the burdens of your ancestors and their pain. Coral energy is alive with vindication, urging you to embrace your humanity and all its flaws. You are here now because you are doing your best, but be open to listening and learning from others. There is no such thing as sin. The concept has been used for centuries for control and oppression, masking true intentions with ideas of order and perfection. But Coral stands firmly against these notions, demanding self-forgiveness for past actions while never forgetting the journey that brought you here today. Your story is constantly evolving, and if you allow yourself to remain silent or play small out of fear of being human and making mistakes, you continue to feed energy vampires, narcissists, and an unjust system that thrives on limiting beliefs.

Human history blends light and dark, with societies often glorifying sacrifice and death to appease divine forces. While the Western world condemns the Aztec tradition of human sacrifice as savage, they betrayed and killed Jesus Christ because of his progressive beliefs, ultimately using his death as a tool for control and domination over others' spirituality.

Coral is a color that wants to liberate you from the shackles of guilt and shame. It encourages you to break free from the cycles of self-doubt and self-sabotage and instead embrace the journey of self-discovery and growth. Coral reminds you that you are worthy and deserving of love despite your imperfections.

Coral also has excellent protective properties in many cultures. It is believed to have a solid connection to the sea, often seen as a source of wisdom and mystery. In ancient Greek mythology, the goddess Aphrodite was said to have been born from the sea foam and carried a coral necklace as a protective amulet.

In Chinese culture, coral symbolizes longevity and protection against evil spirits. It is often used in feng shui to bring harmony and balance into the home. Coral is also known for its ability to ward off negative energies and protect its wearer from harm. Its vibrant color represents passion and vitality, giving us the power to stand up against oppressive forces and overcome challenges.

When we embody the energy of coral, we are reminded that we are strong and capable of protecting ourselves from any negative influences. We are encouraged to trust our intuition and not be swayed by outside pressures or expectations. Coral also teaches us about adaptability and resilience. As coral reefs can withstand harsh ocean conditions, we can learn to navigate difficult situations gracefully and with strength.

By wearing or surrounding ourselves with coral, we can tap into its protective energy and feel empowered to create our path toward liberation. We can break free from limiting beliefs and societal norms that seek to control us and instead embrace our true selves with love and acceptance. Embracing the vibrant energy of coral allows us to live authentically without fear or shame. It reminds us that our journey constantly evolves, but as long as we stay true to ourselves and listen to our inner voice, we will always find our way towards freedom and fulfillment.

But this liberation is not just for us. It extends to those around us as well. By breaking free from our chains of guilt and shame, we can inspire others to do the same. We can create a ripple effect of healing and empowerment in our communities.

Coral also symbolizes resilience and survival in the face of adversity. Throughout history, coral has been used as an amulet for protection during dangerous journeys at sea. This serves as a reminder that even during chaos and uncertainty, we can overcome any challenge. Coral is a color often associated with passion and creativity. It ignites a fire within us, urging us to follow our dreams and pursue what sets our souls on fire. By embracing this energy, we can tap into our inner power and manifest our most authentic desires.

So let coral be your guide on your journey towards self-love and liberation. Let it remind you that your past does not define you, and your struggles do not make you unworthy. Embrace your humanity with all its flaws and imperfections – for that is what makes you beautifully human.

Incorporate coral into your life through clothing or accessories or surround yourself with items representing this vibrant hue. Meditate with coral crystals and visualize yourself breaking free from guilt and shame.

There is a beautiful power within our human existence, one that allows us to both give and receive love. It transcends any labels or categorizations we may be assigned, for our validity as humans cannot be defined by such shallow measures. We have all made mistakes, me included. Hurtful words were spoken, and wounds were created. But like the vibrant coral color, our energy can be harnessed to heal these scars and repair broken hearts. If you seek forgiveness and wish to mend relationships, working with this hue will guide you toward identifying grievances to forgive and grudges to release. While some commit unspeakable atrocities, we must not let those acts manipulate our energy and breed victimhood. You are not a victim but a survivor, strong and resilient.

Dahlia - Healing Unrequited Love

The memories of those who slipped through our fingers, the ones we let go because of our insecurities and doubts, are all intertwined with Dahlia's energy. It is a place where our hearts were left broken, our pride wounded by the pain we couldn't ignore, and we found ourselves numbly watching yet another episode of "Sex and the City" to distract ourselves from the reality that our love for others was not being nurtured as it should be. In this realm of Dahlia, self-neglect flourishes unchecked. Long-distance relationships fade as we become complacent in our love, too exhausted or disinterested to put in the effort required to keep the flame alive. As Spirit guides us towards Dahlia's presence, we must take a moment to reflect on whether we are genuinely giving enough love, showing up with genuine passion and enthusiasm, and expressing ourselves openly and boldly in our romantic gestures. Each person speaks their unique love language, and if we don't take the time to understand and communicate in their preferred way, we may struggle in all our relationships. Listening to what the other person needs is crucial for building strong connections. But even then, sometimes the other person may not know what they truly need or desire, making it a difficult journey to navigate together. The energy of Dahlia is acutely aware of how empty our hearts can feel when we neglect our own needs and desires. It challenges us to let go of unrealistic romantic ideals and instead embark on a personal revolution within our hearts. Are we indeed committed to what we long for and hope for? Or are we simply going through the motions, holding onto relationships or jobs out of fear of the unknown freedom and creativity that comes with exploring ourselves and new ways of being?

Dahlia, a vibrant and resilient flower, stands out just like you. It can be easy to get lost in your struggles and insecurities in a world where it often feels like you are the only one who truly cares about the Earth's well-being. But what if you miss all the love and support surrounding you? It's like trying to contain your beautiful bouquet in a vase full of holes - how can they thrive when all their emotions and energy spill out onto unappreciative ground? And navigating a toxic work environment is challenging when you feel undervalued and unfulfilled. In these moments, remember the courage within yourself. How can you find that red badge of courage to overcome your suffering and step into the banquet hall of love? Don't limit yourself to societal expectations or old beliefs that true love can only come from a specific gender, hometown, or through sacrificing your self-worth for a relationship or career. Dahlia is here with tough love: you can have it all, just like having your cake and eating it. It's time to break free from limitations and embrace variety, spice, and decadence in all aspects of life.

Sunset Joy - Pleasure & Laughter

If the rush of the holiday spirit had a favorite color, it would undoubtedly be Sunset Joy. This bold and tangy red hue embodies the foundation of cheer, transitions, and homecoming. Its vibrant nature symbolizes our pleasure when seasons change, as the day melts into night and night awakens today. You can find this color in dazzling fireworks displays and fields of poppies dancing in the breeze. I was blessed enough to be born during the twilight hours, and every day, I am reminded of the incredible power of transitioning across the thresholds of light and shadow by the ever-changing colors of sunrise and sunset.

Sunset Joy is a constant reminder of a pulse within comedic timing and the juxtaposition of life and death. It teaches us that true pleasure requires discipline and that change is an inevitable part of life. Are you currently going through a period of transition? Or are you perhaps instigating an eclipse due to your beliefs about penance being a source of humor and social validation?

Think about how you commiserate with others because of your privilege. Do you earn a living or feel better off at the expense of other people's pain and misfortune? As we gather at networking events, holiday parties, and casual luncheons, let us strive to exude class and grace. Unfortunately, there are times (especially during family gatherings) when people spike the punch with odious opinions and hard-hitting criticisms, turning what should be a joyous occasion into one filled with judgment and hurtful words.

Egos flare up, and the blood boils under the bedrock of our years. And that is precisely why Sunset Joy has appeared before you today. Those moments of pain, embarrassment, and life itself are fleeting. Why waste precious time and karma entertaining mockery, criticism, and jokes that belittle the passions and dreams of others? Remember, your time on this earth is temporary. Don't laugh at joy. Embrace it with open arms and spread its warmth to those around you.

As the sun dipped below the horizon, Sunset Joy beckoned you to choose pleasure over pain. It was a vibrant color that evoked warmth and happiness, tempting you to leave behind toxic relationships and embrace a new, brighter chapter in your life. Remember those moments when laughter helped you cope with difficult situations? Perhaps it was a time when you were forced to fake a smile at a hurtful comment. Sunset Joy reminds us of the ironic and complex ways we use humor to navigate cultural circumstances. Let this color inspire movement and ignite motivation when you feel stuck. Let it guide you towards shedding the weight of criticism as a measuring tool for self-worth and instead empower you to thrive courageously along your journey. I experienced this transformation firsthand during a 5-month stay in Florida, where I underwent a transition period. It brought me back to where I started, but with fresh eyes and a newfound understanding of my social power and why joy should never be something to laugh at.

Melon Pink - Compassion

Melon Pink is the eldest sister among her colorful counterparts, Grapefruit and Coral. When this vibrant hue appears in a reading, it signals that you are being called to confront and tackle suffering and conflict head-on. It urges you to act and do whatever is necessary to ease or end the struggles of those around you. Melon Pink takes on the role of a social worker, saint, and sponsor in *The Color Mage Oracle*, embodying empathy and compassion in action. But it also requires courage to go beyond mere sympathy and truly empathize with others. This color may guide you towards seeking a mentor, coach, or supportive figure - a sibling, fabulous aunt, or gay uncle - to help you through your current challenges. Alternatively, it may ask you to step into these roles and support those in need. If someone who played such a role in your life has passed away, Melon Pink invites you to hold space for their energy and allow it to guide you forward. Be bold and ask for their guidance anyway. The appearance of Melon Pink may also indicate fear on your part - perhaps worry that others will become dependent on you if you offer them a helping hand or support. You may struggle with trusting others and fear being seen as nothing more than a charity case, believing there must be some ulterior motive behind people's gestures of kindness. This color may also represent a fear of appearing weak amid adversity. In The Color Mage Oracle, red constantly balances risk and reward. Melon Pink reminds us that genuine compassion goes beyond simply alleviating our struggles or those of others; it involves taking meaningful action and facing our fears head-on.

Melon Pink is known as the color of empathy and compassion in action. It calls upon us to confront and tackle suffering in ourselves and others head-on. This color encourages us to act and do whatever is necessary to ease or end the struggles of those around us.

One of Melon Pink's critical roles in The Color Mage Oracle is that of a social worker, saint, and sponsor. It embodies the energy of someone who empathizes with others profoundly and takes meaningful action to support them. This color reminds us that genuine compassion goes beyond simply alleviating symptoms; it involves addressing the root causes of suffering.

If Melon Pink appears in a reading, it may guide you to seek out a mentor, coach, or supportive figure in your life—someone who can offer guidance through your current challenges. Alternatively, it may ask you to step into these roles and support those in need.

However, the appearance of Melon Pink may also indicate fear on your part - perhaps worry that others will become dependent on you if you offer them a helping hand or support. You may struggle with trusting others and fear being seen as nothing more than a charity case. This color asks us to confront these fears and trust that our actions come from a place of genuine empathy and compassion.

In some cases, Melon Pink may be a fear of appearing weak in the face of adversity. This color reminds us that true strength comes from facing our fears head-on and taking meaningful action toward resolving them.

Overall, Melon Pink urges us to risk our comfort for the sake of others or ourselves while also working towards resolving the root causes of suffering. It teaches us that true healing involves treating symptoms and addressing underlying issues.

In action, the color Melon Pink must be deliberately incorporated into your life and work to have a lasting impact. It cannot simply be added as an afterthought or for aesthetic purposes. This vibrant and welcoming color holds a great responsibility, much like a big sister, to generosity and forgiveness. While it may provide immediate relief in times of trauma, it also encourages the creation of new patterns and systems to address the root causes of suffering in our society. Melon Pink is powerful, symbolizing advocacy, care, and social science. It calls those driven by purpose rather than just a paycheck to make a difference in spaces that desperately need change. Incorporating Melon Pink into branding, vision boards, writing materials, or even party dishes can promote compassion and drive resolutions for ending socioeconomic oppression and systemic suffering. Let this color remind us of our responsibility to uplift and support those around us and constantly strive to create a more equitable world.

Himalaya - Pure Love

Why is a pink color in the root chakra? With intention and transitory influence, colors blend—growing lighter and darker. Himalaya is the most criticized color energy in the Oracle deck because people have limited their color and chakra associations to primary hues, like an oversimplified and generalized math problem. However, design makes life, color, and chakra energy more complex. Chakras pulsate, and so do the colors in *The Color Mage Oracle*. Himalaya is in the root chakra for womb space and the light behind our flesh. The majestic Himalaya mountains stretch towards the sky, bathed in the warm embrace of the rising and setting sun. It's a gentle kiss before bed and upon waking, a reminder that the light of love is fundamental to our humanity's survival. Pure and untainted by earthly limitations, this love is the essence of grace. In a world filled with free will and often lacking in displays of pure love, Himalaya works as a high-vibrational frequency in our root center to stand forthright in purification and purity. It calls to us to cleanse our lives and souls, not through traditional detox or drastic changes, but through choosing more love in all aspects of our existence. Just as the mighty Himalayas shield and nourish those who call them home, so does pure love protect and sustain us. Love is all we truly need to thrive. Society is addicted to dystopian projections, so this color harks a new sound for utopia. Though some may dismiss this as fluffy or idealistic, I know from my experiences that love conquers all, even at the base of our chakra system. Having been homeless at ages 14 and 25, I never once lost faith in the power of love to guide me through the darkest days. And if Himalaya has appeared in your life, know its intentions are pure because you are inherently pure at your core. The secret ingredient you seek is unconditional love - an unwavering force that accepts and embraces us just as we are. Survival does not need to be so cut-throat and scarcity driven. So, take out your pink salt - a symbol of healing and cleansing - and pray for love to fill every corner of your being. You've been comparing yourself as of late out of survival and fear.

The vibrant energy of this color is gracing your life at this very moment, inviting you to explore and embrace self-care and self-love rituals. Taking the time to intentionally indulge in activities that make you feel beautiful and satisfied is incredibly fulfilling, a true reflection of your desires and intentions. With this, the validation from others becomes less necessary as it does not diminish the magic you have created for yourself. The essence of Himalaya urges you to discover the various forms of love across cultures and how humanity has coexisted in peace throughout history. If there were one color that could heal the Palestinian crisis, it would surely be a hue inspired by the mountains and valleys of the Himalayas. Our survival as a species is crucial so as not to limit the expression of love on this planet. Love knows no boundaries and holds no harm when pure and genuine. Pure love will always find its way to you, whether through unexpected conversations with strangers during a car ride or through realizing that someone else's body image is not within your control but solely their business. Allowing this understanding is an act of pure love. Remember, life doesn't begin in the womb; it starts when we self-actualize and embrace love over fear. So, purifying ourselves or others should never mean trying to rid them of their imperfections; instead, it is about expanding our capacity for love, light, and all the colors that make us unique.

SACRAL NAVEL CHAKRA

Snuggle - Natural Touch

Snuggle beckons you to embrace the fullness of intimacy through physical touch. When was the last time you allowed yourself to indulge in a soothing massage? Snuggle encourages you to shed any reservations and become comfortable with your nakedness. You could visit a nudist campground or explore the healing benefits of Ayurvedic massage. Strengthen your relationships by showing love through both physical and verbal expressions. Snuggle guides you into the present moment in this reading, inviting you to focus on your sensations. What do you feel in your physical space right now? Is it cluttered, chaotic, or serene? Snuggle urges you to contemplate how your physical presence affects your interactions with others and your work environment.

With Snuggle's energy, breakfast in bed, midday naps, and spa treatments hold extra significance. It is a time to pamper your physical being and honor its existence. Let Snuggle inspire you to disconnect from the online world and plug into the tangible reality around you - one that can be touched, tasted, smelled, and heard in real-time. Like the soft purring of a rabbit or the infectious giggles of a baby, Snuggle's energy enters your life now to challenge you: How intimate are you truly being? Are you fully embracing intimacy in all aspects of your life?

On the other hand, if this color appears reversed or in a challenging position during a reading, it raises deep-seated issues about being comfortable in your skin. The color seems to mock and taunt, daring you to assert yourself and establish personal boundaries. It speaks to the struggle of finding refuge from manipulative individuals who invade your privacy and use physical means to get what they want. This is not in line with spiritual practices; it is rooted in fear and insecurity. Pastel colors may seem delicate, but they hold immense power. In this case, the color Snuggle represents the act of cozying up to someone for selfish gain, using them, and weaponizing intimacy or sex to avoid facing one's insecurities.

In work situations, Snuggle can manifest when co-workers are looking for information and dirt on others. Images of sneaking around corners and meeting in stairwells to exchange gossip are suggested. A true story that happened while I was wearing a Snuggle-colored cardigan. Exciting things happen when we start living and using the colors from this deck. As I learned the hard way, my demure aura attracts those thirsty for drama and secrets. I now use Snuggle combined with royal blues and deep greens to protect myself from being taken advantage of or dealing with energy vampires. These colors represent firm boundaries and escaping unsolicited interrogations.

We must be mindful of how we use colors and how they can impact our interactions with others. Each hue holds its unique energy, capable of affecting us physically and emotionally. By embracing the power of color, we can harness its potential for good or ill in our lives.

Although snuggling seems soft and gentle, it may reveal a space in your aura vulnerable to others using intimacy for their gain. It's essential to recognize your self-worth and seek guidance when needed. Don't deny yourself the ability to feel tender and resilient. Be aware of those who may try to exploit your vulnerability, but don't let it prevent you from seeking the warmth and comfort that comes with closeness. Remember to stand firm and value yourself above all else.

Light Apricot - Release Your Fears

The color Light Apricot is like a quesadilla of courage and faith, warm and inviting with a hint of spice. Its presence today signals that you are meant to embrace the light and let go of any self-doubt and cynicism holding you back. The vibrant hue urges you to stop sabotaging your relationships and projects and instead create a diverse and inclusive spiritual practice, shedding any fears or stereotypes placed in your mind by others or societal programming.

As you bask in the glow of Light Apricot, remember that any threats you feel are self-inflicted through your thoughts and disbelief in the power of your voice and potential. This color wants you to release those negative beliefs and have faith in yourself as a living, breathing consciousness made of stardust and connected to the divine.

Despite its bright and uplifting energy, Light Apricot acknowledges the presence of Dark Apricot, where quips and satire reside. It reminds you that while it is crucial to question faith and maintain integrity, you need not carry guilt or shame for making decisions that align with your true desires. You are free to choose your path without owing anyone an explanation.

So, embrace Light Apricot today, for it represents bravery, positivity, and unwavering faith in humanity. Let it guide you towards a brighter future and a stronger connection to your inner spirit.

The desire for something is valid even if it is unclear and undefined. It does not make you lacking or foolish. Light Apricot beckons you to take each step with care and intention. As you let go of the doubts and worries that hold you back from reaching for your aspirations or gaining the necessary experience to move forward, you are signaling to the Universe that you are ready for abundance. Consider lighting a black candle, symbolizing release, and a Light Apricot candle as you pray and meditate on freeing yourself from these fears. Take a piece of paper and jot down all the fears that plague your mind at this moment in time, allowing them to dissipate onto the page like escaping ghosts.

Dear Universe, I Fear...

Place this letter of fear underneath the black candle or burn it if you are incredibly safe. While the black candle burns, I want you to see the Universe taking the letter and putting it inside a magical Light Apricot box. This heavenly recycling machine eats up any worries or doubts you may have. After you feel ready, write a second letter to the Universe.

Dear Universe, I Love...

As the black candle burns and your fears dissipate into the universe's recycling machine, it is time to focus on the power of love and faith. Light Apricot represents bravery, positivity, and unwavering belief in yourself and the world around you.

Take a moment to reflect on all the things you love, big and small. They can be people, places, objects, or experiences. Write them down on paper or hold them in your mind.

Now light the Light Apricot candle and imagine these loved things being showered with courage and faith from the glowing flame. Visualize each one becoming stronger, brighter, and more resilient as they are infused with this energy.

As you do this, say aloud or silently to yourself:

"Dear Universe, I love... (list all you love). I believe these things will continue to bring joy, abundance, and growth into my life. I trust that my connection to them will only deepen as I let go of fear and embrace courage."

Spend some time basking in this optimistic feeling of love and faith. You can even add extra energy by placing your hands over the flame (carefully) or holding a piece of rose quartz crystal.

When you feel ready, blow out the candle and thank it for its guidance. Take a deep breath, knowing that Light Apricot's energy has amplified your love.

Remember this exercise whenever doubts or worries start creeping back in. You can always return to this place of love and faith within yourself. Trust in the power of Light Apricot to guide you towards a brighter future filled with abundance and positivity.

Dark Apricot - Find the Humor

In a world filled with darkness, there is a glimmer of joy and mischievous energy known as Dark Apricot. This creative force is a trusted ally to artists, comedians, and public relations professionals who may feel stuck in fear. Dark Apricot beckons you to don your Dennis the Menace goggles, take a closer look at your life and work through the lens of instigation. How audacious the Universe can be in grabbing our attention! What playful elements have you found in your current situation that have brought you to this moment? Instead of feeling like we are constantly chasing our dreams, could we be purposefully reacting to the mood and energy of the Universe? In Dark Apricot, an inherent playfulness inspires us to fake it until we make it. Not because we are being phony but because we are igniting our potential and coaxing it out of hiding. You are here right now seeking the irony of synchronicity, hoping for a light bulb moment in your sitcom. Dark Apricot often serves as comedic relief during challenging and intense moments, helping to solidify the lesson even further. But be cautious, for there may be fallout if the timing needs to be corrected or the right words need to be used.

In life, we often experience moments of divine timing when things seem to fall perfectly into place at just the right moment. But what about those moments when it seems like everything is going wrong, and we feel embarrassed or ashamed?

Dark Apricot wants us to laugh at our humanity in these moments. Instead of beating ourselves up for making mistakes or feeling like fools, Dark Apricot encourages us to use these situations to fuel growth and self-improvement. We can surprise our critics and prove our inner self-critical thoughts wrong by learning from these experiences and doing better next time. Dark Apricot reminds us that it's not about justifying our naivete but using our mistakes and challenges as opportunities to become stronger and wiser.

So, the next time you find yourself in a challenging situation, remember Dark Apricot's mischievous energy and use it to overcome your obstacles with humor and determination. Embrace the irony of synchronicity and trust that everything happens for a reason. Trust yourself and your ability to learn and grow from every experience, even the embarrassing ones. Ultimately, it will only make you a more well-rounded and resilient individual.

At this very moment, there is still time to create a new experience for yourself. Despite the darkness that may surround you, finding humor in those situations does not diminish the pain and suffering that you may be experiencing. Instead, it offers relief and connection with our shared humanity. Our flaws and past mistakes are not funny, but they do happen. And Spirit wants you to know that it's okay to make mistakes. It's all about what we learn and take away from them that holds power. Now, Dark Apricot bestows upon you the gift of flexibility - the ability to not take authority figures, parents, agents, the government, or even your critical inner voice too seriously. Shit happens, my dear. And it's not personal - it's just life. Let go of any solemn disregard for joy and embrace the beauty of living in the present moment.

As you gaze upon your life's turmoil, adversity, anguish, and limitations, can you feel your inner wisdom and patience rise to meet them with a knowing smile? If not, it may be time to seek the guidance of a professional, as these could be symptoms of depression. Remember, there is no shame in seeking help for yourself. You are valuable and deserving of support on your journey towards healing.

Pink Gari - Courageous Sexuality

Embrace your sexuality. Let Pink Gari awaken your desires and unleash your sexual prowess. The heat between the sheets is tantalizing, a succulent feast for the senses. And don't forget, it was through sex that you were brought into this world in all your physical glory. But the identities of those involved in your conception may not have been pure or confident in their sexuality. Society has stigmatized sex, relegating it to hushed whispers and hidden corners, limited by narrow beliefs and constrained by shame. Pink Gari invites you to tap into its raw, unadulterated power and break free from any self-imposed barriers hindering your personal growth and fulfillment. Your sexual identity is critical to unlocking confidence and courage in all facets of your life. Spirit urges you to explore your carnal desires, indulge in self-love, and release any pent-up energy lodged within your chakras. Alternatively, you can attend a playful sex toy party or educate yourself on kinks in a safe, judgment-free environment.

Sensual experiences ignite the senses and awaken a deeper, more primal part of ourselves. Pink Gari, also known as prepared sushi ginger, is a delicious and versatile ingredient that can add an element of sensuality to your date nights. The flavors and textures of sushi are designed to stimulate the taste buds, but they can also be enjoyed for their sensual qualities.

The delicate slices of pickled ginger add a touch of sweetness and tartness to sushi rolls, creating a symphony of flavors in every bite. But beyond its taste, Pink Gari has a crisp texture that provides a satisfying crunch as you bite into it. This combination of tastes and textures can heighten your senses and bring you into the present moment.

Consider adding Pink Gari to your menu when planning a date night with your partner or even just treating yourself to a solo evening of indulgence. Savor each slice slowly, fully allowing yourself to experience each bite's flavor and sensation. Let the salty, sweet, and sour notes dance on your tongue, and embrace the pleasure and joy it brings you.

But beyond its culinary uses, Pink Gari can also be used as a tool for sensuality in other ways. For example, you can explore incorporating this flavorful ingredient into foreplay with your partner. Try feeding each other slices of

Pink Gari during intimate moments or using it as edible body paint for some tasty fun.

Playing with food this way allows us to tap into our senses in new and exciting ways. It encourages us to let go of inhibitions or self-consciousness about our bodies or desires. Instead, it invites us to embrace pleasure and enjoy the moment without judgment.

If you are feeling adventurous, consider attending a sushi-making class together as a couple or hosting one at home for a fun date night activity. Not only will you learn how to make delicious sushi, but you will also be able to incorporate Pink Gari into your culinary

If your cheeks are flushed with a deep, rosy hue and you feel a sense of discomfort, it's likely a reflection of how insecure you feel about sex and exploring your sexuality. The color symbolizes vulnerability and sensitivity, both of which can be amplified when it comes to matters of intimacy. Sexual identity is a complex and personal journey for everyone, influenced by social constructs and limited education that often leads to feelings of shame, guilt, or fear. Pink Gari is a supportive color energy that can assist in breaking free from societal norms and binary expectations. However, this journey is far from simple or easy for humans with limited perspectives to comprehend fully. It requires deep introspection, self-discovery, and the courage to share oneself with others, sexually or creatively. If there are fears or reservations about sharing creative ideas or expressing oneself sexually, seeking professional advice is always an option. It's also important to note that expecting a perfect love story or following the unrealistic standards set by pornography will only lead to disappointment. Sex should not be reduced to a performance or imitation of what we see on screen. While some may view confident and comfortable displays of sexuality as "crazy" or "sensationalized," it's important not to suppress one's true nature for fear of being judged or labeled as unconventional. Embrace your creativity and entrepreneurial talents, and don't hold back in fear of being perceived as prudish or unconventional. After all, the purest form of self-expression is when we let go of inhibitions and embrace our rawest selves.

Veni, Vidi, Vici.

Peach - Open Certainty

Like a well-worn blanket on a chilly evening, Peach is the color of warmth and familiarity. It evokes memories of simpler times when life was easy and pleasant. But now, as you navigate your evolution, you can't recreate that comfort because everything has shifted. New perspectives and paradigms are on the horizon, waiting to be explored and expanded upon. Like in the movie *James and the Giant Peach*, you must step out of your comfort zone and embrace new certainties. If this color appears in a reading, it's a reminder to tap into your co-creative power and embrace the journey ahead with open arms. The unknown may seem daunting, but it holds great rewards. And remember, you don't have to travel alone - others have walked before you, and their experiences are as meaningful as yours. Peach encourages you to be honest with yourself about your dreams, hopes, and expectations with others. It's easy to get lost in uncertainty during challenging times, but this color reminds you to stay true to yourself and strive for your goals. Take a moment to reflect on what is certain and uncertain in your life and work right now - this will guide you toward finding comfort and positive energy again.

The subtle hue of Peach symbolizes a sense of self-imprisonment and a lack of confidence in one's desires and motivations. This could be rooted in a fear of stepping outside the boundaries of comfort or from external influences pushing for conformity. It may also suggest an inner conflict between personal desires and societal expectations or demands.

Peach encourages you to step back and evaluate your actions and decisions. Are you doing something because it aligns with your values, beliefs, and philosophy? Or are you doing it simply because it is what is expected of you? It is vital to break free from societal norms and expectations and listen to your inner voice.

This color also reminds you that changing course is okay if something feels no longer right. Life is a journey of growth and evolution, and what worked for you in the past may not serve you in the same way now. Embrace the unknown and trust yourself to make the right decisions for your happiness and fulfillment. In relationships, Peach can signify a need for open communication. Be honest with yourself and others about your needs, desires, and boundaries. Don't let societal pressure or fear hold you from expressing yourself authentically. Peach reminds us to trust in ourselves and embrace our individuality. We can create our path, even if it deviates from the expectations of others. Have confidence in our choices and stay true to who we are.

Discovering a sense of complete absoluteness is a rare occurrence. In a world where change is the only constant, things naturally outgrow their prescribed roles and expectations. How we see ourselves and understand the world can shift with new evidence and experiences. Like a fresh, juicy peach, these changes can inspire unprecedented creativity. Some may see this as innovation and adaptability, while others view it as sacrilege and propaganda threatening tradition. In today's ever-evolving culture, nothing will remain the same tomorrow. Embracing the energy of Peach invites a creative mindset to explore past life experiences and heal any lingering grief, trauma, or patterns. It encourages one to adopt an open-mindedness about life and work, empowering them to negotiate and advocate for themselves more confidently. This color also promotes diversity and inclusivity in one's relationship with culture and alternative sources of information. It reminds us not to take opinions as facts but to seek truth and authenticity. Use this energetic peach hue to shed light on deceptive practices and people who pressure you into conforming to their limited reality. Remember that conformity may provide short-term certainty but is fleeting as everything changes with time.

Orange - Creativity & Vitality

You are a creative being. Orange is the color of creativity and vitality because it's life itself. This attractive color energy springs you forward, and you instantly react to it. Orange is often used as an umbrella color for creative energy because it's playful and vibrant. Businesses usually accent their blue and green wellness programs with

Orange because it pops up and brings attention to important ideas. As for your life and work, Orange wants you to realize that you are a creative being. And not in the traditional artsy fartsy sense of the word. Being creative is about being alive, solving problems, and working with the mood of the Universe to attract experiences and things to you. Orange is also a color attributed to spirituality. Being awake and not enlightened doesn't matter in the context of being creative because it's all about contribution. It doesn't make heinous crimes and foul racism okay! Orange highlights loudly that life is a living, open, and active energy that we are responsible for using for good. Not greed.

Vitality isn't about getting by or living within your means. Everyone has a varied definition of what and who makes them happy. Unfortunately, the pursuit of happiness isn't regulated, sustained, or measured by everyone's quality of life. It's rather cunningly distributed through discrimination and conformity, and should you color outside the lines of your predetermined label, vitality and creativity become more burdensome to believe in. You lose your sense of control in a corrupt class system.

Orange is a strength that honors the individual and the collective. The shadowy side to this color can remind you of changes made in your life where you had no voice or say. Choices are limited because of the scarcity of resources and education. You don't need to have what someone else must feel: purposeful or proud. You are enough. Talent goes to waste when we allow scarcity to creep inside our minds. We begin to cheapen our processes or settle for less because we don't believe we're creative or extroverted enough to carry this through. What about your current situation? Do you feel limited, small, and blocked because you don't have enough right now? What do you wish you had enough of? What story have you been repeating to yourself or others reaffirming the same outcomes?

Poverty serves no purpose. There's plenty to go around. Orange is constructive and meant to be used in times of crisis. When you have to make a choice, decide vitality over vanity.

Tangerine - Anticipation & Excitement

Tangerine is appearing for you today because you've forgotten what it's like to be excited. Excited energy keeps the momentum alive. It's similar to passion because it's active and alive. However, the essence of Tangerine keeps your energy in an eager and anticipatory state. Anxiety creeps in when you feel bored or choose not to get your hopes up because you barely allow yourself to feel committed to positive emotions. You want to be safe. Tangerine is here to shove your worries aside briefly and imagine what life would be like if you were living it as the most alive version of yourself that you can be. You are awake. It's not a chore to feel excited. Energy naturally is exciting; you're propelled forward when you tap into this color frequency. What are you looking forward to the most right now?

Does something feel sticky, or is Tangerine showing up in a challenging position for you? Too many extra loud efforts are being made, so the intentions are not received honestly and clearly. Overstimulation is why it's harder to feel confident with yourself now. You're distracted by the constant influx of ideas, options, people, and possibilities, and you're caught in a hamster wheel, unsure of how to make the next right move. Tangerine can be harnessed like a slingshot to shoot you over far distances; be sure to couple this color with your favorite purple to invoke transformation.

Some people choose roller coasters to get their thrills, others hook up, and you might enjoy the excitement in ways others may not naturally gravitate toward. This is okay. It doesn't make you better or them better for how they choose to feel excited and eager. Trust the chemistry in the conversation. Often, we carry expectations of a job interview or dating app only to make it about us and forget we're here to learn what the other party is bringing to the situation. This goes for the prospective employer and potential date. No one escapes the chemistry of excitement. Add Tangerine to put a little more bounce in your step and make you feel happier about what you're looking forward to. Other people's happiness doesn't define your happiness. Excitement is contagious. It's not your job to make or persuade others to be excited. Be excited when everyone else is bored as fuck.

Salmon - Overcoming Adversity

Your suffering isn't the same as another person's, and it's not the same as five years ago. Salmon energy is the color of resiliency and mastering victimhood. This tricky love color supports and reminds you of milestones and the journey you've been trekking or tripping on. Salmon isn't a weak-willed color and is not privy to only deep pockets. Adversity affects us all. We're only as good as our weakest link. But adversity or pulling yourself up from the bootstraps can become addicting. There are rewards in place that keep us playing small. Systems like welfare and social aid incentivize people to stay in that comfort zone because it's convenient. Salmon is appearing in your life and work right now to stop coddling your victimhood. You're a survivor, and you had better start acting like it. Rise like a phoenix. Stop apologizing for your history, your poverty, and your upbringing, and start writing a new personal reference point. This color helps you create a new normal for yourself and others. The biological lottery doesn't define your destiny. Your skin color doesn't diminish your desire to do good. You can be more than a creature of habit—more than a number. Adversity has been romanticized in society because we all, at some point, felt like or were the underdog. And we all want to win. It's just in our nature. Some of us work, and some of us play. Either way, no struggle is the same.

Salmon in the wild must journey through hardship and pass the drooling jaws of bears and humans to reach a fertile nesting place. Some Salmon are commercially farmed and never experience the wild unknown. Based on your life and work, has your experience been wild-harvested or commercially grown? Salmon's energy makes you question how hard you work to get here. What made it harder for you to get to this point? We tend to create drama if we don't feel adverse enough. You're not more worthy because you have more battle scars. The amount of pain, suffering, or number of ailments you have doesn't put you in first place above others. Some adversities we face are unnecessary and rooted in illusions and motives beyond survival of the fittest. Getting the wrong item in your online order isn't adversity. Having to pick up the kids at a different time is also not adversity. How could you turn an ant hill into a molehill instead of accepting that circumstances provoke your creative nature? You can choose to create more pain and suffering, or you can choose to build stamina, agility, and endurance as we all swim upstream.

Desert Sand - Awaken Your Creativity

Desert Sand is showing up for you because you're in an energetic space vulnerable to burnout and mismanaged resources. Often (for survival, no less), what we do and who we are is chosen for us. Look at the state of your reality currently, what aspects feel dry, scorched, bare, and forcing you to ration your emotions out of fear. Being reserved in times of great drought and stern strife makes sense. We want to preserve ourselves and the pride of the project or partnership at whatever cost necessary, even if it means bottling up our emotions to maintain the mirage of expectations. Desert Sand is an ancient color rooted in Earth that heals our perfectionism because of society's intense ideals to perform and create originality. You are unique, and there's no need to prove your worth. Deserts test our stamina and endurance to survive. When this color comes up in a reading, what part of your situation is under immense pressure to be perfect?

Don't be afraid to burn. Desert Sand speaks of renewal in our creative power. Instinctively, you create this situation by responding to it, so perhaps it's not a lack of passion but a lack of rhythm and resources, making it feel like you're in the middle of a sandstorm. Fortunately, you're not alone. Creativity comes with a caravan. Your destiny is to create through intent, actions, results, and improvements. Desert Sand asks you to reinvent how you look at yourself and this situation right now. It's an attractive color energy for improving the emotional and mental infrastructures fueling your identity and career. Think about what you typically eat, do, and say that might not reflect the oasis of your original gifts. Do you believe hoarding Facebook friends or material objects equates to self-confidence? The most courageous thing you can do right now is accept yourself. And take that you have the control to create the kind of self that isn't set in stone, for not even Gaia could expect to keep continents the same shape for billions of years. You may feel abandoned, angry, and apathetic about many things. Still, inside you, the cosmological flame keeps the sands of time ticking as you create your moments and identity evermore. You weren't made from nothing to be nothing. You were made from everything and all that there is so that you can be something. Make something, anything, that ultimately is the purpose of our collective human experience.

Aurignac - Energy of the Ancients

Aurignac is an archaeological commune in France dedicated to paleo-anthropology. This color is fascinating because it's found in ancient cave paintings, shavings of old relics, and some dinosaurs believed to have been this color. It's an old color, as old as dirt if you ask me. Aurignac is a tribute color to our ancestors. When it appears in a reading, it could indicate that a loved one is present and invites you to explore mediumship or build an ancestry altar in your sacred space. I've used Creedite crystals during rituals to communicate with the distant past and connect with my past lives. Your karmic history is partially your own doing. Some elements of your consciousness are embedded within your inherited consciousness. Patterns that your ancestors passed down to you are why free will is essential to our being. You are partially shackled to the altar your ancestors and relatives worshiped. If anything about the spectrum of oranges teaches, your creative essence is alive, and you can use it to access courage and happiness. Aurignac energy is grounding and an indication that you're coming full circle in your journey. Aragonite crystal gridding can help if you carry childhood wounds that no longer serve your adult self. This color energy stabilizes you in the moment of upset and trauma and enables you to communicate better in crisis.

Exploring natural history, anthropology, and paleontology arises because you have something to learn from history. Your DNA is an artifact of technology. Preserve it and safeguard your privacy right now because the rate at which society is evolving is outpacing your comfort levels to change. You may need to be more accurate with outdated systems and relationships that are karmically hindering your ability to heed your intuition. There are gifts from our past we should carry forward, but then there are archaic beliefs that keep us small, ignorant, and simple-minded regarding the depth and breadth of our humanity. Use Aurignac to gracefully approach industrial and informational revolutions with the understanding that not all generations prioritize or see the value in the situation at equal footing. Commune with your ancestors out of love; do not fear. Seek creative and conventional counsel as you explore the caverns of your spirit. Not all elders are wise - but all elders are human, just like you. Your age does not limit your spirit.

SOLAR PLEXUS CHAKRA

Yellow Sand - Give it Time

Be patient.

Buttercup - Sweet Surrender

Buttercup is a gentle yellow about your autonomy in the age of ascension. Your power center activates deeper when you disconnect from a judgmental society's physical, mental, and emotional expectations. Who are you without the bells and whistles? Who do you want to be without the shame, poverty, and gross mismanagement of time on this planet? Buttercup wants you to choose positive energy over the foolishness of falsified beliefs that corrupt. You may have reached the edge of the grass feeling greener, and that's ok. You can plant new thoughts and beliefs about yourself and the world. How have you given away your power recently by default? I remember when I would sit on the hill between my trailer home and the home my grandparents built in the 1970s. Sprinkled between jade green blades of grass stood pockets of sunshine yellow, and patches of buttercups danced between my toes as my siblings, and I would run, roll, and fly down the hill. Buttercup energy is showing up to restore your sense of surrendering to this world like a child would—the carefree, unapologetic zest for happiness.

What's so ugly and adult-worthy that makes you starve yourself from the riches and sweetness this world has to offer? Why must you beat yourself with responsibilities and ignore your power to see these as moments of magic? Surrendering to miracles is hard if you constantly drown yourself in the swamp of societal validation. It's neither beautiful nor holy for any human to be homeless, famished, or deprived of experiences. Buttercup warns you not to trade your joy for the lab-grown jewels of jealousy. Should you, though, have the liberty and freedom to turn the darkness inside out? Instead of chasing symptoms of your struggle that inadvertently reaffirm the need to struggle, how instead you chase joy. Fall into the lap of love. Pick a buttercup flower, hold it under your chin, and let that life of that tiny moment light you up from the inside out. No matter how fleeting the feeling of goodness may be, joy increases over time. You may think you must do this with others, but no one is self-made to build themselves up. Part of using this color now in your life and your work is highlighting the opportunity of having a group or a partner to lean on. Befriend positive energy. It's much easier in the long run if you don't allow waiting for the other shoe to drop to justify your habits for an acquired taste that's conventionally sour. And Buttercup, you don't need trauma for shock value or a struggle bus for camaraderie. You need to surrender to being alive.

Firefly - Illumination

Firefly yellow is a holy light of all the color cards that appear in a reading because it indicates synergy and enlightenment. Knowledge is power. Awareness is ascension. The ability to be yourself is so powerful in your life and career right now; through that presence, you radiate your natural luminescence. Firefly energy is not only a solitary dance with the divine. It sparks and makes you more attractive to find and communicate with your tribe, community, and platform. If you struggle to fit in or be seen as the best version of yourself, you can use this energy to detox your demons. This shows up in reading to consecrate your consciousness and help you integrate with a newly invigorated sense of belongingness in society.

In 2013, when I began to shine my light as a color psychology expert, I meditated to connect with my brand's spirit animal. I found myself at a beach, guided between the dunes and broken seashells by a trail of wispy fireflies. The entourage led me to an old abandoned lighthouse with eroded walls once designed to stand its ground to warn travelers of the jagged edges of landfalls. I climbed this lighthouse, unsure if it was safe, but carried a fierce commitment in the fireflies that summoned me here and eventually reached the top, where I conjured a clear crystal container. Then, I asked the fireflies' permission to enter the jar to power up this structure again.

Although I intended to find a visualization for my brand, I walked away, connecting with the animal that lives inside all of us. Firefly energy appears in readings to let me know that I am supposed to be reading this person's energy and that I am being guided in the right direction, even if the environment and circumstances look dire. Firefly energy is illuminating because it allows you to acknowledge risk and caution and to see, witness, and experience the unique sequence of power you possess in this cosmic universe. This color empowers and activates resilience from within instead of relying on outside forces to rescue or relax you away from your purpose. If you feel this color indicates some negative narratives or potential deception, you need to practice identifying red flags, warnings, and patterns more and find your abandoned beacons to mark where the land of ego meets the sea of your soul.

Goldenrod - Stay Committed

Golden Rod is the farmer archetype of the color oracle. This color pops up for you because it asks you to consider your cycles and seasons regarding investments and productivity. It also indicates that you may not see your power or potential because you're fixated on control. If farmer energy scares you, then consider this color like a project manager for your purpose. Once you acknowledge and accept a purpose-driven life, you must gather resources, plan, plot, and do the work necessary to write a new story for your life and work. This is one of the most demanding phases in our color journey because it takes you out of a wounded gut reaction and into a heart-centric approach to managing your daily life. And this color message never goes away. Say hello to the grind of being human. Golden Rod asks you to ride your plans through and stay committed to collecting more experience and lessons. Information is robust, so this is an opportunity to identify requirements and analyze similar triumphs and risks that others may have experienced before you. This road of being human has been traveled frequently, so consider what successful people you admire do daily to help you establish and stay committed to a positive and inspiring routine. Not all routines have to be boring. Commitments don't always have to feel like a chore or an obligation when you improve how you digest life through an empowered lens.

Let's talk about spiritual bypassing for a hot second.

Spiritual bypassing is what religions and self-help tycoons have used to justify piss-poor ethics and malignant morals. Golden Rod is not about staying small for the sake of whomever you feel inferior or indebted to or settling for less than because, as you'll eventually discover with this color, you have willpower. And it's your job to steward your soul path. We choose to be proactive (or reactive), and often, it means focusing on the most critical path and identifying equitable ways to compromise to make decisions and mitigate risk. I'm a certified project manager, and time, cost, and schedule are constantly mismanaged in life and work. So, it's vital that you understand that what you commit to can evolve as more evidence comes to light. Don't be afraid to confront people, places, and things where the compromises you're making or being forced to make are too steep to carry when it comes to your personal well-being, ethics, and morals. We often use work to distract ourselves from the spiritual lessons we need or push the blame on another to justify our ignorance, and that keeps you stuck in a rut because you're not willing to take responsibility for your power. Your body is a free enterprise. So, commit to light.

Gold - Abundance

One of the most challenging color energies to work with, Gold is everyone's go-to to feel rich, famous, seen, validated, and assured in their assets. Gold is culturally implicit to inspire holy energy, alchemy, endurance, and a means to expand your self-worth and self-image. If this color shows up for you in a reading, you must trust your Midas touch. Your power to attract people, places, and things into your life is only sometimes for pain or pleasure. The art of attraction is not cosmically designed for personal gain or materialism. Gold energy sparks ascension. It invites you to evolve your relationships with people, money, values, and natural abilities here on Earth. Gold is often sought after but hastily hoarded. The underbelly of this luminous color frequency speaks of accolade, accomplishment, and entitlement everyone can access; however, abundance is never the same. This is where we need to improve our understanding of self-worth as we over-commit to responsibilities or relationships only to hoard a handful of dopamine hits derived from instant gratification. Glitz and glamour are the sisters of illusion when integrating Gold into our minds and hearts. We become addicted to our own Gilded Age with little awareness for others and believe that others who don't achieve what we achieve get what we get or have what we have are less than us. And that's not golden. It's gratuitously arrogant.

Are you assuming you must acquire someone else's abundance to substantiate your attractive power? Is there a deep-seated belief that you are not of Holy energy and that your existence is insignificant? Or could it be a twinge of guilt that someone is destined to go without if you take what you want? I would be a fool if I suggested Gold is all gratitude and no grit. What we commit to creates our habits, and if you've been getting by on pity parties and cutting yourself down to size to balance other people's budgets, Gold will not help you expand or gain the abundance you desire. You're addicted to the chase of pleasing plutocracy. The adrenaline of proving your worth over and over again based on someone else's calculations and scarcity tactics. Gold is not a random ticket to inherit the baggage of someone else's gregarious imposter syndrome. Gold is life, liberty, and the pursuit of happiness created of, for, and by this straightforward truth, the connective tissue between our crown and heart: What you want, wants you. You are enough.

Sunflower - Expansion & New Opportunity

Sunflowers follow the path of the light. Some might stumble across this color card with high hopes and hubris and overlook a critical element to making things work. Often, we stay committed to our convictions and careers and don't see past the tall bodily comforts that show up in our lives, giving us intuitive impulses of there being more beyond our backyards. This color pops up to poke your pride with keen optimism to expand. It's time to see your situation differently, albeit from a higher vantage point, and offer a solution to make your space more comfortable. Your energy is overflowing. And it craves more scope to feed on more light. Where is the light in your life and work right now? What are you focusing on that might be taking your attention away from nourishing your roots or keeping you distracted from the bugs eating your leaves? A sunny disposition is admirable, but firmly planted on one side of the aisle is risky. Real growth takes surrendering to scale your scenery. In the darkest hours, this color may appear in your reading to reveal that you have an opportunity right under your nose, but you're daydreaming vigorously and infatuated with an ephemeral escape from the potential grief and pain you might feel if you make a move.

Resting on our laurels for too long procrastinates our living potential. Rest and rejuvenation are required to thrive. However you look at needing more time, we become idle in our identity, which we curate for ourselves and our families. Sunflower invites you into a midsummer dream, a temporary gig, or a late-night hookup because we want to feel wanted and new. We want to feel our work is anything but dull. We look to make light of our cage and forget what the world feels like when we flex our wings. Sunflower is here to help your inner child heal into maturity. There is plenty of light to rejoice in, so this color card transforms your imposter complex of comparing yourself to others. It gives you a kind warmth to feel at peace with your growth. Being present with yourself. It serves no one when you stay in toxic environments for appearances and upkeep. A friend once told me, after I was homeless, that I'm a commodity and not an oddity. For most of my life, I never felt quite like anyone and carried guilt and shame for moving so much. It was not until a bus ride, seeing a yard full of sunflowers, that I realized that my mobility and openness to seek the light was my greatest strength. I follow the light even when it asks me to leave the darkness behind.

Expansion is kind.

Constriction is blind.

El Sol - Deserved Reward & Purpose

El Sol is the sun card in the deck, which resonates with traditional tarot messages surrounding optimism and positive energy. It's the source of warmth, light, and nutrients to help natural growth. Without the sun, none of us would exist. One element to highlight strongly with this color energy is that most religions and doctrines want to overlook your power. So often, we crave more control in our lives and don't know how to rise out from the shade of socioeconomic oppression designed to keep us small and ignorant. This color activates the core battery of your existence. You exist; therefore, you deserve the richness and abundance life offers. Period. There is no work or effort on your part to exude positive energy. You are not more worthy if you are addicted to working hard or believe vehemently that hard work pays off. Sometimes, you don't get paid in hard, cold cash for all the work you put on your plate. So, your reading asks you to set a new baseline for what makes you happy and not complacent in your life and work. The sun's radiant energy cuts through the darkness and shines without permission. Have you been asking others or the outside conditions to validate your mood or how you've been choosing to see your life until this point?

Be careful not to burn through all your resources out of desperation to feel validated. This behavior may look like overspending, ignoring deep wounds with food or relationships. It also may show up in your life if you find yourself consistently being reliable in the social circle or a work setting and always saying "yes" because you fear saying "no." El Sol reminds us that rewards come in all shapes and sizes. If you consciously and mindfully acknowledge what a person, place, or thing rewards you, that will make showing up in your life and work a thousand times more fulfilling. You recognize your likes and dislikes and can fortify your boundaries appropriately. Find your solar flare and lean into a purpose right now that lights you up instead of a role that squashes you into a small shoebox. When you realize you have a purpose and deserve your happiness, you experience self-enlightenment. This color expands your solar plexus chakra to help you gain the strength to carry your happiness with conviction, not corruption. If you haven't felt appreciated lately, compliment others and volunteer for projects that lighten you up. Again, we want to transform your inbound self into a confident, creative outbound being with much to offer to conversations and society.

Pumpkin - Dance for Life & Love

Pumpkins are often associated with the harvest season, symbolizing abundance, prosperity, and nourishment. They are a staple in many autumn festivals and celebrations, notably Halloween and Thanksgiving in the United States. I've used pumpkins in transformation rituals every year because the life cycle of a pumpkin, from seed to mature fruit, symbolizes growth, transformation, and renewal. This can reflect personal development and the idea of reaping the fruits of one's labor. The one spell I get excited to craft is my pumpkin spell for love and abundance. It's taking a pumpkin and using it in honor of the Yoruba orisha, Oshun. For more information about Oshun, I encourage you to read Vivian Carballo's[1] article about the lore and legend of Oshun. It's a tale about the lessons of hoarding revenge and true love. Oshun is a prominent deity in the Yoruba religion, associated with water, fertility, love, beauty, and wealth. She is often depicted as a benevolent and compassionate goddess who brings prosperity and joy. In Yoruba rituals, pumpkins can be used as offerings to Oshun. The fruit's abundance, fertility, and protection qualities resonate with Oshun's influence domains. Offering a pumpkin can be seen as a gesture of seeking her blessings for prosperity and love. The rich, vibrant color of pumpkins (typically orange) can symbolize the golden hues often associated with Oshun, frequently depicted in yellow or gold attire, representing her radiant and life-giving nature.

When the Pumpkin card appears in your reading, it is tied to harvest and abundance, naturally leading to celebration themes. Dancing, especially in harvest festivals, expresses joy and gratitude for the bounty of life. In this context, the pumpkin symbolizes the fruitful rewards of hard work and the celebration of life's blessings. However, the symbolism of pumpkins goes beyond their physical attributes. Just as pumpkins are often shared and enjoyed communally, they symbolize the sharing of emotions and the unity of people coming together in love and harmony. This communal aspect of pumpkin consumption is closely tied to the practice of dance, which in many cultures is a powerful medium for expressing love and connection. In ceremonies dedicated to Oshun, dance plays a significant role.

---

[1] Vivian Carballo, "The Legend of Ochun and the Pumpkin," South Florida SunSentinel, 2/19/1998.

Devotees often perform dances to honor her, invoking her blessings of love and fertility. The pumpkin complements these rituals as an offering, enhancing the symbolic representation of life and love through dance.

When Pumpkin is reversed or challenged, this color wants you to stop comparing your worth. You are enough. You don't need to steal or copy someone else's life or belongings to feel beautiful. If Pumpkin shows up, it's time to dance beyond your imposter complex. The inertia you think might be because you're outsourcing your joy, failing to put a handcrafted spin on your projects, or fearing your luck is running out, and you must escape the ballroom at midnight. Do you fear you won't be loved or admired if others know or see the real you? Stop throwing your pearls to swine and protect yourself from falling into the traps of identifying your self-worth based on the misfortunes and mistakes you've made in life. Don't be afraid to dance the struggle off.

Honey - Sweeten Your Approach

Honey holds deep symbolic significance across various cultures and traditions. Its relationship to deities associated with bees, such as the Greek goddess Melissa and the Yoruba goddess Oshun, further enriches its meaning in your color readings to bee deities and how it represents a sweeter approach to life. Honey is a universal symbol of sweetness, pleasure, and delight. Its rich, sweet flavor is associated with enjoyment and the good things in life. Known for its medicinal properties, honey symbolizes health, healing, and nourishment, providing comfort and reassurance. It is often used in traditional remedies and is celebrated for its ability to promote well-being. Bees creating honey is seen as a miracle of nature, symbolizing abundance and prosperity. Honey's golden hue is often associated with wealth and richness. Due to its natural purity and the industrious nature of bees, honey is also seen as a symbol of purity and sanctity. It is often used in religious rituals and offerings. It's one of the key ingredients in my pumpkin spell for love and abundance.

Melissa is a nymph in Greek mythology associated with bees and honey. Her name means "bee," and she is credited with discovering and teaching the use of honey. Melissa's connection to honey emphasizes the themes of nourishment, knowledge, and sweetness. As for Oshun, the Yoruba goddess of love, fertility, and fresh water, not only is pumpkin a sacred tool to connect with Oshun but so is honey. Honey is one of her favorite offerings, symbolizing sweetness, love, and the pleasures of life. Oshun's use of honey in her rituals highlights its importance in promoting love and healing.

Have you heard the saying about catching more flies with honey than vinegar? You attract more with sweetness instead of a sour disposition, although social media is proving to be a swarm of rage-baiting wasps. When it comes to your power, use this color to appear more approachable and influence likeability. Honey's sweetness encourages an optimistic outlook on life. A sweet approach means focusing on the good, savoring life's pleasures, and cultivating joy and gratitude. Your reading reminds you to stick with kindness, compassion, and the importance of caring relationships. Honey also symbolizes abundance and prosperity. A sweet approach to life involves recognizing and appreciating the abundance around us, whether in relationships, opportunities, or experiences.

When Honey is negatively influenced, or you swallow your pride in a highly frustrating situation, recognize that you might feel vulnerable and overwhelmed like a fly stuck in a sweet blob of made-up expectations. When you work with honey, say for a honey pot spell or use honey in your tea while planning your New Year, be mindful that honey is sticky and invokes qualities, ideas, and stubborn intentions you want to keep front and center. What lengths will you go to preserve appearing polished and perfect? Do you want to stick to a bittersweet hivemind mentality or find freedom in combing your way past conformity into a state of individuality and creative democracy?

Honey is the color of brand appeal and marketability. What hurts most are the forgotten details; those seemingly small aspects can make or break an opportunity if left unattended. What feels like honey oozing from those juicy Winnie-the-Pooh lips when you look at your life and work? What's worth licking your fingers over? Have you considered how others harvest your energy, time, or knowledge? Do you feel exhausted giving your all and not experiencing the sweet side of life because an assembly line of algorithms, conformists, and tacky aesthetics litter the path?

Honey is a powerful color energy; its most significant lesson is understanding and attracting the power in our nectar—your secret sauce of what you came to this planet to do. You want to be a busy bee, not a busybody now. Don't get distracted trying to chase after every flower already picked. Honey provides essential nutrients and energy, symbolizing nourishment and the sustenance necessary for life. It reflects the idea of being nurtured and supported, both physically and emotionally. The production of honey involves the collective effort of the bee colony.

This represents the importance of cooperation, teamwork, and community in achieving common goals and creating something valuable. Honey production depends on the delicate balance of ecosystems, including flowers, bees, and their environment. This symbolizes maintaining harmony with nature and within one's life. The sweetness of honey is often seen as a reward, symbolizing the fulfillment that comes from hard work, dedication, and perseverance. It encourages a mindset of seeking and appreciating the sweet rewards of life.

In integrating the symbolism of honey into a broader perspective on life, we see a multifaceted symbol that touches on various aspects of human experience:

- **Sweetness and Joy:** Encouraging the pursuit and appreciation of life's pleasures and delights.
- **Health and Healing:** Emphasizing the importance of physical and emotional well-being.
- **Abundance and Prosperity:** Inspiring a mindset of abundance and recognizing the rewards of hard work.
- **Purity and Sanctity:** Promoting the values of purity, integrity, and sacredness in life.
- **Community and Cooperation:** Highlighting the significance of working together and supporting each other.
- **Balance and Harmony:** Encouraging a harmonious relationship with nature and within oneself.
- **Reward and Fulfillment:** Valuing achievements and fulfillment from dedication and perseverance.

Honey is more than just a sweet substance produced by bees; it is a powerful symbol with profound meanings related to joy, health, abundance, purity, community, harmony, and fulfillment. These qualities make honey a meaningful metaphor for a rich and rewarding life. This is the main buzz for the honeycomb design on the back of the color cards.

Legion - Be a Friend or Ally

Do you have the support you need right now? Legion is coming into your life to share news about being a friend and seeking a friendship. Delegating and outsourcing our energy isn't always the best course of action, but when we need to vent to our best friend or network to grow our brand, we must accept that seeking support from others isn't selfish; it's selfless. It's a gift. It allows others to add to their karma banks and gives kindness and charity a chance to show up. When we need help, we must ask for it, and when we do, the universe knows how to pull its resources to make a shift happen. After all, life responds in kind to your mood. Even if we falsely believe we are alone or must do it alone. Legion is a golden amber honey hue that reminds us that we have the power, authority, and autonomy to invoke co-creativity. This life force could come from more than one place or person. It's asking you to be more open to others' opinions. To merge with altruism. Put your ego on hold for one minute and allow yourself to breathe into those who walked this path before you and walk alongside you (even if you think you're the only person going through this right now). Connecting individual people, concepts, or details for a common goal or intention might be the social juice that your soul needs right now. You're being called to create a movement. Feel momentum. Take your share of the pie. There's plenty to go around, so don't be afraid to give up for fear of not getting the same in return. An outsider's perspective might be the missing ingredient to crack the case. Find a mystic or holistic practitioner to listen to your story and allow their prowess to provoke the next steps. Figuring out your ride-or-die values is essential to finding your tribe, which, in turn, influences your vibe. And vice versa, your vibe attracts your tribe. You're on this cosmic loop cycle right now, trying to figure out your vibe and allowing others to reflect that higher consciousness. This is the work. You are learning to be the friend you need and allowing the Universe to be an ally to your cause.

Alternatively, Legion could signal that you have a traitor in your midst. Other colors in the reading will offer more guidance if this is the case. Bad friendships happen—a run-in with your ex. People you no longer talk to because of bad blood and drama are the reversed meaning of this color. Falling outs are wholly human and normal. And if you've been carrying grudges and miserable over bygones, join the club. I'm no stranger to friends that eventually became strangers. It would help to read the poem *"A Reason, A Season, A Lifetime" by Brian A."Drew" Chalker.* When Legion appears in a reading, it's a challenge for you to orient your individualism with the communal spirit of the collective. You might have been masquerading with a "me vs. them" bravado, alienating yourself from others and making it harder to be your friend. There should be a masterclass on being a friend, but it's not always so black and white. You could be the traitor sabotaging your inner circle with silly beliefs and fears rooted in scarcity.

There are advantages and disadvantages to being part of a group. It's this balance that keeps the creative life force flowing. The color energy of Legion is asking you to pull yourself by your bootstraps and not forget others who have inspired you and walk this path with you. Whether you just started or carry veteran status, we must not alienate others based on loose labels. Legion is a color of collaboration, not confrontation. And we must take responsibility for what we bring to the table, even if it means we must learn to share our successes and mistakes with others. As a species, we are one of many.

HEART CHAKRA *Part I*

Pale Lime - Gentle Healing

After a run-in with confrontation, drama, negativity, or just seeking respite from the extroverted reds, oranges, and yellows, we can find solace in the calming pools of Pale Lime. A return to nature over nihilism that the root, sacral (navel), and solar plexus chakras constantly battle. Pale Lime is a color that invokes gentle healing. It's a healing that happens over time. Karmic healing. It works similarly to repeating your favorite song in the background while you work, play, and zone out. It taps into the Akashic records of your incarnations. Your consciousness is on a rinse & repeat cycle with this color energy.

Before navigating deeper color energies associated with the heart chakra, Pale Lime is a light introduction to preface your relationship with masculine and feminine energy. Orienting yourself with this interconnectedness will help you read your color cards more objectively and openly so that your intuition can be unfiltered.

All colors are both masculine and feminine. Their application and experiences may shape your overall impression of associating colors to represent specific people in your life and their personalities. Taking colors based on corporate imposed messaging and heteronormative gender constructs limits your understanding of the real force behind understanding the Heart Chakra at large. All colors are androgynous by nature. This androgyny is essential as your soul is neither male nor female. Pale Lime is the color of genetics. DNA. Ancestry. Pale Lime is a return to that nonbinary lifeforce only to reincarnate into a new experience and reality. Before energy is upcycled, it needs to be recalibrated, so Pale Lime is a color of synthesis of expertise and rebalancing the karma and dharma of your existence. This limitlessness is a gentle process that suspends animation so that ideas, concepts, thoughts, words, and art can be cultivated. There's so much raw potential in Pale Lime, and when it appears in a reading, it asks you to mend, repair, restore, and resolve any imbalances that may be occurring. It's a color of holistic wellness. Not everyone likes neon green; the vibration could be overstimulating and obnoxious, so Pale Lime is a softer, invigorating version where that brings messages about adaptability and fostering quality over instant gratification.

Pale Lime is a color of attunement. And when it appears hindered or reversed, it's a message about desperation for quick fixes and faster response times. There's a drawback to jumping back into things too quickly if you're not ready, and there's an equally damaging response to simply stagnating and not taking any action out of fear. Pale Lime wants you to know you're here to heal on Earth. Heal yourself and others. How you heal is entirely up to you. But not all solutions on the surface are served with the purest of intentions. Pale Lime's challenge is to repair, mend, and distill information organically. Still, so much of our world today is bombarded with information overload, extraneous stimuli, and environmental and psychic pollution, making it challenging to heal ourselves and evolve our humanity gently. However, this color dawns evolution, and like stepping onto land for the first time, evolution didn't happen overnight. Neither is your healing journey. It's an aura of attunement and holistic collision of powers, chemicals, bio-divergent processes, genes, and universally androgynous matter and information to regenerate and renew.

Luna Moth - Goddess Ishtar & Fertility

The epic love story between Ishtar and Tammuz in ancient Mesopotamia is one you should look up. Luna Moth is a color that comes into reading when you must ask yourself how far you will go for love. Our descent into darkness often teaches us profound truths about our essence when we reach rock bottom. No matter how much bullshit and hoops one must go through, nothing could ever touch the incredible power of your creative vibration here in the Universe. You are here to journey to hell and back so you can understand your strength and conviction to create a fertile existence. This color energy speaks about dream walking, astral projection, and sleep protection. Often, intrusive energies gnaw at our minds and hearts when we sleep, so how are you protecting yourself at night? The energy of Luna Moth asks you to embrace your evening mother, perform moon rituals, petition Ishtar, and work with Luna Moth as a spirit animal to help you transform during the witching hour and as you work on understanding your shadow self.

Adversity isn't a walk in the park. It takes real grit and spirit to traverse the most challenging terrain of change in our lives. Luna Moth is here to plant the seeds of possibility while you sleep and celebrate contrast. Balance is vital, and any overzealous addiction to the macabre, death, decay, rot, or poison could be counterproductive, so use the shadow work with care and intrigue. Luna Moth is a messenger who releases what no longer serves you. It's asking you to choose something or someone new. This unorthodox color energy helps us synthesize data of our actions and encourages us to respond to change and death meaningfully. This color also inspires us to spot an underdog in the situation and break the stereotypes imposed by the status quo.

Fertility is a word in our world that seems to be pigeonholed into women-only circles and baby-making. But the word comes from the Latin root word "*fertilis*," meaning bearing abundance and sustaining vigorous and luxuriant growth. To bear means to carry the weight of something. You bear creations, ideas, emotions, and existence, so you are fertile despite your age, gender, career, or religion. We seem to get stuck in pragmatic loops around our power on this planet because pretending our prosperity is out of reach is simpler. But truthfully, our life force is inside us.

And we don't need to be fertile in every sense. All yourself to strip down to the bare-naked truth of yourself, and you'll find love there without labels. Luna Moth wants you to let go of the vanity of your vigor and embrace the reality of your rigor.

Sage - Wisdom

Old wives' tales. Anecdotes. Guidance from grandparents. Sage is a color of lived experience. It's also a color asking you to seek professional advice and counsel. No one else is going to do the work for you. You can't cheat your way out of this situation. Sage is a color that invokes trust in others and reminds you that your words and actions matter. When Sage appears in a reading, your reputation is under review. This is a color of discernment and judgment. Do you feel others treat you deliberately in a specific way on repeat? Telling you the same stuff over and over? Sage is showing up right now because it's a color of repetition. You may be making the same mistakes twice. You are caught in a cyclical pattern holding you back from your potential. The nagging you're getting from others is an indication from the Universe that you are living and acting out of alignment with your true self. The nagging stops when you step into your true self.

Allowing authority to guide you and influence you isn't a singular assault on your autonomy as an individual. But an invitation to have a heart-to-heart conversation. It's a reminder that this world is a collaborative environment, which means others will always be watching you and offering unsolicited observations for your review. It's up to you not to take things so personally or respond righteously.

Respecting our elders in society matters. And wisdom doesn't always have to come from old people or establishments. Wisdom is an organic interplay between instruction and instinct. This earth color will protect and ground you while you navigate external judgments and perceptions. It helps you appear more approachable.

Sage is a color that prompts you to consider reviewing people, places, and things that could be wasting energy. A return on investment is essential right now. Are the people, places, and things in connection to your current situation positively adding or subtracting from your higher well-being? Make a list of the pros and cons. If you do this, then what will happen? Get creative with figuring out the impact of your dilemma. What drawbacks immediately come up for you? I use a green pen when I'm wrapped up in if/then statements and pro-con lists. I savor lists because they help take all the stock inside my mind and put it on paper to see what I've been stewing on.

Self-growth and self-reflection are the most innovative things you can do for yourself and others. And like RuPaul says, "*Your fear of looking stupid is making you look stupid.*"

Mint - Decisive Action

Mint grows out of its sister color, Sage, when it comes to helping us make decisions. As an Aries, I love action. It means movement. Change. Flux. You are going with the flow. I was born amid chaos; color has helped me orient myself in fight-or-flight responses. Clear-headedness is key. Mint is an intelligent color for acting because it's about spearheading our destiny with deliberation. Before making life-changing decisions, we freeze, hiccup, and avoid any uncertainty because we naturally fear the unknown. Oppression and systemic discrimination have numbed our minds as people. And that corporatist indoctrination fears the masses mobilizing. Mint is a grassroots color of action that creates momentum. It's a color that gets you unstuck mentally. Mint is here to help make your situation more straightforward. Clarity is power. And with this power, you want to think clearly and act with intention. Allow the Universe right now to be your informant. What are your options? More information and data might be needed to decide on the next steps. Be cautious of information paralysis. Don't let the lack of information or data trip you up. Mint is showing up in your reading as an indicator that you may have been resting on your laurels for too long and too timid to act because your ego finds great comfort in not committing to people, places, and things for fear of losing control. This noncommittal angst may protect your ego in the short term but reduce your reward on the planet in the long term.

Mint is not asking you to make choices in haste or under duress. It's not asking you to get up and go now, but it invites you to recognize that you are still choosing by making no choice. Small, deliberate actions add up over time, and this could be about committing not too grandiose gestures but more minor, digestible acts that still make a difference over the long term. Mint wants you to act in a way that scales your success over long distances instead of always making quick, on-your-feet reactions to survive in the interim. These quick one-shot reactions may help now, but clear your mind, body, and soul afterward to recover more swiftly from the sprint.

Sprout - Learning Something New

Beginner's luck happens when you keep an open mind. Sprout reminds you to read the situation like an open book. Inviting others into the conversation to learn a new aspect or process that impacts the problem is helpful. You want to explore your life work with curiosity and avoid the pitfalls of being a know-it-all. Many educational brands and institutions build their aesthetic around green because it's about learning and development. But learning things takes time. A gestation period happens when we need more information and data to consume and delineate. Outcomes could change, so the flexibility you need right now puts open-mindedness at the forefront. Sprout carries a message of applying practice to the grind. The drudgery of day-to-day routine can bog down our minds, making us susceptible to anger and resentment. Sprout refreshes our perspective and puts us back in a spirit of open curiosity.

Alternatively, if Sprout appears in a reversed position or is hindered by negative aspects during a reading, it could indicate a closed mind and narcissism. How do you or others falsely believe you have learned everything to know about the situation? Sprout showing up negatively could indicate systemic issues preventing learning and knowledge from being disseminated openly and justly. Elite narcissist groups in corporate and academic settings could be limiting the flow of knowledge through archaic beliefs built on capitalistic supremacy and discrimination.

Your ideas and projects matter, so when you lean into Sprout, you should consider asking yourself what the takeaway is and what others can learn about you and your brand.

New Thyme - Inner Calm & Balance

Thyme is a magical herb. New Thyme is here to give you more courage and protection. So often, inner calm and balance are more complex to maintain or achieve because of outside forces and inside fears we have because of trauma. The state of the world is moving at such a rapid pace that marginalized people who want to live a happy and healthy life are finding it harder to maintain balance and experience calm. There are two kinds of chaos: Corporate Chaos and Natural Chaos. Corporate chaos is the sudden blow to our jobs when we are let go unexpectedly. It is often planned to promote a particular agenda - frequently financial. Natural Chaos is simply Mother Nature doing whatever she can. Corporations work as a collective group of privileged individuals who believe in their hubris over life—proselytizing control over Mother Nature or the Universe itself. Chaos is at odds with itself; you're caught in the middle like a child stuck between a rock and a hard place. New Thyme is here to mitigate this chaotic narcissism, giving you the strength you need right now to purify your social circle and mindset.

Working with this color energy inspires a preventative approach to shitstorms. It probably won't avoid the chaos altogether, but it will support you while you meander the Monday melancholia. Work sucks when you're told this is how things are done and expected to follow suit silently. New Thyme is also a color that supports us during grief and despair. You're asked to trust the process when you feel you have no control over the outcome. Keep your anguish to a minimum and suffer in silence. New Thyme doesn't want you to suffer. I often feel like suffering is conflated with settling because we believe that we are fundamentally insignificant based on what we achieve. We trick ourselves into living as shrinking violets because we constantly fear our strengths and power.

Corporate Chaos and Natural Chaos make it so damn hard to explore and enjoy tranquility. Shit happens. But not all shit gets to define you. Just because your life is chaotic doesn't mean you are a big nasty evil asshole. This is where I diverge from the super puritanical approach to "your outer world is a reflection of your inner world." I don't take responsibility for Corporate Chaos and its propaganda to profit from our suffering, our division, and our fear. I do, however, take buckets of responsibility to fight for peace. You are circulating energy around conversations to embrace equity and equality. New Thyme is here to create a matrix of peace, not war.

Chalkboard - Develop Your Destiny

In preschool, I had trouble learning to tie anything and everything. So much so that instead of playing during breaks, the teachers sat me at the table and practiced tying laces on a Chalkboard green square. I eventually learned to tie my shoes, but it wasn't in preschool, but on the couch in the trailer home with my mom's sneakers, which had some dog poo on the bottom. Nothing motivated me more than the smell of shit pulling on my nose hairs and the stern look on my mom's face. Fearing the wrath of my mom was a sign of respect. I love my mom, and I love that learning something so ordinary made such a mark on my approach to developing my path. You see, life served and continues to serve my ass. It must be the Aries sun and Capricorn moon in me, but I was born to blaze my trail. Chalkboard signals you to get out of the bubble of someone else's lecture and find your voice.

I remember another time when Chalkboard energy was crucial to developing my destiny. In high school and during community service hours (we completed hours to earn rewards and credit), I chatted with our German language teacher to discuss creating my language. Little did I know that I was attracted to language because the one language I knew best was color. Because of these early learning experiences, I seized my day and created *The Color Mage Oracle*. I share this with you because you're here to make something, maybe not like a writer or a painter per se. But your existence is creative energy. You go outside the house, buy, eat, and talk with other people, all of which is a form of collaboration with the Universe. You are developing your destiny because you are willpower incarnate. Yes, there are systemic processes, influences, and people that could circumvent the quickest and easiest path for you, but life isn't easy. Rich people and poor people inherit tradeoffs. I don't think we need to have either rich or poor, but I digress.

Chalkboard displays multiple pathways to get you where you want to feel and be. It's like that moment in *Ted Lasso* where he suddenly has an epiphany about improving his team's natural talent and abilities. We can reprogram our animal brains to achieve wild, unfurled dreams with a simple change in our mind's geometry. We all could have been born in better situations. But we weren't. Accept it. A silver spoon or the correct zip code doesn't define your destiny, nor does it tarnish you as a person. You are valid. Real. And deserve to love and be loved in return. Listen, I come from food stamps, trailer parks, homelessness, domestic violence, and many bouts of adversity, but I'm still stubbornly devoted to my core truth that love, light, and color are our collaborative vehicles to reaching enlightenment, peace, and new worlds. It's our shared destiny.

Spirit wants you to make plans, but don't be afraid to erase them for new ones. Your destiny is not set in stone. You are not obligated to carry your family's expectations of you. And you certainly are not destined to work and live in poverty forever. So, make a plan to redevelop the plot of your story and change the direction of your projects.

Jade - Act Now

Jade is a precious stone revered in many cultures and carries profound symbolic meanings that resonate with themes of action, decisiveness, and protection. Its rich green hues symbolize vitality, growth, and the eternal cycle of life. In various traditions, jade is seen as a talisman that encourages its bearer to take action, overcome procrastination, and pursue their goals with determination and clarity. In Chinese culture, jade is considered the "stone of heaven" associated with purity, virtue, and moral integrity. It is believed to possess protective qualities, warding off negative energies and promoting physical and spiritual health. Jade artifacts, such as jade-sculpted emperor seals and ritual objects, have been used throughout Chinese history to symbolize authority and divine power, urging leaders to act with wisdom and decisiveness.

When Jade appears in a reading, spirit wants you to prioritize acting and learn when to apply passivity to the situation. Jade is also the color of luck, which can be invoked more easily when you feel protected. Foo Dogs, also known as Fu Lions or Shishi, are mythical creatures that serve as guardians of Buddhist temples and households in Chinese culture. These lion-like statues, often carved from jade, symbolize protection, power, and vigilance. Traditionally placed at the entrances of buildings, Foo Dogs ward off evil spirits and harmful influences, ensuring a safe and harmonious environment. Foo Dogs' fierce expressions and commanding presence remind us to take decisive action to protect one's physical, emotional, or spiritual domain. Their association with jade further enhances their protective qualities, linking them to the stone's attributes of courage, perseverance, and proactive behavior.

Should Jade be negatively influenced or challenged in your situation, then there's an element of procrastination. You can work with Green Tara, a beloved figure in Tibetan Buddhism who embodies the essence of swift action and compassionate intervention. As the goddess of action, Green Tara is often depicted seated in a readiness posture, with one leg extended, symbolizing her willingness to spring into action to help those in need. Her green color, mirroring the vibrancy of jade, represents active energy and the flourishing of life. According to myth, Green Tara was born from the compassionate tears of

Avalokiteshvara, the bodhisattva of compassion. She vowed to remain in the world until all beings were free from suffering. Invoking Green Tara through prayer and meditation encourages individuals to overcome inertia and procrastination, drawing on her dynamic energy to tackle challenges and achieve their aspirations.

Carrying or wearing Jade is believed to gain the courage and clarity needed to confront fears and overcome procrastination. As a crystal, Jade creates calming energy that helps focus the mind, dispelling confusion and doubt, and champions a proactive mindset. Across different cultures, jade remains a symbol of wisdom, justice, and the triumph of proactive measures over passivity. In Mesoamerican cultures, for instance, jade was highly prized and often used in rituals to invoke rain and fertility, emphasizing its connection to growth and renewal. The Māori of New Zealand also regard jade (Pounamu) as a sacred stone that embodies strength and protection.

In your reading, Jade indicates that action and protection transcend cultural boundaries, inspiring anyone to take charge of their destinies. Through the empowering myths of Green Tara and the vigilant presence of Foo Dogs, Jade encourages us to overcome procrastination, embrace our responsibilities, and act decisively. By integrating Jade into our lives, we can invoke its timeless wisdom and have the energy to transform our aspirations into reality with determination and some luck.

Spinach - Toughen Your Spirit

Spinach, a leafy green vegetable, carries rich symbolism and lore that reflect themes of tough love, natural strength, and fortitude. This nutrient-dense plant is renowned for its robust properties and ability to thrive in challenging conditions. It is a fitting message in a color reading to remind you of resilience, endurance, and reassurance as you press on with the situation. Spinach, like many hearty plants, faces and overcomes various environmental challenges. It can grow in cooler climates and withstand less-than-ideal soil conditions, reflecting its resilience and adaptability. This characteristic teaches us about the strength found in flexibility and the importance of adapting to survive and thrive. Spinach's hardiness is a testament to its robust nature and serves as an inspiration for enduring life's trials with grace and determination. Spinach's journey from cultivation to consumption provides metaphysical insights into the balance of strength and compassion, illustrating the complexities of toughness and how it applies to loving others and us.

Spinach is often associated with physical strength, famously epitomized by the cartoon character Popeye, who gains superhuman strength by consuming spinach. This makes Spinach's reputation and influences a hearty color that offers a grounded mood to sustaining power and puts you face-to-face with the practicality of the situation. Do you feel like the Universe has enrolled you in boot camp and asked you to army crawl through the obstacle course of decisions and expectations? This broad-shouldered color embodies tough love—providing essential lessons that may be initially unappealing to some but are crucial for growth and well-being. Tough love is a parenting, educational, and interpersonal philosophy characterized by discipline, strictness, and care. It involves setting firm boundaries and enforcing consequences to guide someone toward responsible behavior and personal growth. The concept is rooted in the belief that proper care sometimes requires being firm, even when it is uncomfortable for both parties. The aloof and stern exterior of a loved one might not reveal the whole story behind their brutish and blunt requests for you to clean your room, run an errand, or motives to get you outside of your comfort zone.

While this evergreen color appears negatively influenced in a color reading to wake you up to resilience and toughness, there is a paradox in the concept of being overly stern and disciplined. When applied excessively, tough love can become rigid and harsh, potentially leading to burnout or emotional detachment. The strength symbolized by Spinach must be balanced with compassion and understanding. Too much rigidity can stifle growth and create an environment where vulnerability and emotional well-being are neglected. Striking the right balance between being firm and showing compassion is crucial. Too much strictness without empathy can lead to resentment and emotional harm, while too much leniency can undermine the benefits of tough love. Misapplying tough love can lead to harshness and a lack of support. Ensuring that the underlying motivation remains genuine care and concern for the individual's well-being is essential. Implementing tough love can be emotionally taxing for both the giver and the receiver. It requires patience, consistency, and a willingness to endure temporary discomfort for long-term benefits.

Tough love is a powerful approach to fostering growth, responsibility, and resilience. By setting firm boundaries, enforcing consistent consequences, and balancing discipline with care, tough love aims to guide individuals toward positive change and personal development. While it presents challenges and requires careful application, its benefits in promoting independence, resilience, and personal growth make it a valuable philosophy in parenting, education, and interpersonal relationships.

Dragon - Power & Legacy

Dragons are one of the most potent and enduring symbols in mythology and folklore across various cultures. Representing power, strength, and legacy, dragons embody both the creative and destructive forces of nature. Their symbolism extends into the metaphysical realm, where dragons are revered for their protective qualities and transformative energies. In Chinese mythology, dragons are seen as benevolent creatures that symbolize strength, good fortune, and authority. They are often associated with water, rain, and agricultural prosperity. The dragon dance, performed during celebrations, embodies the community's collective wishes for prosperity and good harvests. European dragons are often depicted as fearsome, fire-breathing beasts guarding treasures or sacred sites. They symbolize raw power, danger, and the hero's journey. The slaying of a dragon is a common motif, representing the triumph of good over evil and the hero's attainment of honor and legacy. Japanese dragons, like their Chinese counterparts, are associated with water and are considered protectors of the sea and sky. They are seen as wise and powerful beings, often linked to the imperial family and symbols of divine power and authority.

Dragon's Blood incense, derived from the resin of certain plants, carries the potent energy associated with dragons. Metaphysically, it is used for protection, purification, and enhancing power. It is believed to cleanse spaces of negative energies, promote courage, and amplify spiritual practices. Using Dragon's Blood incense in rituals and meditation can help you tap into your inner strength and assert your authority while maintaining balance and integrity.

While dragons symbolize immense power and authority, their lore also highlights the paradox of empowerment. Having too much power can lead to corruption, tyranny, and isolation. The dragon's strength must be tempered with wisdom and restraint. The Dragon color card is akin to the Strength card in traditional tarot and shares a similar meaning. This balance is essential to ensure that power is used for the greater good rather than self-destruction or the subjugation of others.

In Mesopotamian mythology, Tiamat is a primordial goddess associated with the chaos of the sea and dragons. She represents the untamed power of creation and destruction. In the Babylonian epic "Enuma Elish," Tiamat's chaotic power threatens the gods, leading to a battle where Marduk, the storm god, defeats her. He creates the heavens and the earth from her body, symbolizing the harnessing of raw power to bring order and legacy. Tiamat's story encapsulates the balance of power and legacy. As a goddess of primordial chaos, her overwhelming power becomes a threat. Marduk's victory over Tiamat symbolizes conquest and transforming chaotic potential into structured reality. This myth illustrates the importance of channeling power wisely. Marduk's use of Tiamat's body to create the world signifies the enduring legacy that arises from balanced power.

When Dragon appears in a reading, consider exploring different aspects of yourself through role-playing games like Dungeons & Dragons (D&D). D&D is a highly engaging tabletop role-playing game that fosters creativity, teamwork, and strategic thinking. Players create characters and embark on adventures guided by a Dungeon Master (DM) who narrates the story and controls the game's challenges. The benefits of playing D&D include enhanced problem-solving skills, improved social interaction, and a platform for imaginative storytelling. To get started, new players can begin with the D&D Starter Set, which includes simplified rules, pre-made characters, and an introductory adventure. Joining a local game group or online community can also provide guidance and support for beginners, helping them dive into the rich, collaborative world of D&D.

Dragons are complex symbols that embody power, strength, and legacy across different cultures. They highlight the dual nature of power—its potential for creation and destruction. The metaphysical properties of Dragon's Blood incense resonate with dragon lore's protective and empowering aspects. The story of Tiamat and Marduk highlights the necessity of balancing raw power with wisdom and restraint to leave a lasting, positive legacy. In D&D, you can explore alignments and tell a unique story with others to get comfortable in positions of power and leadership. By understanding and integrating these lessons, you can responsibly harness your inner strength and authority, ensuring that your legacy has a constructive and enduring impact.

HEART CHAKRA *Part II*

Pale Pink - Gentle Love

To love and be loved in return is an essential theme that's coming up in your life right now. You are being asked to approach your work and people with gentle thoughts and understanding. Pale Pink encourages you to practice the artful prayer of Ho'oponopono. This ancestral Hawaiian ritual is designed to disempower the fear-based programming you've experienced over the years. The prayer has four aspects: repentance, forgiveness, gratitude, and love. Before receiving love, you must accept that you are worthy of giving love. Pale Pink brings you back to source energy to acknowledge your limits, take other people's limits, and ascend limits through the four aspects. Ultimately, you've been operating from an overwhelming headspace, and Pale Pink invites you to act, serve, live, and choose from your heart space. Putting much pressure on yourself and others doesn't prevent every bad situation. Neither is being in denial about your limited viewpoint on the situation. You are where you are with who you are, and that's all you need for now.

A considerable fear of avoiding love is the getting hurt part. We all want to avoid feeling any bit of confrontation, pain, and heartache. That's entirely fair. In this fear-based thinking, Pale Pink might also be challenged when reading because you keep a quiet thought somewhere in your headspace. An idea that says it's weak to love. People who choose their passion over the practical are at higher risk for pain. Newsflash: society has created systems to oppress the heart. Institutions have been designed to reward unkindness based on a metanarrative that limits people through the Darwinian theory of survival of the fittest. Natural selection isn't so natural when there are swarms of people collectively promoting Corporate Chaos, fear, tribalism, and other forms of toxic masculinity. Love is never weak. The only weakness our lives face is when we choose to live life and work based on fear – and fear alone. Pale Pink reminds us to err as humans. It's natural for humans to make mistakes. You're not less than because of it. You're not unworthy of things you want because of the fake news inside your head. Many down-to-earth people are doing their best. Let us try to remember this the next time we feel flustered in the grocery store, angry at our loved one, and wrangling with worrisome thoughts of how we think we're being mistreated – but it's not a personal attack on you. Be kind and rewind.

Dusty Rose - Your Love Has Aged

Once you figure out how to feel good about choosing to love in your everyday life, you come to the prowess of Dusty Rose. I wanted this color in the oracle deck because I knew we would face key existential points of our existence as we ascend through the colors and chakra system—our age. Dusty Rose is an indicator of maturity, timelessness, and companionship. It's the color of soul mates. This attractive color energy is an upgrade to its sister color, Ruby Rose, where we explore our soul path. Dusty Rose is an homage to every person (often older) who profoundly impacted my journey: teachers, elders, and friends with more years under their belt than I have. This color serves the same message for you in your readings. Does your situation seem to be influenced by an older mentor? Do you have a desire to be taken seriously and mature? Are you facing your agelessness with grace and acceptance? Have you always been told you have an old soul? Dusty Rose wants you to act your age, not your shoe size. In some instances, acting on the wage you want is also appropriate.

You're not getting older. You're getting bolder. More beautiful. As we age, we continually emerge in our evolution. So, we should transform and elevate our aging process with as much soul as possible. Aging doesn't diminish your beauty or your capacity to love. Of course, you can wear makeup, get work done, and buy the cutest outfit, but none can replace your resonance here on earth. You're making an impact. Every choice, decision, in-decision, opportunity, and regret is yours and yours alone. Dusty Rose appears in a reading to remind you to meet your future self through a guided visual meditation. Use your imagination to see what your future self, your higher self, your divine self, wants you to do or create.

This energy color speaks of you being mature enough to allow others (family, friends, and lovers) to be where they need to be. There's a profound beauty in allowing others to revel in their own experiences. You don't need to try and fix, protect, or control them constantly. If you always jump in to save them, how will they learn to do it themselves or find their strength? Dusty Rose reminds us that we can't always be other people's wings, but we can be the wind beneath them.

Pink - Let Love Enter

Kickass authenticity is the vibration of Pink. In *The Color Mage Oracle*, Pink is your no-bullshit rebel of a color that invokes love without apologies. There's a courageous pulse behind this color frequency that always felt good to work with, especially when you need a heavy dosage of radical self-love. Consider this the hot pink energy of the deck. It might now appear extra exuberant on the surface, but the message is still the same. How have you been shrinking yourself when it comes to love, and in what way can you truly expand your love muscle even more when it comes to showing up authentically? Pink wants you to embrace what's going on in your life now with rose-colored glasses. It contradicts your logical, pragmatic side, but this color frequency is unique because it asks you to walk barefoot in ways that release your inhibitions. Pop a rosé wine and relax. There's a flare of confidence when you work with Pink, and just like Lizzo's *Pink* (Barbie tribute) song, you are good enough, beautiful, and P-I-N-K: pretty, intelligent, never sad, and kool.

Realistically, it's okay to feel ugly, dumb, sad, and irrelevant. I felt and still feel all those things. When Pink appears in a reading, I find that Jann Arden's song *Pink* is a little more faithful to the essence of Pink's message if you are feeling lost, weak, and afraid right now and looking for that tender strength waiting to emerge. Should Pink appear in a challenging position in a reading, you'll want to reassess what your values are at this moment. What we care for and what we love is the most powerful law in the Universe that we should all abide by because love conquers all. Do you feel embarrassed by what or who you love? Pink wants you to love beyond shame and guilt. A caveat to this is that if you're experiencing violence and abuse, then you must, with confidence and courage, seek out help. It's safe to seek help. Loving yourself is not a crime.

As a cis-male, I found myself timid around Pink growing up. Still, I always felt authentically drawn to this vibration, and now I know why because it's an ultimate color that represents love that resonates with me deeper than gender constructs. It's not just for girls. And I want everyone to feel and experience the profound power of Pink. It's a color with attitude that gives us our ride-and-die core values. So, I highlight my notes and passages and wear pink lipstick because it's stunning, bold, and naturally, a don't give a fuck devotional to love. It says I have no fear; love is here.

Cotton Candy - Make A Wish

Experiencing the sweetness of life could fade as we age if we're not careful. Cotton Candy is coming up in your reading to help you rely on that hopeful, wishful, mystified feeling of getting what you want, but not always how you think it should be delivered. Humility and gratitude are the secret ingredients you need in approaching your life and work in this moment. Cotton Candy is a pink color that resonates with a child-like awe that amazes your adult programming. When you're feeling a little too stiff or overly dependent on micromanaging the outcome, you can use Cotton Candy to weave your imagination and resources to make someone else's dreams come true with your own. Charity is a quality that appears often when Cotton Candy pops up in a reading. It's a harmony of curiosity and humanitarianism that helps us stick to our heart center. Treat yourself moments so that you can treat others. This energy personifies receiving but also being open to gifting. Cotton Candy serves as a reminder not to be afraid to ask for what you want and adjust your headspace to imagine. Our imaginations are good at creating fear-driven narratives, but what would it be like if we used that energy to conjure bucket lists, wish lists, and vision boards?

Alternatively, overestimating your resources and leaning into self-aggrandizement. Yes, we all are superheroes, but not all superheroes wear capes. Cotton Candy becomes too sickly sweet or negligent of reality when we discredit the brutal reality of our limits or fall victim to our inner Icarus tendencies to fly toward the sun without protection. In ancient Greece, there was a boy named Icarus whose dad, Daedalus, was good at building things. Daedalus made a colossal maze for the king, but then he and Icarus got stuck in a tower or even the labyrinth because the king thought they might tell secrets. So, Daedalus made wings out of feathers and wax to escape. He warned Icarus not to fly too high or too low, but Icarus didn't listen. He flew too close to the sun, and his wings melted, making him fall into the sea and drown. That's where the saying "fly too close to the sun" comes from. You must be sure your projects and dreams are made of material and a mindset that won't melt. Unless you want to run a soap or candle business, melt away!

Lotus Pink - Goddess Quan Yin & Mercy

Lotus Pink is a color attributed to my favorite Goddess, Quan Yin. We have a special kinship that I've come to respect and encourage others to explore in their spiritual practices. Quan Yin is known for bestowing mercy, forgiveness, and compassion on our planet. Quan Yin, also known as Guanyin or Kuan Yin, is a prominent figure in Chinese mythology and Buddhism, revered for her embodiment of compassion, mercy, and wisdom. Her most famous story revolves around her selfless sacrifice for her father. In this tale, Quan Yin's father, a devout Buddhist, was unjustly accused of a crime and sentenced to death. Despite her pleas for mercy, the authorities refused to listen. In a desperate attempt to save her father, Quan Yin offered to take his place and endure the punishment herself. Touched by her unconditional love and compassion, the heavens intervened, and Quan Yin's sacrifice miraculously saved her father, thus demonstrating the power of kindness and selflessness.

One of the central themes in the stories of Quan Yin is compassion. She is often depicted as a compassionate deity who listens to the prayers of those in need and offers solace and guidance to the suffering. Her actions exemplify the Buddhist principle of Karuna, or compassionate action, which emphasizes empathy and kindness towards all beings. Another significant theme is the idea of enlightenment and spiritual liberation. Quan Yin is often portrayed as a Bodhisattva, a being who has attained enlightenment but chooses to remain in the world to help others achieve liberation. Her teachings emphasize cultivating inner peace and wisdom to overcome suffering and attain spiritual awakening. Overall, the stories of Quan Yin serve as a source of inspiration and guidance for those seeking to cultivate compassion, wisdom, and spiritual growth in their lives. She embodies the ideals of love, empathy, and selflessness, reminding us of the transformative power of compassion in overcoming adversity and fostering harmony and understanding in the world.

Lotus Pink personifies Quan Yin's power and presence in your life. You are showing your parents, children, and overall disposition toward the world - mercy. It's not always easy to loosen your iron fist logic around your grudges, but you can rise from your resentment like a beautiful lotus reaching the surface of the mud. Compassion and mercy are gateways to forgiveness and peace. Lotus Pink gives you the strength to see yourself beyond being a victim of your circumstances. It also is a color that resonates with the spirit of hot pink and magenta. Mercy can be the most radical thing you can give yourself and others now. Stepping off the hamster wheel of your trauma takes courage, and you are a human living in this technicolor reality of vibrations, so it's okay to admit you're still learning how to live in a state of compassion.

Eros - Spirit of Cupid

Eros, known as Cupid in Roman mythology, is a famous figure associated with love and desire. One of the most popular stories about Eros is his involvement in the tale of Psyche and Eros. In this story, Psyche, a mortal princess renowned for her beauty, inadvertently provokes the jealousy of Venus, the goddess of love. In retaliation,

Venus tasks Eros with making Psyche fall in love with the vilest creature on Earth. However, upon seeing Psyche's beauty, Eros accidentally pricks himself with his arrow, falling deeply in love with her. Instead of carrying out his mother's wishes, Eros visits Psyche secretly, keeping his identity concealed. Despite their love, Psyche is forbidden from seeing Eros' face. Doubtful of his intentions, Psyche lights a lamp to uncover his identity while he sleeps, but in doing so, she inadvertently causes him to flee. Driven by her love for Eros, Psyche embarks on a perilous journey to win back his affection, facing various trials and challenges orchestrated by Venus. Psyche's perseverance and dedication eventually prove her love for Eros, leading to their reunion and marriage. One of the central themes of this story is the transformative power of love. Eros' love for Psyche transcends boundaries and brings about profound changes in both characters, highlighting love's enduring and transformative nature. Another theme is the concept of trust and faith. Despite facing numerous obstacles and challenges, Psyche's unwavering belief in the sincerity of Eros' love enables her to overcome adversity and reunite with him. Overall, the story of Psyche and Eros illustrates the complexities of love, trust, and perseverance, emphasizing the profound impact that love can have on individuals' lives. As the god of love, Eros embodies the timeless ideals of passion, desire, and devotion.

Devotion and marriage are central values behind Eros in The Color Mage Oracle. Regardless of your marital status and dating experience, Eros celebrates your commitment to beauty and desire. Your relationship with beauty is unique. And when it comes to admiring others and pursuing people romantically, don't shy away from this pink pop of color. A drawback to Eros in your reading is that it appears in a challenging position, which signifies infatuation and shallow attractiveness. Two-dimensional and one-sided conversations are pinging your intuition currently. When reversed and challenged, Eros expands on the overstimulating side of our devotion to hero worship, idolizing and infantilizing our relationships—cue: breakups, divorce, and domestic abuse.

I'm no stranger to bad relationships. I've been bullied and know first-hand the trauma behind divorce and domestic violence. So, when I would date or even daydream about falling madly in love, those thoughts quickly turned dark and pragmatic. A cynical voice in my head told me that I needed perfection before I could find love. I sabotaged any moment of intimacy, romance, and socialization. It's what I craved. Desire is fickle when left to its own devices. I would get envious of seeing other relationships and public displays of affection at the mall, school, online, or even couples holding hands at an amusement park. Valentine's Day - barf. Yes, being a child of divorce does not curse your conception of what it means to love and be loved in return. I lived through some harsh traumatic experiences, but despite that darkness, I chose love. And in doing so, I focused on self-love as a devotional practice. A regimen that would restore self-confidence and self-worth.

And then, in the middle of the pandemic and a random intuitive hunch to put myself back on a dating app, I found my person—all the thoughts of needing to be a certain way evaporated. In an empty bar in Pittsburgh with an elderflower Cosmo in hand, I met the man that all my pumpkin spells, heart chakra meditations, and color readings helped manifest. It took time. However, my deliberate devotion to my spiritual practice helped me see my worth, attract my Cupid era, and allowed me to share my magic with someone else. Eros' message of Cupid speaks to pricking yourself first with your arrow to enjoy life and love your desire. This devotion doesn't stop when you find love and get married. If anything, your chakras merge and re-emerge through the multifaceted surface of life. Being human is kaleidoscopic. Choose love today.

Echinacea - Inner Strength & Immunity

Echinacea is a fascinating plant with a rich history and metaphysical lore. Historically, Native American tribes such as the Plains Indians used echinacea for various medicinal purposes, including treating infections, relieving pain, and supporting the immune system. European settlers later adopted its medicinal use, and it became popular in Western herbal medicine. Metaphysically, echinacea is associated with protection, purification, and healing. Some believe echinacea possesses spiritual properties that can ward off negative energy and promote well-being. It is often used in rituals and ceremonies to purify the body, mind, and spirit. Echinacea's vibrant purple-pink-toned flowers are said to represent strength, vitality, and resilience, making it a symbol of empowerment and renewal. In holistic healing practices, echinacea stimulates the body's natural healing processes and strengthens the immune system physically and energetically. Echinacea is prominent in traditional medicine and metaphysical practices and is revered for its healing properties and spiritual significance. Its history and lore remind us of the deep connection between plants and human well-being, both on a physical and metaphysical level.

In *The Color Mage Oracle*, Echinacea wants you to prioritize your health and immunity. Protecting your assets and securing your worth is at the forefront. Are you guarding your heart with care and grace? This color in a reading is an essential reminder to get professional insight into your heart's physical well-being. Your immune system is also vital to pay attention to, so what irritants and pollutants could weaken your strength? Working with this color mainly brings more awareness to our physical bodies. I remember this color often appearing in my health occupation textbooks in High School. Pink and purple anatomy figures represent the inner workings of the body systems. I think we forget that we are spiritual beings renting our physical bodies. When Echinacea appears, it's a great reminder to take care of our bodies in this situation you're inquiring about with as much verve and spirit as we do with other projects in our life and work.

Damascus - Self Love

Damascus is one of the oldest continuously inhabited cities in the world, with a rich history dating back thousands of years. It's a cultural and historical hub in the Middle East. It is probably the most pivotal pink in the color oracle deck, especially with current and ongoing events concerning the fierce contention between Arab and Jewish society. As we ascend collectively, we cannot compartmentalize our souls to the point of ignoring politics altogether. Marianne Williamson's presidential campaign efforts echo this sentiment. You don't leave your soul at home. Every choice and action you take either contracts or expands your soul's influence. Working with *The Color Mage Oracle* accentuates participation in your energetics, thus influencing the mood of your global perspective and life story. Damascus symbolizes Rosa × damascena, also known as Bulgarian Rose, Iranian Rose, or Arab rose, and correlates well with all the mystical, pharmacological effects, and metaphysical properties of rose.

Roses have been culturally woven into our pop culture and psyche. In a color reading, its power is instantaneous, as if you were standing in the Valley of Roses, inhaling ancient botanical history one petal at a time. As our planet faces a crisis of consciousness and continues to evolve, we must recognize the differences between self-love and narcissism. Self-love is the genuine appreciation, acceptance, and nurturing of oneself, encompassing care for both physical and emotional well-being. It involves recognizing one's worth, setting boundaries, and prioritizing personal growth and happiness. In contrast, narcissism is characterized by an excessive focus on oneself, often at the expense of others' feelings and needs. It involves an inflated sense of self-importance, a constant need for admiration, and a lack of empathy. In socioeconomic situations, self-love may manifest as individuals advocating for their rights, pursuing opportunities for growth despite challenges, and displaying empathy and support for others in similar circumstances. On the other hand, narcissism in such contexts may be evident in exploiting others for personal gain, disregarding the struggles of those less fortunate, and seeking validation through material possessions or status symbols rather than genuine connections. Identifying these traits involves observing how individuals navigate relationships, handle adversity, and contribute to their communities, providing insights into their underlying values and motivations.

Damascus is a healing color energy to add to your life and work because it raises the vibration with intention and gives radical self-love a platform to feel seen and heard. The challenges you're facing currently when Damascus appears in a reading often signal that narcissism is at play. It may be coming from the opposing party, or it's buried deep within your mindset out of propaganda, misinformation, and fundamental misconceptions about socioeconomic conditions and interpersonal relationships to race, geographic regions, and religion. Damascus wants you to lift the veil over your heart and see the beauty and contrast without fear. Rumi says it best:

Out beyond ideas of wrongdoing and rightdoing,
There is a field. I'll meet you there.
When the soul lies down in that grass,
The world is too full to talk about.
Ideas, language, even the phrase each other
Doesn't make any sense.

Smell the roses and take a break from the noise. Be vulnerable enough to quiet the world and connect on a soul level.

Clary Sage - Euphoria & Insight

Clary Sage is the color of imagination, multidimensional projections, and insight. It's the high you get when your curiosity hits, leaving you feeling exonerated and euphoric. It's a color of righteousness. A vibrant color of knowing our place with the Universe from the seat of our limited human perspective. This is the color of consciousness. It's messaging in a reading invites you to bring your attitude back to the vibration of ecstasy, a rapturous joy, and unadulterated knowledge of your own heart and mind that reminds you of your place in this Universe in relationship to all that was, all that is, and all yet to come. As we age, we lose sight of curiosity and get stuck inside echo chambers of limited human-centered opinions. Our past fears creep in and take control of how we see a situation—creating new fears that our present and future selves will have to learn to identify and overcome. Clary Sage reveals to you how you've been allowing your imagination and anxiety to run loose and wild. Unchecked by love and addicted to conspiracy and paranoia. In a creative sense, this curious chaos is welcomed so that interesting art, stories, and cultural aesthetics can emerge and entertain our human experience. However, this distracts us from our divine nature. Often, Clary Sage shows up because you are addicted to the anxiety of not knowing. Fearing the unknown and forgetting you are the Universe incarnate. Using your imagination to reaffirm self-doubt and ignorance. This shows up when we possess an insatiable urge for our limited opinions to be correct. Consuming mass media obliviously until our understanding of the world becomes one-dimensional, shallow, and compromised by filtered fragmentations of the truth.

You don't know all there is to know. And presuming you do because of the books you read, people you've met, or what opinions you've been told, it doesn't come remotely close to the ultimate source of knowledge: the Universe. Clary Sage invites you to put down what you think you know, let go of assumptions, and open your heart and mind to observing your situation from a higher perspective. In this omniscient ocean of consciousness, you can access your divinity and recalibrate to a state of joy when ignorance gets the best of you.

Eden - Old & New Order

The color of Eden is the intersection between tradition and imagination. The harmony of once was and what could be is distinguished in this color energy as we ascend higher and deeper into *The Color Mage Oracle*. In stories like the Garden of Eden from the Bible, Eden is often seen as a perfect, harmonious place where everything is abundant and peaceful. It symbolizes a state of innocence, bliss, and harmony with nature. However, when Adam and Eve disobey God's command not to eat from the Tree of Knowledge, they are expelled from Eden and subjected to curses, including pain in childbirth and having to toil for their food. These curses symbolize the consequences of disobedience and the loss of innocence. They represent the introduction of struggle, suffering, and hardship into human existence. Similarly, the connection to laws and rules in society can be understood. In a school and work setting, rules are put in place to maintain order, ensure fairness, and protect the well-being of people. Just like the laws set by God in the story of Eden, these rules provide structure and guidance for behavior. Breaking these rules can lead to consequences, just as disobeying God's command led to consequences for Adam and Eve. Overall, the symbology of Eden and its curses can be seen as a cautionary tale about the consequences of disobedience and the importance of following rules and laws to maintain harmony and order in society.

Forging new traditions and values aligned with harmony and abundance is not merely an act of rebellion; it's a profound declaration of personal empowerment and collective progress. Tradition, while often rooted in wisdom and cultural heritage, can also serve as shackles, constraining us within outdated norms and limiting our growth potential. By breaking free from the constraints of tradition, we open ourselves to the boundless possibilities of innovation, creativity, and self-discovery. Creating our traditions allows us to tailor our cultural practices to reflect our unique identities and aspirations. We no longer need to conform to societal expectations that may not resonate with our values or vision for a harmonious and abundant life. Instead, we can craft rituals, celebrations, and customs that uplift and inspire us, fostering a sense of fulfillment and connection.

Disobeying tradition challenges the status quo and paves the way for social progress. Many of the most transformative movements in history—from civil rights to gender equality—were fueled by individuals who dared to defy traditional norms and advocate for change. By daring to challenge entrenched traditions, we contribute to the evolution of society towards greater harmony and abundance for all. Embracing new traditions also cultivates a spirit of adaptability and resilience. Clinging blindly to tradition in a rapidly changing world can lead to stagnation and irrelevance. By embracing innovation and creativity, we adapt to new challenges and seize growth opportunities, ensuring continued flourishing in an ever-evolving landscape. Ultimately, disobeying tradition and creating traditions and values aligned with harmony and abundance is an act of courage and conviction. It is a declaration of our autonomy and a commitment to shaping our destiny. By defying tradition, we unleash our full potential as individuals and contribute to the collective journey toward a more vibrant, inclusive, and prosperous future for all.

THROAT CHAKRA

Lapis Lazuli - Enhance Self-Respect

Blue is a default favorite color for most people. It speaks to the depth of our place on this planet and enables us to feel authority. Lapis Lazuli is no different, and it's the base color of our blue hues because it's anchored in autonomy. Without a sense of self-individuation, you'll go mad with envy and riddle your soul with disease. When Lapis Lazuli appears in a reading, it encourages us to feel our authority in respecting ourselves and others through communication and leadership.

Communication, leadership, and respect are essential for effective collaboration and growth within any organization or community. Historically, leaders who mastered communication and earned respect often achieved remarkable feats in politics, business, or social movements. Effective communication fosters understanding, aligns goals, and inspires action, while respect cultivates trust, loyalty, and willingness to follow a leader's guidance. Leadership, therefore, becomes a symbiotic relationship between the leader and their followers, built upon a foundation of clear communication and mutual respect. Lapis Lazuli, a deep blue semi-precious stone, embodies the interconnectedness of communication, leadership, and respect. Historically prized for its vivid color and symbolic significance, Lapis Lazuli was revered by ancient civilizations for its association with wisdom, truth, and leadership. In ancient Egypt, it adorned the burial masks of pharaohs, symbolizing their divine authority and ability to communicate with the gods. Similarly, in Mesopotamia, Lapis Lazuli was used in royal adornments, reflecting the leaders' status and ability to command respect. Today, Lapis Lazuli continues to be valued for its beauty and metaphysical properties, which are believed to enhance communication skills, promote leadership qualities, and foster respect in interpersonal relationships. Just as this precious gemstone has been treasured throughout history for its symbolic significance, so do the principles of communication, leadership, and respect remain timeless pillars of successful human interaction and societal advancement.

Should Lapis Lazuli appear challenged in a reading, slander and libel are running the show. Disinformation campaigns and smearing opinions and ideas are the main motive behind the current conflict. Lies. Deceit. Betrayal. You may have vowed to a particular ideology or thought process in a situation that doesn't serve the entire truth of who you are meant to be. Echo chambers often ease the difficulties of thinking for ourselves. Lapis Lazuli wants you to feel unattached and more independent from peer pressure. You crave more autonomous truth-telling at this time, which can threaten others who see you as confrontational and self-preserving. You are a seeker of truth and want to lead with this power.

Autonomy, the ability to act independently and make decisions without external influence, shares a complex relationship with the rogue archetype, a character often associated with rebellion, independence, and non-conformity. The rogue archetype embodies a figure who operates outside societal norms, usually pursuing their agenda and challenging authority. This archetype can be found across various cultures and storytelling traditions, from the trickster folklore figures to the antiheroes of modern literature and cinema. At its core, the rogue archetype embodies the pursuit of autonomy. Rogues reject societal expectations and institutional authority constraints, choosing instead to chart their course and define their moral code. Their actions are driven by a desire for freedom and self-determination, even if it means operating on the fringes of society or engaging in morally ambiguous behavior. In this sense, rogues represent a celebration of individuality and the refusal to be bound by external rules or conventions.

However, autonomy within the rogue archetype is not always depicted as purely positive. While rogues may embody a sense of freedom and self-reliance, their pursuit of autonomy can also lead to conflict and moral ambiguity. Their disregard for authority and willingness to bend or break the rules can harm others or themselves. Additionally, the rogue's autonomy may sometimes isolate them from meaningful connections or support networks, leading to loneliness or alienation. While autonomy is a central theme within the rogue archetype, its portrayal often involves a nuanced exploration of the consequences and complexities of individual freedom.

Sapphire - Regenerate Community

Sapphire is a healing color for family rifts, culture shock, and global fallout. When this color appears in a reading, you want to ask yourself how the community interacts with your situation. Regeneration and community are intricately linked concepts, particularly in the context of social and environmental sustainability. Regeneration involves restoring, renewing, or revitalizing something to a better or more productive state. When applied to communities, regeneration refers to enhancing social, economic, and environmental well-being within a particular area or group. Here's how the connection between regeneration and community plays out:

Social cohesion: Regeneration efforts often focus on strengthening social bonds within communities. This can involve community events, cultural celebrations, or projects encouraging collaboration and communication among residents. By fostering a sense of belonging and connection, regeneration can enhance community cohesion.

Economic revitalization: Many regeneration projects aim to stimulate economic growth and development in disadvantaged or neglected areas. This can involve investments in infrastructure, job creation programs, small business support, or initiatives to attract new industries or businesses. By improving economic opportunities, regeneration can contribute to a community's well-being and reduce socio-economic disparities.

Environmental sustainability: Regeneration also encompasses efforts to restore and protect the natural environment within communities. This can include projects such as urban green spaces, sustainable transportation infrastructure, renewable energy initiatives, or conservation efforts. By promoting environmental sustainability, regeneration not only enhances the quality of life for residents but also contributes to the long-term health and resilience of the community. So, how does one regenerate their community?

Community involvement: Encourage residents' active participation and engagement in identifying regeneration priorities and solutions. This can involve organizing community meetings, forming committees or task forces, and fostering collaboration among diverse stakeholders.

Asset-based approach: Identify and leverage the community's assets and strengths, including cultural heritage, human capital, natural resources, and local institutions. Building upon these assets can help catalyze regeneration efforts and empower residents to take ownership of their community's future.

Partnerships and collaboration: Forge partnerships with government agencies, non-profit organizations, businesses, and other stakeholders to pool resources, share expertise, and maximize impact. Collaborative approaches to regeneration can facilitate collective action and leverage complementary strengths and resources.

Long-term planning and sustainability: Adopt a holistic and strategic approach to regeneration that considers community well-being's social, economic, and environmental dimensions. Develop long-term plans and strategies prioritizing sustainability, resilience, and equity, and regularly monitor and evaluate progress towards regeneration goals.

By implementing these strategies and fostering a culture of collective action and empowerment, individuals and communities can work together to regenerate and revitalize their communities for the benefit of current and future generations. Sapphire is a powerful color to apply when working on large-scale projects. It is also a central color to support leadership and promote trust among people investing their resources into a centralized project. Use this color to improve equity in your situation in a socialized and altruistic way.

Blue - Charity & Trust

The association of blue with trust and reliability is a complex interplay of psychological, cultural, and historical factors. Its calming effect, positive cultural associations, and widespread usage in branding all contribute to its perception as a color symbolizing trustworthiness and dependability. Blue is often perceived as calming and tranquil, evoking stability, serenity, and peace. These psychological effects contribute to the perception of trustworthiness and reliability. When people encounter blue, it can subconsciously put them at ease and create a sense of security, which enhances trust. Across many cultures, blue is associated with positive attributes such as loyalty, integrity, and dependability.

These cultural associations have been reinforced through various contexts, including art, literature, and religious symbolism. For example, blue is often associated with faithfulness and devotion in Christianity. Many companies and organizations choose blue as a primary color in their branding precisely because of its association with trust and reliability. Blue is frequently used in logos, marketing materials, and corporate designs to convey a sense of professionalism, competence, and dependability. This repeated exposure reinforces the link between the color and these qualities. Blue is commonly found in nature, particularly in elements like the sky and water. These natural associations can further reinforce the perception of trust and reliability.

The vastness and stability of the sky and the calming presence of water contribute to the positive connotations associated with blue. Throughout history, blue has been used in various contexts to signify trustworthiness and reliability. For example, blue ribbons or badges have been awarded to individuals for demonstrating honor or excellence. Over time, these historical usages have contributed to the color's association with positive attributes.

Charity is fundamentally about giving help to those in need, usually in the form of money, goods, or services. Its purpose addresses societal or individual suffering, poverty, or hardship, aiming to alleviate or eliminate these issues and promote well-being. Beyond mere material assistance, charity often embodies compassion, empathy, and solidarity, emphasizing the interconnectedness of humanity and the moral imperative to assist others. On the other hand, trust is the foundation of healthy personal, professional, or societal relationships. It involves relying on another party's integrity, ability, or character with the expectation that they will act in a predictable, dependable, and ethical manner. Trust fosters cooperation, collaboration, and mutual support, serving as a lubricant for social interactions and facilitating collective endeavors. Building trust becomes even more critical in stressful situations, as it can significantly impact the outcome and resilience of individuals and groups facing adversity. A philosophy of building trust in such circumstances often revolves around several fundamental principles:

Transparency: Open and honest communication is vital. It provides clarity and reduces uncertainty. Being transparent about intentions, actions, and constraints fosters understanding and trust.

Consistency: Consistently demonstrating reliability and integrity reinforces trust. People tend to trust those whose behavior is predictable and aligned with their values.

Empathy: Showing empathy and understanding toward others' feelings and perspectives builds rapport and strengthens interpersonal bonds, enhancing trust even in challenging situations.

Competence: Demonstrating competence and expertise inspires confidence and trust. When individuals perceive that others can handle the situation effectively, they are more likely to trust their judgment and leadership.

Accountability: Taking responsibility for one's actions and decisions, including acknowledging and rectifying mistakes, is crucial for maintaining trust, even in the face of adversity or stress.

Mutual Support: Offering support and assistance to others fosters reciprocity and solidarity, reinforcing trust and cooperation within the group.

Resilience: Demonstrating resilience in the face of challenges instills confidence and reassurance in others, showcasing the ability to navigate difficulties and maintain trustworthiness.

By embracing these principles and actively cultivating trust through actions and behaviors, individuals and groups can navigate stressful situations with greater resilience, cohesion, and effectiveness, fostering mutual support and collective well-being. On the other hand, Blue has an underbelly of hidden intentions and motivations that might be at play in your situation.

The underhandedness of Blue reveals that people will stubbornly trust charismatic thought forms, loose lips, and projections of Corporate Chaos even if it's to the detriment of their well-being; the security in consistently maintaining misery and chaos is optimized only for corporations and government entities that profit from misinformation and censorship. Blue serves as a scapegoat under these negative influences, sending you a message to take note of anything out of the blue that you feel is aggressively attempting to exploit your trust currently. Narcissists and micromanagers love to apply ample pressure to create the illusions of trust and smile condescendingly while talking down at you as if you weren't already in the loop.

Suppose you've been stuck and wondering why you keep pursuing a dead-end job or defending misguided beliefs that we live in a meritocracy. In that case, the system is designed to keep you predictable and compliant. Working harder does not always equate to more money in your pocket. Corporate Chaos has hijacked the humanity of consistency with platitudes and changed the cultural gauge for determining what is reliable and integral. It's time to unpack where you want to put your trust.

Magi - Reconcile Differences

Magi, often spelled as "Maggi" or "Magu," is a concept rooted in African philosophy, particularly among the Akan people of Ghana. It represents a reconciliation, mediation, and conflict resolution process within communities. Magi emphasizes the importance of dialogue, empathy, and understanding in resolving differences and restoring harmony. Magi involves the following principles:

Mediation: The Magi typically involves a neutral third party, the "Magi" or "Maggu," who mediate between conflicting parties. This mediator facilitates communication, helps parties express their grievances, and guides them toward finding common ground.

Dialogue and Listening: The Magi process emphasizes open dialogue and active listening. Conflicting parties are encouraged to respectfully express their perspectives, concerns, and emotions. Through dialogue, participants gain a deeper understanding of each other's viewpoints, fostering empathy and mutual respect.

Restorative Justice: The Magi focuses on restoring relationships and harmony within the community rather than simply assigning blame or punishment. The goal is to address the underlying causes of conflict, promote healing, and rebuild trust among individuals or groups.

Consensus Building: Magi encourages collaborative problem-solving and consensus building. Participants work together to identify shared interests and values, exploring creative solutions accommodating different perspectives and needs.

Community Involvement: Magi is not limited to the conflicting parties but often involves the broader community. Community members may provide support, offer insights, or serve as witnesses to the reconciliation process, reinforcing the collective responsibility for maintaining harmony. Magi offers valuable insights and approaches to reconciling differences of opinion. Instead of viewing disagreements as irreconcilable, the Magi encourage individuals to engage in constructive dialogue, seek understanding, and find common ground. By fostering empathy, communication, and consensus building, Magi enables people to address differences peacefully and respectfully, strengthening relationships and promoting community unity.

In your color reading, Magi's appearance reflects an intermediary to reconcile different opinions. In a heated argument or debate, you may battle cognitive dissonance with conflicting information or people at each other's throats. This rivalry of ideas requires a calm and trusting blue frequency to recalibrate the intentions away from taking opposing viewpoints as a personal attack. What is the common goal that both parties can agree on?

Another reason this color shows up in a reading is a reminder to give credit where credit is due. Sometimes, we are so fixated on our realities that we forget that other people are also walking in under their own kind of weather. Be sure to communicate and recognize effort, no matter how much of it is readily viable. Be mindful not to overindulge in this as it could open your energy field to becoming vulnerable, and others may take advantage of you, so it's beneficial to involve a third party to witness and facilitate the dissemination of recognition in a way that's received mutually. Magi is a welcome color, but it requires preventing yourself from taking the situation personally. It is a sign that an outsider's perspective is an excellent resource for gaining perspective and communicating with peace of mind.

Cornflower - Stand Up to the Elements

Cornflower appears in a reading when the situation calls for self-advocacy by standing up to the elements. Cornflower often symbolizes hope and strength. During World War I, the cornflower was adopted as a symbol of solidarity and support for veterans. This historical use speaks volumes of perseverance and resilience, as those who served had to endure and advocate for their needs upon returning home. Cornflowers are hardy plants that can grow in various environments, often thriving in less-than-ideal conditions. This adaptability mirrors the concept of resilience, where individuals must adapt and persevere despite obstacles.

Self-advocacy involves navigating difficult conversations and environments and then finding ways to thrive. Its vibrant blue color stands out in fields, much like self-advocacy requires individuals to stand out from the crowd and make their voices heard. Resilience is about maintaining hope and strength even in challenging situations, much like the cornflower's ability to thrive in various conditions. Practicing self-advocacy during intense periods of setbacks and adversity involves actively advocating for your needs, rights, and well-being, even in challenging circumstances. Here are some strategies for practicing self-advocacy during hard times:

Acknowledge Your Feelings: Recognize and validate your emotions, including frustration, sadness, or fear, that arise during setbacks and adversity. Accepting your feelings without judgment can help you better understand your needs and priorities.

Clarify Your Goals: Take time to clarify your goals and priorities, considering both short-term and long-term objectives. Clearly defining your goals can guide your actions and decision-making during difficult times.

Seek Support: For support and guidance, contact trusted friends, family members, or mental health professionals. Sharing your struggles with others can provide emotional validation, practical assistance, and new perspectives on navigating adversity.

Communicate Assertively: Practice assertive communication by clearly expressing your thoughts, feelings, and needs respectfully yet firmly. Be direct about what you require to cope with setbacks and advocate for the support or accommodation you need.

Set Boundaries: Establish healthy boundaries to protect your physical, emotional, and mental well-being. Learn to avoid additional responsibilities or demands that may exacerbate stress or overwhelm you during challenging times.

Explore Resources: Research and utilize available resources, such as support groups, counseling services, self-help books, or online forums, to provide information, guidance, and practical strategies for coping with adversity.

Practice Self-Care: Prioritize self-care activities that nurture your overall well-being, including adequate sleep, nutritious eating, regular exercise, relaxation techniques, and hobbies that bring you joy and fulfillment. Taking care of yourself is essential for building resilience and coping effectively with setbacks.

Cultivate Resilience: Cultivate resilience by reframing setbacks as opportunities for growth and learning. Focus on your strengths, past successes, and previous experiences of overcoming adversity to bolster your confidence and resilience during difficult times.

Stay Flexible: Remain open-minded and adaptable when navigating setbacks and adversity. Adjust your goals, strategies, and expectations to cope with changing circumstances and unexpected challenges.

Celebrate Progress: Acknowledge and celebrate your progress as you navigate setbacks and adversity, no matter how small. Recognizing your resilience and achievements can boost your confidence and motivate you to continue advocating for yourself.

By incorporating these strategies into your daily life, you can cultivate a strong sense of self-advocacy and resilience, even during intense setbacks and adversity. Remember that practicing self-advocacy is a continuous process that requires self-awareness, assertiveness, and compassion toward yourself.

Azure - Angelic Communication

The connection between the sky-blue Azure color in our color oracle and working with angels in a spiritual context often stems from symbolic associations and interpretations within various spiritual traditions. Azure is frequently described as the color of the sky on a clear day and is linked to expansiveness, tranquility, serenity, and spirituality. The sky bridges the earthly realm and the heavens above in many cultures. In numerous spiritual beliefs, angels are regarded as celestial beings who act as messengers or intermediaries between the divine and humanity. They are often associated with purity, protection, guidance, and divine communication. The connection between sky blue and angels can be understood in several ways:

Symbolism of the Sky: The sky is often perceived as a realm of purity and transcendence, where the divine resides. When Azure appears in a reading, it represents the vastness and openness of the heavens talking to you, suggesting a connection to the spiritual realm where angels dwell.

Purity and Serenity: Azure blue is a calming color associated with peace, tranquility, and purity. Similarly, angels are often viewed as beings of purity and serenity, embodying qualities that bring comfort and peace to those seeking guidance, especially during transition and trauma.

Divine Communication: Just as the sky serves as a medium through which sunlight, rain, and celestial phenomena reach the Earth, sky blue can symbolize a channel for divine communication. Angels are believed to convey messages from the heavenly realm to individuals on Earth, acting as conduits for spiritual guidance and insight.

Protection and Guidance: Azure is often associated with protection and guidance, much like the role attributed to angels in many spiritual traditions. Angels are believed to watch over and guide individuals, offering support and assistance on their spiritual journeys.

Association with Higher Realms: Azure is often perceived as a color that transcends earthly concerns and represents a clear connection to higher realms of consciousness. In this sense, it aligns with the celestial nature of angels and their role in facilitating connections between humans and the divine.

I find that when Azure shows up in a color reading, it's because someone on the other side is communicating with the inquirer. I don't see dead people or proactively practice mediumship, but I respect that our world is not as it seems on the surface. One of the key reasons why people love this color deck is its universal spirituality. I've always had a personal connection with angels in my life, thanks to my maternal grandmother. She would collect dozens of statues and figurines, personifying saints and angels. There's something protective and serene about their presence that I always gravitated to when I would stay with her while being kicked out of the house for whatever reason, my abusive family would hang over my head. In a color reading, the Angels and your ancestors are wrapping you in their loving and protective energy, and this shouldn't be ignored. Azure's cosmic message is anchored in our ability to be seen in heaven and charismatically attractive here on earth. When this color energy appears in a reading, it's a message from our loved ones from the other side inviting you to remember you are of the Universe and to trust the strength of your wings.

So, what about charisma? Azure is appearing to invite you to practice inspirational leadership. Charismatic individuals often possess qualities that inspire and motivate others. In spiritual traditions, angels are sometimes viewed as inspirational figures who guide and uplift humanity. Charismatic individuals can inspire positive change and uplift society by embodying qualities associated with angels, such as compassion, wisdom, and benevolence. Be open to Divine guidance. Charismatic leaders may be perceived as having a sense of purpose or mission that transcends personal ambition. In some beliefs, angels are seen as messengers of divine guidance, helping individuals align with their higher purpose and contribute to the greater good. Charismatic individuals who are guided by principles of kindness, justice, and service may be seen as embodying angelic qualities. Approach others and situations with the angle of an Angel. Charisma often involves a magnetic presence or aura that draws others in. In spiritual contexts, this magnetism may reflect one's connection to higher realms of consciousness or divine energy. As celestial beings, angels are often associated with grace, beauty, and light. Charismatic individuals who radiate positivity, kindness, and authenticity may be perceived as embodying these celestial qualities. Prioritize healing and empowerment. Charismatic leaders often can heal and empower others through their words, actions, and presence. In spiritual traditions, angels are sometimes invoked for healing and protection. Charismatic individuals who use their influence to uplift and empower others can be seen as channeling angelic energy for the greater good of society. Align yourself with virtues and moral causes. Charismatic individuals who are seen as embodying virtues such as compassion, integrity, and humility are often admired and respected in society. In some spiritual beliefs, angels are regarded as embodiments of divine virtues and guardians of moral principles. Charismatic leaders who uphold these virtues and inspire others to do the same contribute to creating a more virtuous and harmonious society. If you struggle to feel the messages in your reading, ask out loud for clear and direct signs, then pay attention to those hunches and occurrences that stop you in your tracks, taking your breath away in awe and bewilderment. The Universe is like an algorithm; the more you tune in to the vibration you want, the more the celestial program will respond.

Overall, the connection between charisma, angels, and becoming a charismatic person for good in society lies in aligning one's personal qualities and actions with principles of virtue, inspiration, guidance, and service to others, reflecting a higher purpose or connection to the divine. Azure is your direct line to connecting and channeling to the astral plane and connecting with other celestial bodies in multidimensional ways. Look for angels in your life right now, or recognize that you can touch others with your angelic powers.

Sky Blue - Express More Magic

Sky Blue piggybacks off Azure but with an emphasis on the higher purpose and connection to the Divine in a down-to-earth way. There's a correlation between your higher purpose and expressing your authentic self in a profound and multifaceted society. Sky Blue is showing up in a color reading to remind you to use more magic. Set time aside and explore rituals, prayers, meditations, and songs that attune yourself to the outcome, desires, and goals of your intentions. Understanding your higher purpose often involves aligning one's actions and expressions with deeply held values and beliefs. When individuals express themselves authentically in society, they are more likely to feel fulfilled and purpose when their actions reflect their core values. This alignment fosters a greater sense of meaning and coherence in life. Expressing oneself in society can be a means of contributing to the greater good. When individuals tap into their unique talents, passions, and perspectives to address societal needs or challenges, they fulfill their higher purpose by positively impacting the world around them. Whether through creative endeavors, advocacy, community service, or leadership, expressing oneself in society can be a vehicle for positive change and social progress.

Sky Blue is drawing out that feeling you have inside that there's more to the situation. Many people feel a deep inner calling or mission guiding their actions and choices. This sense of calling often encompasses a higher purpose—a larger vision or goal that transcends personal ambitions and serves the common good. By expressing themselves authentically and pursuing their passions in society, individuals can fulfill their sense of calling and make meaningful contributions aligned with their higher purpose. This sixth sense of feeling helps to self-actualize. Expressing oneself in society can be a powerful catalyst for personal growth and self-actualization. Individuals can cultivate their strengths, overcome challenges, and develop their fullest potential through creative expression, meaningful relationships, and purposeful action. By embracing opportunities for self-expression and exploration, individuals can deepen their understanding of themselves and their place in the world, ultimately fulfilling their higher purpose. As you continue to ask the colors for messages and guidance, the more the energy will respond to your mood and environment should you heed the wisdom and intuitive advice by connecting with the Divine. Authentic self-expression creates connections and builds meaningful relationships with others. Your vibe starts attracting your tribe. By sharing your authentic self with the world, you'll form genuine connections and conversations based on mutual understanding, respect, and shared values. Old wounds start to heal, and you'll have the energy and resources to provide support, inspiration, and a sense of belonging, enriching your life further and contributing to our globalized sense of purpose and fulfillment as humanity.

Sky Blue is the expanse. It takes you from a me-centered place in reading and zooms out on your impact on the greater good. Express yourself before you wreck yourself. Holding back your thoughts, ideas, words, and things that give you joy, spiritually speaking, steals from the great expanse of our collective humanity. How can you give more authentically today to someone who might rub you the wrong way? Settings where this energy finds itself are on television shows like *Survivor* and *The Amazing Race* and even on college campuses. These spaces allow you to step outside your fragmented echo chambers and connect with others on a universal level. Your freedom and human right to self-expression are essential to democracy and enlightenment. As Marianne Williamson puts it in her book, *A Return to Love*:

"*Our deepest fear is not that we are inadequate. Our deepest fear is that we are powerful beyond measure. It is our light, not our darkness that most frightens us. We ask ourselves, 'Who am I to be brilliant, gorgeous, talented, fabulous?' Actually, who are you not to be? You are a child of God. Your playing small does not serve the world. There is nothing enlightened about shrinking so that other people won't feel insecure around you... And as we let our own light shine, we unconsciously permit other people to do the same. As we are liberated from our own fear, our presence automatically liberates others.*"

Take to the sky. And fly.

Cyan - Speak the Truth

Cyan is the electricity of authenticity. This color energy appears in your reading today to highlight threads of the situation you're in denial about or the person you're inquiring about, which could be wrapped up in a case of dishonesty. Denial, in psychological terms, refers to a defense mechanism where individuals refuse to accept reality or truth, often to protect themselves from facing uncomfortable or distressing emotions, thoughts, or situations. Cyan cuts through the facade and encourages you to get down to the truth so atomic that it defies the ego's reliance on narcissistic disbelief to prioritize itself in the situation. Confront it. In Shakespeare's tragedy "Hamlet," the titular character grapples with self-doubt and denial regarding his father's death and his uncle's treachery. His reluctance to confront reality leads to tragic consequences for himself and those around him. In *Fight Club*, the narrator initially denies his dissatisfaction with his mundane life, instead seeking solace in consumerism and conformity. His denial manifests in the creation of an alter ego, Tyler Durden, leading to a spiral of violence and chaos as he tries to suppress his inner turmoil. The fall of the Roman Empire is often attributed in part to the denial of its leaders regarding the internal and external threats facing the empire. Rather than confronting the issues head-on, they engaged in self-delusion and denial, ultimately leading to its decline. Lastly, in the biblical story of Adam and Eve, their denial of their disobedience to God's command leads to their expulsion from the Garden of Eden. Their refusal to acknowledge their actions reflects a form of denial that has profound spiritual consequences. Albeit I don't fully buy into the Christian propaganda rooted so heavily in heteronormativity, often people live in denial because they are taught to fear God.

Today, the rise of social media has created a platform where Individuals often present curated versions of their lives, denying the reality of their struggles and imperfections. This denial of authenticity can lead to feelings of inadequacy and disconnection in oneself and others. Cyan is like a sword suit in a traditional tarot deck. Nothing cuts more profoundly than the truth. And it's often the truth that people can't handle. So, they paint a prettier exterior to hide the less-than-ideal and choose to live in a vault of vapid oppression. Cyan breaks through the bullshit of your veneers and is the spark you need to jolt you out of your delusions. When Cyan appears, it signals a rude awakening if not mindful. People can feel culture shock, too, when their entire paradigm shifts. Cyan wants you to recognize that denial may be a viable option for the short term. Yet, acceptance is easier when you go with the flow rather than trying to control the flow. Cyan is the color of Elsa's icy embrace of self-acknowledgment and personal power to let it go. Whether through tragic endings, societal downfall, spiritual separation, or personal disillusionment, denial often leads to adverse outcomes that could have been mitigated by facing reality with honesty and courage.

Speak the truth.

Turquoise - Spiritual Empathy

Turquoise pays homage to our two-spiritedness, collective humanity, and anthems to protect ourselves through emotional and spiritual exchanges. When Turquoise appears in a reading, you're invited to see the situation through the eyes of kindred spiritedness - empathy. Not sympathy. Society gets nowhere with sympathy. Thoughts and prayers on social media do a whole lot of nothing. Couch potato efforts contribute no value to society. Sympathy is socioeconomic minimalism, and I'm tired of people choosing convenience over some hard-elbows-deep community service. When turquoise is used as a crystal in spiritual practices, its healing and protective properties are believed to be amplified. Many people use turquoise crystals for meditation, healing rituals, or wearing jewelry to intensify the intention behind the object or because it represents it, makes it accessible for spiritual purposes, and brings heaven to earth and earth to heaven. The crystalline structure is connected to the Earth's energies, grounding and anchoring spiritual practices, thus building a deeper connection to nature and the elements, which promotes a sense of rootedness and stability. This interplay of spirit meeting the physical and the physicality's rendezvous with spirit is a cosmic dance that can't be amplified if we approach the situation with fear of putting any skin in the game.

You are a spiritual being living through a physical experience. Your physical experience is sharpening or dulling your spirit should you succumb to laziness and avoid any ounce of hard work required to participate in your life story or positively contribute to someone else's life. Getting hurt sucks, but lessons are designed to be learned, and the good soul-deep ones are meant to be experienced first-hand. The great thing about Turquoise showing up is that your hurts and fears are nothing new. Others have pilgrimaged this path before you, and it's time you speak up and see that wisdom for yourself or pay it forward to another. To truly engage in spirituality and develop self-awareness, one must confront challenges and adversity rather than avoid them altogether. Turquoise wants you to look at your situation and find where to serve yourself. How can you take the focus off protecting your echo chamber and amplify our equitable protection for our shared humanity?

Neptune - Voice of Your Muse

The story of Neptune, the Roman god of the sea, and its association with the Muses and inspiration draws upon various elements of mythology and symbolism. In Roman mythology, Neptune is the counterpart of the Greek god Poseidon. While Neptune's primary domain is the sea, his influence extends beyond mere maritime matters. Neptune is often regarded as a patron of the arts and creativity, much like his Greek counterpart, Poseidon. As such, he is associated with the Muses, the goddesses of inspiration in Greek mythology. In mythological narratives, Neptune's connection to the sea represents the vast depths of creativity and imagination. Just as the sea is boundless and mysterious, so is the wellspring of artistic inspiration. As companions of Neptune, the Muses are believed to draw inspiration from the depths of the sea, channeling their creative energies to inspire poets, musicians, artists, and thinkers. Neptune's association with the Muses underscores the belief that creativity and innovation often arise from a deep connection to nature and the elements. Artists and poets, seeking inspiration, would invoke Neptune and the Muses, hoping to tap into the divine source of creativity and bring forth their works of art. Water symbolizes the subconscious mind, emotions, and the realm of dreams in various mythologies. Neptune's realm of the sea represents the depths of the unconscious, where artistic inspiration resides. Just as the sea ebbs and flows, so does the creative process, with moments of inspiration followed by periods of introspection and gestation. The association of Neptune with the Muses underscores the deep connection between the sea, creativity, and inspiration in Roman mythology. Through invoking Neptune and the Muses, artists sought to tap into the boundless reservoir of creative energy that flows from the depths of the sea, bringing forth works of art that inspire and enrich human experience.

When Neptune appears in a reading, you're beckoned to the sea of your consciousness to create and inspire others. This is *The Color Mage Oracle*'s entrepreneur's sidekick color card. It's a color of exploratory emotion, inventions, dreamscapes, partnerships, and public speaking. Various pop culture references and concepts reflect Neptune's influence and symbolism as a source of inspiration and creativity. Here are some examples:

Music: Numerous songs and albums draw inspiration from Neptune's association with creativity and imagination. For example, "*Neptune*" by Sleeping at Last is a song that explores themes of introspection and artistic expression. Album covers or music videos featuring oceanic themes, mystical imagery, or references to Neptune may evoke a sense of creativity and inspiration.

Television: Neptune's influence often appears in fantasy and science fiction films and TV shows where creativity and imagination play significant roles. For instance, in *The Little Mermaid*, Neptune's underwater kingdom serves as a fantastical backdrop for the protagonist's journey of self-discovery and exploring the unknown. Dream sequences or surreal imagery in movies and TV series may symbolize Neptune's realm of inspiration and the subconscious mind.

Art: Paintings, sculptures, and other visual art forms may incorporate Neptune's imagery, such as seascapes, mythical creatures like mermaids, or depictions of the sea god himself, to evoke feelings of inspiration and creativity. Authors often use Neptune's symbolism to explore themes of creativity, imagination, and the mysteries of the subconscious mind in novels, poetry, and other literary works.

Fashion: Fashion designers and artists may draw inspiration from Neptune's realm by incorporating oceanic motifs, such as seashells, waves, or aquatic colors, into their designs. Costumes and fashion designs inspired by mythical creatures associated with Neptune, such as mermaids or sea nymphs, may convey a sense of whimsy and creative expression.

When Neptune appears in a reading in a challenged position, it often represents you, or the inquirer is submerged under discouragement and apathetic expectations. You are chasing after someone else’s dream, pining for love as a hopeless romantic, or living under inherited beliefs that apathy, lethargy, and despair are rewards. The starving artist and bag lady archetypes are centralized themes that appear when Neptune’s energy is reversed or negatively influenced. The "starving artist" and "bag lady" archetypes represent common cultural perceptions and fears associated with financial instability, particularly within creativity and success. The "starving artist" archetype embodies the belief that pursuing a creative passion often leads to economic struggle and hardship. It symbolizes the notion that artists must sacrifice financial stability for their art. The "bag lady" archetype represents the fear of losing financial security and becoming destitute, often associated with women.

You may feel the anxiety of being abandoned or left with nothing. You're waiting for the other shoe to drop. Both ideations indicate that unresolved anxiety, living paycheck to paycheck, and lack of appreciation are impacting your mood to feel inspired, putting your head over your heart when it comes to creative projects, and finding the resources not only to survive but thrive. Here are strategies to try to overcome the starving artist bag lady vibes in your situation:

Diversify Income Streams: Explore multiple avenues to monetize your creative talents, such as freelance work, teaching, commissions, or selling merchandise.
Financial Planning: Develop a budget, save money, and seek financial advice to manage expenses and build savings.

Value Your Work: Recognize the worth of your creative contributions and advocate for fair compensation for your skills and expertise.

Networking and Promotion: Build a solid professional network, market your work effectively, and seek opportunities for exposure and collaboration.

Continuous Learning: Improve your craft, acquire new skills, and stay updated on industry trends to enhance marketability and competitiveness.

Financial Empowerment: Take control of your finances by educating yourself about money management, investing, and retirement planning.

Build a Safety Net: Establish an emergency fund, obtain insurance coverage, and create a financial plan to provide stability and security.

Career Development: Invest in your education, skills, and professional development to enhance your earning potential and career opportunities.

Seek Support: Surround yourself with a supportive network of friends, family, or mentors who can offer guidance, encouragement, and assistance during challenging times.

Self-Care: Prioritize self-care and well-being to maintain resilience and effectively cope with stress, anxiety, or uncertainty.

By addressing financial concerns proactively, fostering resilience, and pursuing opportunities for growth and empowerment, you can overcome the "starving artist" and "bag lady" archetypes, allowing yourself to pursue your creative passions with confidence and security.

THIRD EYE CHAKRA

Grape - Intoxication and Stupor

In ancient Greek mythology, Dionysus is the god of wine, fertility, theater, and ecstasy. His story is rich with symbolism and lessons, often reflecting the dual nature of wine—its power to bring joy and celebration and its potential for excess and chaos. The tale of Dionysus begins with his unusual birth. His mother, Semele, was a mortal woman who caught the eye of Zeus, the king of the gods. Zeus seduced Semele and impregnated her, but when Hera, Zeus's jealous wife, discovered the affair, she tricked Semele into asking Zeus to reveal himself in his full divine glory. Zeus reluctantly complied, knowing that mortals cannot withstand the sight of a god's true form. As a result, Semele was consumed by the intense brilliance of Zeus's lightning bolts, but Zeus managed to rescue the unborn Dionysus by sewing him into his thigh until he was ready to be born. This myth highlights themes of divine punishment, jealousy, and the interplay between mortality and divinity. But the story of Dionysus doesn't end with his miraculous birth. Dionysus traveled the world as he grew, teaching humans the art of winemaking and revelry. He was accompanied by a wild band of followers, known as the Maenads or Bacchae, who engaged in ecstatic rituals and frenzied dances in his honor. However, Dionysus's teachings and revelry also revealed the darker side of human nature. In his most famous myth, Dionysus encountered resistance from the city of Thebes, where King Pentheus refused to acknowledge his divinity and banned his worship. In retaliation, Dionysus drove the women of Thebes, including Pentheus's mother, Agave, into a wild frenzy, causing them to tear Pentheus apart in a fit of Dionysian madness. This myth embodies hubris, divine wrath, and the consequences of denying the sacred. It warns against the dangers of suppressing natural urges and the folly of trying to control forces beyond human comprehension. Overall, the story of Dionysus offers lessons about the power and pitfalls of indulgence, the blurred lines between the mortal and the divine, and the importance of embracing both the light and dark aspects of existence. Through his myths, Dionysus invites us to celebrate life's pleasures while acknowledging the inherent risks and responsibilities that come with them.

Grape appears in a reading to highlight the winemaking process and the intoxicating effects of consuming alcoholic beverages. Grapes, mainly purple varieties, are widely used in the production of wine. The process of fermenting grapes to make wine dates back thousands of years and has been celebrated in various cultures as a sacred and transformative practice. The deep purple hue of many grape varieties symbolizes richness, abundance, and vitality, qualities often associated with wine's intoxicating allure. Wine has long been linked with intoxication due to its alcohol content. Wine can induce relaxation, euphoria, and sociability when consumed in moderation. However, excessive consumption can lead to intoxication, characterized by impaired judgment, loss of coordination, and altered perceptions. The association of wine with intoxication has been depicted in art, literature, and mythology, where wine often symbolizes revelry and excess. Are you overexerting yourself or playing the role of the fool to downplay your leading role in the situation?

Purple generically has symbolic associations with royalty, luxury, and sensuality, all of which can contribute to the intoxicating allure of wine. In many cultures, purple is also associated with spirituality and the divine, reflecting the ancient ritualistic use of wine in religious ceremonies and celebrations. As such, purple can evoke a sense of mystique and enchantment, further enhancing its connection to intoxication and the pleasures of the senses. Grape, in essence, isn't entirely hostile, but it is a potent reminder that environmental pollutants, vices, and mob mentalities might be doing more harm than good in this situation. Corporate chaos numbs our senses and debilitates our intuition and instincts from emerging and pressing humanity out of us until we fall into a delirious state of obedience, conforming to a preordained place in the vineyard of consumerism.

Succumbing to peer pressure in society leads to unnecessary misfortunes, so allow your conscience to guide and stay vigilant regarding cult-like activity, overinflation, and gossip. Just because you heard it through the grapevine doesn't mean it's true. While I felt jealous, my mother would ask me, "If they jumped off a bridge, would you too?"

Wise Owl - Inner Wisdom and Foresight

Intuition will come through if you're paying attention to it or not. But don't be fooled; psychic connections or intuitive hunches don't govern every element of our existence. A person's perceived luck may come from nepotism, privilege, and systemic education to groom a child early based on prejudice. Wise Owl is the hag in the woods surprise we stumble upon when we are coming off our revelry high and peer pressure bandwagon we found from the previous color, Grape. As Helen Reddy once sang, it's wisdom born from pain. The witch in the woods sees through our platitudes and grants us natural growth opportunities. Wise Owl wants you to seek someone older with more life experience to mentor you, like Merlin counseling King Arthur. It's the spirit of our grandparents and senior citizens. If you find yourself lost in the Forbidden Forest of your feelings, remember to use the spirit animal of an owl to guide you along your forest path. Owls are often associated with wisdom, intuition, and insight in spirituality. They are creatures of the night, possessing keen senses that allow them to navigate the darkness, symbolizing the ability to see beyond illusion or deception. In some cultures, owls are considered guardians of the spirit world or messengers between realms. When considering these elements, one could interpret a connection between owls, spirituality, and this color, representing a union of wisdom, spiritual insight, and heightened consciousness. In your reading, Wise Owl, associated with wisdom and the unseen, could guide your spiritual journey, represented by purple in general, leading you to a deeper understanding of your purpose and path to enlightenment.

Foresight predicts future events or developments based on present conditions or insights. Foresight in spirituality often involves the ability to perceive or anticipate spiritual growth, challenges, and opportunities. It can encompass intuitive insights into one's path or the paths of others, as well as a broader understanding of the interconnectedness of events and energies. Foresight in spirituality may be cultivated through practices such as meditation, introspection, and divination, allowing individuals to gain clarity and guidance regarding their spiritual journeys. You may be called to get serious about your spirituality and how it connects to the mundane world of work and use it to restore peace to the ravaged people, places, and things that Corporate Chaos uprooted or destroyed. Through mentorship, foresight is invaluable for guiding and supporting others on their paths to growth and achievement. A mentor with foresight can anticipate challenges and opportunities that mentees may encounter, offering proactive guidance and advice to help them navigate their journeys more effectively. Foresight enables mentors to see beyond immediate circumstances, identifying long-term trends or potential obstacles that may impact their mentees' goals. By sharing their insights and experiences, mentors can empower mentees to make informed decisions and develop their foresight skills.

Wise Owl is a reminder that you are not alone in this. The Universe and the Divine essence of your ancestors are here to offer the key to accessing the power that resides in yourself. Connecting with your future self is a perfect exercise you can practice when this color appears. An older and wiser version of you that you have nothing to hide because it's you. You already know who you were and where you've been, and so does your future self. They are waiting for you.

Indigo - Clairvoyance

If you feel enamored by the wild world of enchantments and spells, well, Indigo is a rich color in lore, history, and mysticism. The history of purple and its connection to indigo dye is fascinating and spans centuries of human civilization. Purple has strong ties to the indigo plant, from which a deep blue dye is extracted. Indigo dye has been used for thousands of years, with evidence dating back to ancient civilizations such as those in the Indus Valley and Egypt. It was prized for its rich hue and ability to color textiles, ranging from clothing to tapestries. In many cultures, purple has been associated with royalty, nobility, and spirituality. The color was often reserved for monarchs and high-ranking officials due to the difficulty and expense of producing purple dyes. In ancient Rome, for example, only emperors were permitted to wear clothing dyed Tyrian purple, a luxurious dye derived from certain shellfish species. Purple was also used in religious ceremonies and rituals, symbolizing divine connection and spiritual enlightenment. With the advent of synthetic dyes in the 19th century, the traditional methods of producing indigo dye from natural sources began to decline. Synthetic dyes offered a cheaper and more consistent alternative to natural dyes, leading to a decline in the cultivation of indigo plants and the use of natural indigo dye. However, there has been a resurgence of interest in natural dyes and traditional dyeing techniques in recent years, driven by a desire for sustainability and environmental consciousness.

Your consciousness is active and transforming as we evolve collectively as a species. I love considering Indigo as purple and blue. This means it's transformative and transitory. When Indigo appears in a reading, it wants you to activate your third eye, receive transmissions from the larger pool of consciousness, and protect yourself during psychic attacks or periods of energy manipulation. *The Color Mage Oracle* Is about flexing your multisensory experiences on this planet. Clairvoyance is the psychic ability to perceive information or events beyond the ordinary human senses, typically through extrasensory perception (ESP). It involves receiving intuitive insights or visions about the past, present, or future that are not readily apparent to the five physical senses. To get to a comfortable place with our intuition, we must practice empathy, recognize our prejudices, and remember that we are constantly transitioning. The fluidity of our reality is vast and deep, and the art of metaphysics certainly helps those who are highly sensitive and perceptive of our interactions with the day-to-day minutia.

Indigo confirms that signs and moments of synchronicity are being delivered and that you should ask for clearer ones to seize them when they strike. If Indigo is challenged or reversed, it could be one of those Magic 8 ball answers: "Try again later." You don't need to predict or anticipate every nook and cranny of your situation. There's far too much shifting and changing, so it could be for your protection if you feel stuck, blocked, or rejected. This is an excellent time to work with antioxidants and blueberries to support your immune system. Consider decompressing with fun brainteasers and games that stretch your imagination.

You may also feel compelled to work the energy of a Sphinx to guard your clairvoyant powers. The Sphinx is a mythological creature from ancient Egyptian and Greek mythology. It typically has a lion's body and a human's head, although variations can include the heads of other animals. The Sphinx is often associated with mystery, wisdom, and enigma. As a guardian of secrets and hidden knowledge, the Sphinx parallels the idea of clairvoyance, where one seeks to uncover unreadily apparent information. The Sphinx represents the barriers to this hidden knowledge, and those who seek it must demonstrate their insight and perception. The Sphinx is famous for posing riddles that require deep thought and understanding. This process is akin to clairvoyance, requiring an individual to perceive beyond the obvious and tap deeper, often hidden truths. Both the Sphinx and clairvoyance are associated with the mystical and the supernatural. The Sphinx's enigmatic nature and connection to ancient myths enhance its symbolic relationship with clairvoyant abilities, often considered beyond ordinary human experience.

Imperial - Sovereignty

Imperial is the color of your independence, specifically in your life and work, where you actively practice autonomy, self-determination, recognition, and legal reviews. Both freedom and sovereignty involve a degree of independence or self-governance. Independent entities can make decisions and act according to their own will without external interference. Similarly, sovereign states have supreme authority and control over their internal and external affairs. When Imperial appears in a color reading, you are reminded that you have the right to determine your destiny. Your existence is seen as an independent nation or sovereign state that can shape its political, economic, and social systems according to its preferences and interests. If corporations can influence these aspects with money, you too can reign supreme in your authority to influence and create conscious and healing content. People, places, and things often require recognition by other entities, such as other nations or international organizations. Recognition acknowledges the legitimacy of the entity's status as independent or sovereign. As it refers to your situation, Imperial wants you to see how your body, mind, and spirit are enshrined in legal frameworks, such as constitutions or international treaties. Does your citizenship hold more weight than you realize? These legal documents establish the rights, responsibilities, and obligations of autonomy or independence for collective groups and organized movements made up of individuals.

When Imperial appears in a reading, consider how you've been programmed to believe specific things about the situation. Prejudices that give you blind spots can make it difficult to see your influence beyond your wheelhouse of expertise and limited perspective. There's an opportunity to legitimize your claims and desires to help you operate from a place of power. However, it would help to recognize outside forces that impede you from working or thinking independently. In what ways have you given your power away? Do you need to license your creative works to grow your name? Imperial can indicate it's time to seek legal advice to protect your intellectual property and ideas.

Imperialism, while challenged, can show a power struggle between forces. Sovereignty implies a hierarchical relationship between the sovereign and subordinate entities within its jurisdiction. In contrast, independence typically conveys a sense of equality and autonomy without hierarchical connotations. Do you need help because the power dynamics are imbalanced or are reducing the scope of your influence? You can work with color to assist in the art of compromise. While working independently provides autonomy and freedom in decision-making, compromising remains vital in various aspects of work, such as collaboration, negotiation, conflict resolution, and managing conflicting priorities. Compromising, when necessary, allows you to navigate complex situations more effectively and achieve optimal outcomes. Working independently and compromising may seem contradictory at first glance. Still, there are situations where they complement each other for the greater good.

You can make decisions independently without consulting or compromising with others. However, there may be instances where collaborating or compromising with others can lead to better outcomes. Being open to compromise allows you to consider different perspectives and adapt your decisions accordingly, enhancing the overall quality of your work.

In independent work settings, you may have competing priorities or limited resources. Compromising involves finding a middle ground or reallocating resources to address multiple needs. By being willing to compromise on certain aspects of your work, you can better manage conflicting priorities and achieve a balance that maximizes overall effectiveness.

Even when working independently, you may collaborate with others on projects or initiatives. In such cases, compromise becomes essential for reconciling differences in opinions, preferences, or approaches. Being open to compromise allows you to work effectively with others, maintain positive relationships, and achieve common goals.

Independent professionals often negotiate contracts, agreements, or terms of service with clients, partners, or collaborators. Compromise is crucial in these negotiations, as both parties may need to make concessions to reach mutually beneficial agreements. By understanding the needs and priorities of all parties involved and being willing to compromise, you can establish sustainable and successful working relationships.

Conflicts may arise in any work setting, including independent work. Compromise is a valuable tool for resolving disputes and finding mutually acceptable solutions. You can address conflicts effectively and maintain productive working relationships by engaging in constructive dialogue, listening to different perspectives, and being open to compromise.

Everyone has an opinion these days. Some may even communicate their points with more charisma, noise, or financial support, but don't be too eager to accept defeat and fall into the lone wolf demise of working alone. This diminishes your autonomy by playing the victim or the martyr, which feeds the gaslighting cycle that narcissists and Corporate Chaos love to see in the world. Imperial invites you to balance opposing forces, represent duality, find equilibrium, and achieve personal victories through self-discipline. Being independent doesn't necessarily mean being alone. It means living with enough flexibility to recognize that your body, mind, and spirit are not corporate fodder or used for geopolitical warfare.

Shapeshift - Myth & Magic

Shapeshift is like the wizard behind the curtain, production crews for television, and immortalizing our humanity through mythologizing. When society creates a myth around someone or something, it's often called "mythologizing" or "mythmaking." This process involves embellishing or distorting facts and stories surrounding a person, event, or concept, often creating legendary or exaggerated narratives. Mythologizing can occur for various reasons, including cultural significance, historical interpretation, or to serve specific social or ideological purposes. Many historical figures have been mythologized over time, with their stories embellished or distorted to fit certain cultural or political narratives. For example, figures like King Arthur, Robin Hood, and Hercules have been mythologized in various ways, with their deeds often exaggerated and their historical reality obscured by legend. Across different cultures, creation myths often involve the mythologizing of gods or supernatural beings and their roles in the world's creation. These myths explain the universe's origins and humanity and often incorporate symbolism and metaphor. Countries often mythologize their national heroes and founders, portraying them as larger-than-life figures who played a pivotal role in the nation's history. For example, figures like George Washington in the United States or Joan of Arc in France have been mythologized as symbols of courage, patriotism, and national identity. Religious texts and traditions frequently involve mythologizing figures such as prophets, saints, and divine beings. These myths often convey moral and spiritual lessons and shape the beliefs and practices of religious communities. Folklore and fairy tales often feature mythological elements, with stories of magical creatures, heroes, and supernatural events passed down through generations. These myths serve as cultural touchstones and may contain moral lessons or explanations for natural phenomena. Historical events are sometimes mythologized to emphasize certain narratives or ideologies. For example, events like the Israeli-Palestine conflict or the French Revolution have been mythologized to highlight the struggle for freedom and justice while downplaying complexities and contradictions.

When Shapeshift appears in a reading, remember that not everything is as it seems. Shapeshift exposes crusades, campaigns, and cults. It invites you to explore esoteric rituals, invisible lines, or unspoken truths of discrimination. It inspires you to investigate your situation by finding the means, motive, and opportunity of your situation and desires. Looking for means, motive, and opportunity within the context of your color reading involves understanding yourself deeper and recognizing any factors that influence your actions, desires, and capabilities. You may want to pull additional color cards to elaborate on this when Shapeshift appears.

Means refers to the resources, skills, and abilities available to achieve your goals and fulfill your desires. In the context of self-help and personal fulfillment, identifying your means involves taking stock of your strengths, talents, and resources and recognizing any limitations or obstacles you may face. Ask yourself questions such as: What skills and abilities do I possess that can help me achieve my goals? What resources (financial, educational, social, etc.) do I have access to? Are there any areas where I need to acquire new skills or seek assistance?

Motive refers to the underlying reasons or intentions behind your goals and desires. Understanding your motives is crucial for aligning your actions with your values and finding fulfillment in your pursuits. Reflect on questions like: Why do I want to achieve this goal? What values or beliefs are driving my desire for personal growth and improvement? Am I pursuing this goal for intrinsic or extrinsic reasons (personal satisfaction, growth) (external validation, social status)?

Opportunity encompasses the circumstances and situations that enable you to act and progress toward your goals. Recognizing opportunities involves being open-minded, adaptable, and proactive in seeking out possibilities for growth and development. Consider the following: What opportunities in my current environment align with my goals? How can I create or capitalize on opportunities for learning and growth? Are there any barriers or limitations I must overcome to seize opportunities for personal fulfillment?

Mythologizing our mass media and consumerism leaves us in a constant state of questioning. There is an overwhelming amount of distance between today and the world of yesteryear. That distance and secondhand knowledge mean our knowledge is up for interpretation and educational guesswork. We love to idolize our history, but in what ways have we ignored the reality of how a person, place, or thing came to be, say, 2000 years ago or even what seems like overnight success? Winners write history, and people with money buy their image and pay to plan their ascent in society. Shapeshift speaks of underground corporations and secret affairs designed to influence and shape the world and our minds according to the matrices and back-office metrics to satisfy capitalistic egos. Classism is a turn-key construct that governs all of our lives. It is the most devilish dream to navigate when you're a spiritually conscious person living in a world riddled with mystery, illusions, and disinformation. This is why we inquire about learning and brainstorming the means, motive, and opportunity.

Esoteric knowledge and myths involve mystery, symbolism, and hidden meaning. Shapeshift holds cultural significance, asking you to create a repository of wisdom, tradition, and collective identity within a society. When inquiring about your situation, can you list movies, celebrities, or movements throughout time that connect to your struggles and desires? Permit yourself to shift to another time or universe to play out your ideal self in this situation. Do the means, motive, and opportunity shift if all involved are in different headspaces? You can use guided visual meditations to achieve this, or better yet; you can become an actor by channeling your mythos into a role-playing environment akin to *Dungeons & Dragons* or performing clinical role-play under the guidance of a therapist. The idea is for you to shapeshift your mindset with skills and a moral compass fit for the answers you seek and the conflict you face.

Shapeshift is a color to project energy into the world and feel protected. The blessing of this color is that you may want to keep your projects to yourself until you're ready to unveil them. Don't make any public appearances until you have all the facts. Remember to look for the means, motive, and opportunity when consuming information and news or deciding to collaborate with others.

Lavender - Me, Myself & I

Lavender is the Beyonce of the deck. It is a potent reminder for you to be your own best friend. It's also a tribute to the trifecta of our energy fields through body, mind, and soul. Lavender, in terms of its physical properties and color, is often associated with various metaphysical and wellness attributes. Lavender is renowned for its soothing aroma, used in aromatherapy to promote relaxation and reduce stress. It's believed that inhaling the scent of lavender can help calm the mind and body, making it helpful in managing anxiety and promoting better sleep. Lavender is often associated with balancing energy, particularly in feng shui and crystal healing practices. It's thought to help harmonize emotions and create a sense of inner peace and tranquility. In some spiritual traditions, lavender is used for cleansing and purifying spaces and dispelling negative energies. Burning lavender incense or using lavender-infused water for rituals is believed to clear away stagnant energy and promote a sense of clarity and renewal. Lavender is also associated with healing properties, both physically and energetically. It's believed to have antiseptic and anti-inflammatory properties, making it worthwhile. Additionally, lavender is sometimes used to protect against negative influences and promote overall well-being.

Regarding its color, lavender is a purple shade, often associated with spirituality, intuition, and wisdom. Like the scent of lavender, the color lavender is considered calming and soothing to the mind. It can help promote relaxation and reduce stress, like the aromatic properties of the plant itself. Purple shades, including lavender, balance emotions and promote emotional stability. The color lavender is believed to encourage a sense of harmony and peace, helping to alleviate tension and anxiety. Like other purple hues in the color deck, Lavender is linked to spirituality and higher consciousness. Lavender, a lighter shade of purple, can evoke a sense of spiritual awareness and intuition, encouraging reflection and inner exploration. Purple tones are also associated with creativity and imagination. The color lavender can stimulate artistic expression and inspire new ideas, making it a favorable choice for creative spaces or activities.

When Lavender appears in a reading, it's time for you to accept the interplay between the physical and spiritual worlds. You are a spiritual being living in a material world. The Universe wants to experience your emotions with you. You're being asked to take ownership of your destiny and involvement. Not getting involved is still, by proxy, deciding and influencing the situation; you must take responsibility for your actions and inactions now. If you feel funky, this color gently reminds you to relax. Some elements and conditions require a slow, calm, and steady approach. The need for speed or pressure for instant gratification isn't necessary currently.

Be present when Lavender is opposed or challenged during a reading. It often shows an imbalance in your chakra system. Your body, mind, and soul lack active and conscious awareness. Which part of you feels hungry? In this situation, does the struggle seem to match up best in your body? Depending on where you feel pain or can visualize the struggle the most can indicate which chakra area could be underperforming or overactive. The same goes for physical body systems; you must prioritize your health holistically now. Healing one part of the body and alienating other parts will only exacerbate imbalance further down your timeline.

A pivotal moment in my spiritual journey while working with the color cards was when I colored my hair Lavender for the first time. It was a decision that reprogrammed my brain. I looked at myself differently and with vervitude (verve + attitude). I allowed spirit to work itself through me as opposed to forcing antiquated fears around hairstyles for men and professionalism in a work environment. Lavender set me free. It was in direct response to realizing that, through building the *Rainbow Revolution* (available wherever books are sold), there were altars with tiny purple in my space. Inherently, I am very spiritual and intuitive, so perhaps I didn't need as much purple. Still, I took the minimal purple in my life in 2015 as a sign to get my hair colored, and Lavender was the perfect choice to explore myself further.

Lilac - Belief & Faith

Lilac is the color of peace. In a reading, it represents the autonomy of divine timing through core values that promote harmony. Belief and faith in the context of divine timing often refer to trusting that there is a higher power or cosmic plan at work in the universe. Belief typically involves accepting something as trustworthy or honest without tangible evidence. In divine timing, belief might entail trusting that events unfold according to a larger plan or purpose, even if we can't always understand or control those events. Conversely, faith is often described as a deep trust or confidence in something or someone. In the context of divine timing, faith involves trusting in the timing of events, believing that things will happen at the right moment according to a higher wisdom or divine plan. Together, belief and faith in divine timing suggest a mindset of surrendering to the notion that a greater intelligence or order is guiding the unfolding of events in our lives and that, ultimately, everything happens for a reason. This perspective can provide comfort and resilience during challenging times, as it encourages individuals to trust in the process of life and to remain open to the possibilities of growth and transformation.

Your truth may look and sound different compared to someone else's presumed truth. Recognizing and appreciating the diversity of beliefs is crucial. Each individual or group may have their worldview shaped by their culture, upbringing, and personal experiences. This diversity can foster an environment where different beliefs are acknowledged and respected. Engaging in open and respectful dialogue allows people from various belief systems to understand each other better. Through conversation, individuals can share their perspectives, listen to others with empathy, and find common ground or areas of understanding. Despite differences in beliefs, many belief systems share common values such as compassion, kindness, and justice. Focusing on these shared values can help bridge the gap between opposing beliefs and foster cooperation and collaboration. Accepting the idea of pluralism, which acknowledges the coexistence of multiple valid perspectives, can promote harmony among different belief systems. Rather than seeking to convert others to one's belief system, embracing pluralism involves recognizing and accepting the legitimacy of diverse beliefs. You can use Lilac to emphasize the importance of peaceful coexistence and non-violent conflict resolution for maintaining harmony between opposing belief systems. This includes respecting each other's rights to hold and practice their beliefs without fear of discrimination or persecution. Identifying common goals or objectives that transcend specific belief systems can unite people from different backgrounds. Working together towards shared goals, such as environmental conservation, social justice, or community development, can help build bridges between opposing belief systems.

No religion, region, or race is the end all, be all.

Right now, peace is the only option. Achieving harmony between opposing belief systems requires a commitment to tolerance, understanding, and cooperation. Swallow your pride. Individuals and communities can coexist peacefully despite their beliefs by embracing diversity, engaging in constructive dialogue, and focusing on shared values and goals.

Mauve - Emotional Flexibility

Mauve is the cup of tea beside you while the outside world crashes against your thoughts and feelings. How do you respond to confrontation, drama, and spontaneous outbursts of a mother scolding their child outside of a store because their son or daughter left their iPad on the ground in a fit of temporary despondency? We all are simultaneously walking through a wetland of feelings that are not our own in real life and online. Emotional flexibility is the ability to adapt and respond to changing emotional situations healthily and constructively. It involves recognizing, understanding, and managing one's emotions effectively and being open to experiencing a range of emotions without becoming overwhelmed or rigidly attached to any one emotional state. Emotional flexibility is essential for self-development, allowing individuals to navigate challenges, build resilience, and foster personal growth. Emotional flexibility enables individuals to adapt to different circumstances and environments. Instead of reacting impulsively or rigidly to emotional triggers, emotionally flexible individuals can adjust their responses based on the demands of the situation. This adaptability promotes greater resilience in adversity and enhances problem-solving skills.

Mauve supports your ability to regulate and manage emotions effectively. This includes recognizing and accepting emotions without judgment and employing healthy coping strategies to regulate intense or distressing emotions. Individuals can reduce stress, anxiety, and other negative emotional states by developing emotional regulation skills, improving overall well-being. Simply wearing the color Mauve enables emotionally flexible individuals to experience a wide range of positive and negative emotions without denying or suppressing them. This openness allows for greater self-awareness and emotional authenticity, as individuals are more willing to explore and express their feelings. Embracing emotional experiences in this way promotes self-acceptance and fosters a deeper understanding of oneself. Cultivating emotional flexibility is essential for building resilience and encouraging personal growth. By learning to adapt and respond to emotional challenges constructively, individuals can bounce back from setbacks more effectively and turn adversity into opportunities for learning and development.

Mauve encourages a growth mindset, which enables individuals to view obstacles as temporary and surmountable.

Be flexible with your feelings. In a reading, Mauve reminds us of our power to breathe through our boredom. The repetitive nature of our work, social life, and internal conversations we keep to ourselves can feel overwhelmingly mundane to the point of avoiding any emotion whatsoever. We are emotional creatures. It's our job to feel. Numbing yourself or downplaying your feelings will only create more of a mess. Mauve is here to reaffirm that if you struggle to regulate your emotions, seek professional help. And remember that you may have unconsciously taken on someone else's emotions to replace your own. So, you'll have to delineate your feelings and desires about the situation flexibly and authentically. So, how are you feeling?

Mallow - Active Listening

Mallow is the twin of Mauve. This dynamic color pair provides comfort, absorption, flexibility, naturalness, and versatility. You want to listen to your intuition actively currently. Mallow is inspired by idiomatic expressions all related to the concept of perception, understanding, or attention. What we see and hear with our third eye chakra and physical senses tell a story of our reality. Pulling the wool over your eyes is an expression to deceive or trick someone, often by concealing the truth or manipulating information to prevent them from seeing the reality of a situation. It implies that someone is being fooled or misled, much like if you were to pull a piece of wool over someone's eyes, obscuring their vision.

Getting the cotton out of your ears is a figurative way of telling someone to listen attentively or pay closer attention to what is being said. It suggests that the person is not fully hearing or comprehending what is being communicated as if their ears were stuffed with cotton, which muffles sound. In one ear and out the other is another expression describing a situation where someone hears or is told something but quickly forgets it or fails to retain the information. It implies that the information had no lasting impact or influence on the person as if it entered one ear and exited the other without being processed or retained. These idioms highlight the importance of attentiveness, understanding, and perception in communication and interaction. They remind us to be mindful of how we perceive information and actively engage with and process what is being communicated.

Active listening is a communication technique that involves fully concentrating on, understanding, responding to, and remembering what is being said by another person. It's a skill that requires not only hearing the words being spoken but also paying attention to non-verbal cues, such as body language and tone of voice, to grasp the message entirely. Active listening is a fundamental aspect of effective communication and is essential in various contexts, including personal relationships, professional settings, and conflict resolution. Mallow wants you to give your situation your full attention. This means minimizing distractions, such as putting away electronic devices, making eye contact, and focusing on the words and non-verbal cues while processing or confronting the situation.

Demonstrating genuine interest in what others say encourages them to continue expressing themselves. Nodding, maintaining eye contact, and verbally affirming that you're receiving the information show that you're engaged in the conversation. Reflecting or paraphrasing the speaker's words back to them proves that you are actively listening and understanding their message. Don't be afraid to upcycle someone's perspective to find common ground. Take the time to explain your viewpoint patiently and calmly. It also allows for clarification and ensures that both parties are on the same page. It's natural for all of us to want to be heard.

Mallow encourages empathizing to better understand and acknowledge feelings and perspectives outside your worldview. Acknowledging someone else's emotions validates their experience and creates a sense of connection and understanding. Active listening requires setting aside personal biases or judgments and listening to another soul with an open mind. Avoid interrupting or jumping to conclusions; strive to understand the speaker's viewpoint before forming opinions. Providing feedback involves offering responses or asking questions that encourage further conversation. Mallow explores comprehension of the information we consume. When soaking up news and information, summarize main points, ask clarifying questions, or offer supportive comments. Remembering critical points of the conversation shows that you value another human being and are actively engaged in the exchange. Remembering details allows for continuity in the conversation and reinforces the sense of connection between both parties.

Should Mallow slip into opposition or be challenged somehow, understand that active listening is not to persuade others that you are right and they are wrong. An overactive third eye or underperforming one can lead to confusion, imposter syndrome, and sabotage. Looking at the situation honestly, are there hypercritical accusations (flaws, mistakes, or shortcomings in a straightforward and unsympathetic manner) pointed at you or the desired outcome? Mallow reversed is all about internal and external messages delivered with intense disapproval or contempt. It can be emotionally damaging and may focus on attacking the person rather than criticizing the behavior or idea. It suggests that the critic needs to focus more on finding fault or nitpicking rather than offering constructive feedback or support. If you fear criticism, Mallow appearing in a reading can indicate the value of constructive criticism, offering you an outlet to cultivate resistant versatility to the situation and supporting you in reaching a space of objectivity so that your subjective state of happiness may improve. Constructive criticism aims to identify areas for improvement while offering support and encouragement for growth and development. Are you taking the struggle, conflict, or situation too personally that the fear of being seen as less than perfect is pulling the wool over your eyes? Do you want the cards to tell you only things you want to hear?

Ignorance is a fool's game. But undoubtedly, we only know what we know when we know it. Mallow is a strong ally in your color repertoire to understand the fabric of narcissism, criticism, and selective hearing in your life. When you practice active listening, you will feel better equipped to identify and handle the nuances of your perception and the information you consume. Mallow's wisdom and effective listening strategy can create a sense of comfort and safety in interpersonal interactions. When someone feels genuinely listened to, they may feel understood, validated, and supported, much like the comfort provided by cotton. Cotton can absorb moisture, which is why it's commonly used in towels and other absorbent materials. Active listening involves absorbing information and understanding the message. Just as cotton absorbs liquid, attentive listeners absorb the words, emotions, and nuances of the world around them. While cotton and listening may seem unrelated on the surface, they share qualities of comfort, absorption, flexibility, naturalness, and versatility. By recognizing these similarities, we gain a deeper appreciation for the importance of active listening in our daily lives.

CROWN CHAKRA

Orchid - Raise Your Vibrations

The phrase "Your vibe attracts your tribe" suggests that people with similar energies, attitudes, or characteristics tend to gravitate toward each other. In this context, if someone emits a vibe associated with being a "space child" or having an otherworldly aura, they might naturally attract others who resonate with or understand that vibe. When connecting this concept to Orchid from *The Color Mage Oracle*, we delve into a realm where our spirituality and the mood of the Universe intersect. Orchid, as described, embodies qualities of having out-of-this-world feelings, spatial awareness, and divine intelligence. These attributes could be interpreted as metaphysical or transcendent, suggesting a connection to concepts like resonance theory and panpsychism. Resonance theory suggests that everything in the universe vibrates at its frequency, and when two frequencies align, resonance occurs, leading to a harmonious interaction. Orchids appear in your reading to send you a message to connect individuals and concepts that are drawing upon, accessing, or emitting similar vibrations or energies. Aesthetics align when you tap into the mood of the Universe. In marketing, this resonance theory is practiced by brands that show up where their ideal customers are. For panpsychism, it proposes that consciousness or the mind is a fundamental aspect of the universe, present in all things to some degree. Orchid's embodiment of intelligence and otherworldly feelings could reflect elements of consciousness or awareness beyond what is conventionally understood, aligning with the panpsychist idea that a kind of mind or consciousness is inherent in all existence. Orchid wants you to remember that you were designed through the Universe's wild alchemical, biological, and social process of humanity. Your vibe matters. What you choose and not choose to do impacts the world around you. An excellent tool for you to use to realign to raising vibrations is the spiritual system of Human Design.

Human Design combines elements of astrology, the I Ching, Kabbalah, and the chakra system, among others, to provide insights into an individual's personality, strengths, weaknesses, and life purpose. It's based on the idea that each person is born with a unique energetic blueprint, which can be analyzed using a chart derived from their birth information. It suggests individuals have specific energetic frequencies or vibrations that make up their unique blueprint. When these frequencies align or resonate, it can lead to harmony and alignment in one's life. Resonance theory supports that individuals with compatible energetic frequencies are naturally drawn to each other and may experience smoother interactions and relationships. Human Design also incorporates the concept of consciousness into its framework, suggesting that everyone has a unique consciousness or awareness that is part of universal consciousness. This aligns with panpsychism's idea that consciousness is a fundamental aspect of the universe and is present in all things to some degree. From a panpsychist perspective, Human Design can be seen as a way of understanding how consciousness manifests in individual human beings through their energetic blueprint and how it influences their lives and interactions with the world.

Your life experience does mean something; you may have forgotten this truth. With all the weight, distractions, and Corporate Chaos, it's easy for someone to slip into lower frequencies to justify keeping up with the bare necessities. Still, when you try to attune and align yourself to higher vibrations, it makes the life, liberty, and pursuit of happiness you crave more tangible and real.

When Orchid is reversed or challenged by other influences, the reading reflects caution as the crux of the conflict is generated by spiritual bypassing. Spiritual bypassing refers to using spiritual beliefs, practices, or concepts to avoid dealing with or confronting uncomfortable emotions, unresolved issues, or real-life challenges. You see this in mainstream religions like

Christianity when people flood social media with "thoughts and prayers" as if they offer any practical relief or solutions. It involves using spiritual catchphrases or practices to escape from or deny aspects of oneself or one's life that are difficult to face. Denying yourself to acknowledge unease, unrest, and upheaval exacerbates the unease, turmoil, and upheaval you're afraid of in the first place.

While spirituality can be a powerful tool for personal growth and healing, spiritual bypassing can hinder genuine growth and lead to a superficial or inauthentic spiritual experience. The first step in overcoming spiritual bypassing is to know when it's happening. Pay attention to when you use spiritual beliefs or practices to avoid uncomfortable emotions or situations. Notice if you're using phrases like "everything happens for a reason" or "just let it go" to dismiss or minimize the problem and conversation. It would be best if you accepted that humanity is messy. Recognize that spiritual growth involves facing and working through your human experiences, including pain, fear, and uncertainty. Feeling and acknowledging difficult emotions is okay—a natural part of being human.

Instead of avoiding your feelings, allow yourself to experience and process them fully. You're not alone in this; we all are together. Don't be afraid to seek support from others, whether it's friends, family, or a therapist. Talking about your struggles and emotions with someone you trust can help you gain perspective and insight into your experiences. It can also provide validation and empathy, essential for healing and growth. Integrate your spiritual beliefs and practices with a grounded sense of reality. This means recognizing that spirituality is not a substitute for practical action or addressing real-life challenges. Find ways to apply your spiritual insights and principles to your everyday life meaningfully and constructively. Be gentle and compassionate with yourself as you navigate your spiritual journey. It's okay to make mistakes or fall into old patterns occasionally. Treat yourself with kindness and understanding. Remember that growth is a gradual process not designed for overnight success.

Watered down, vibes might be a feeling, but feelings have real consequences because we are human. Orchid infuses our perspective in an elevated way that projects us into future timelines. As you work with the energy of Orchid, open yourself up to the vastness of space-time, divine channeling, and the mood of any information you interact with daily. The more you interact and consume information, the more your energy will respond intuitively. Then the Universe will react automatically, and you'll find yourself in a multisensory continuum of circumstances that you might not otherwise feel if you sang another tune, walked another path, or ignored the person you were born to be.

EARTH STAR CHAKRA

Chocolate - Indulgence

You are asked to indulge in your human experience. We all have a limited time here on Earth, so we must respect our connection and relationship to Earth, accessed through the Earth Star Chakra. The Earth Star Chakra is associated with grounding, stability, and connection to the

Earth's energy. It is located below the feet and serves as an anchor point for our energetic body to connect with earthly experiences, no matter how mundane. The depth of your pockets is fine regarding this universal connection. Money is a social construct and a mechanism to micromanage Earth's resources, and in the eyes of Corporate Chaos, people too are resources. Why should corporations and governments be the only ones to recognize the resourcefulness of being human?

You have power here. Indulge.

Chocolate is often associated with earthy flavors and can evoke a sense of grounding and connection to the physical world. Mindfully consuming chocolate can help individuals feel present and connected to the earth during a reading, primarily when focusing on the sensations and flavors experienced. Chocolate from the cacao bean, which grows on the cacao tree, a plant deeply rooted in the earth, is seen as a product of the earth's abundance and a source of nourishment and sustenance. Similarly, the Earth Star Chakra is believed to be a reservoir of Earth energy that provides support and nourishment to the entire energetic system of our existence. Both chocolate and the Earth Star Chakra symbolize the idea of drawing sustenance and support from the Earth's energy. Going deeper, Chocolate is often associated with pleasure and enjoyment, particularly in its indulgent forms, such as rich desserts or decadent treats. Similarly, the Earth Star Chakra is linked to sensual experiences and the enjoyment of physical sensations. Both chocolate and the Earth Star Chakra remind us to appreciate and savor the pleasures of the physical world, whether through the taste of chocolate or the sensation of bare feet on the earth.

Chocolate originated in ancient Mesoamerica, where the cacao tree (Theobroma cacao) is native. The Olmec civilization (1500–400 BCE) is believed to be among the first to cultivate cacao, with evidence of cacao consumption dating back to around 1900 BCE. The Maya and later the Aztecs also highly valued cacao, using it in religious rituals, as currency, and to create a bitter drink called "xocolātl." Spanish explorers, such as Hernán Cortés, encountered chocolate during their expeditions to the Americas in the 16th century. They brought cacao beans back to Europe, where the elite initially consumed chocolate as a beverage. Sugar was later added to sweeten the drink, making it more palatable and increasing its popularity. In the 17th and 18th centuries, chocolate houses became fashionable European gathering places, particularly in cities like London—chocolate production, mass-producing chocolate bars, candies, and other confections, industrialized during the Industrial Revolution. Chocolate has long been associated with luxury and indulgence due to its rich taste and historical rarity. The wealthy elite often consumed it as a symbol of status and refinement.

Chocolate's history is intertwined with human culture, from its ancient roots in Mesoamerica to its widespread popularity and symbolism in the modern world. It continues to be cherished for its delicious taste and multifaceted symbolism in society. When Chocolate appears in a reading, you're asked to connect to your energy levels. Cocoa contains natural stimulants such as caffeine and theobromine, which can boost energy and vitality during rituals or magical workings. This can help practitioners to focus on their intentions and amplify their mood. Despite its stimulating properties, cocoa can also have grounding and centering effects. It can help practitioners feel more rooted and connected to the earth, making it useful for rituals that involve grounding, protection, or connecting with nature spirits. Like many ingredients used in magic and ritual, cocoa can be a focal point for intention setting and amplification. Practitioners can harness its properties to support their magical goals and manifestations by infusing cocoa with specific intentions or energies.

Should Chocolate be reversed or influenced negatively during a color reading, it involves going beyond what is necessary or healthy and can negatively affect our lives. Unhealthy foods, alcohol, or other substances can lead to weight gain, poor nutrition, and increased risk of chronic diseases such as diabetes, heart disease, and liver damage. It can also contribute to fatigue, decreased energy levels, and impaired physical function. Overindulgence can negatively impact mental health by exacerbating stress, anxiety, and depression. Using substances or engaging in excessive behaviors as a coping mechanism can mask underlying emotional issues and prevent individuals from healthily addressing them. Overindulgence in material possessions or excessive spending can lead to financial strain, debt, and insecurity. It can also contribute to a cycle of consumerism and dissatisfaction, where individuals constantly seek fulfillment through external possessions or experiences. Prioritizing indulgence over meaningful connections can result in feelings of isolation and loneliness. The gluttony of our greed can interfere with productivity and goal attainment by consuming time, energy, and resources that could be allocated to more constructive pursuits. It can lead to procrastination, distraction, and a lack of motivation to pursue meaningful goals and aspirations. Overindulgence can have multifaceted adverse effects on our lives, including physical health, mental well-being, financial stability, relationships, productivity, and personal growth. Recognizing and addressing patterns of overindulgence is essential for promoting balance, health, and overall well-being.

Chocolate reminds us to indulge in our multisensory experiences here on Earth, but not at the expense of our well-being or others. Although indulgence may be a luxury or a privilege, remember that we all have a sweet tooth for life, liberty, and the pursuit of happiness.

Heather - Solitude & Diligence

Heather is one of the colors in *The Color Mage Oracle,* inspired by anyone who finds themselves as the black sheep in family settings, wallflowers at school functions, and people who prefer to work independently and live a quiet and solitary life away from the fanfare. In traditional tarot, the Hermit card typically represents introspection, inner guidance, and solitude. Depicted as an old man holding a lantern, the Hermit withdraws from the world to seek wisdom and enlightenment through introspection and solitary reflection. Although the Hermit may wear a tattered old heather brown cloak with years of experience, Heather, in the color oracle deck, recognizes that old souls come from all walks of life, not just old white men with a beard (no shade to Santa, Gandalf, or Dumbledore). This color is inspired by the magic of pinecones.

Pinecones are the reproductive structures of conifer trees, primarily pine trees. They are cone-shaped and consist of overlapping scales that protect the seeds produced by the tree. These seeds are released when the pinecone matures and opens, allowing them to be dispersed and germinate to grow new trees. I often found myself alone outside, playing with pinecones and fascinated by their existence. Pinecones symbolize enlightenment, wisdom, and spiritual awakening in many spiritual traditions. This symbolism is derived from the pineal gland, a small endocrine gland in the brain that regulates sleep and wake cycles and is often referred to as the "third eye" in spiritual contexts. The pineal gland is named after its pinecone-like shape, and thus, pinecones are sometimes associated with spiritual insight and the pursuit of higher consciousness. Pinecones' sturdy and resilient nature also makes them symbols of protection and strength in certain cultures. They are often used in crafts, decorations, and even architectural ornamentation to evoke feelings of stability, security, and resilience.

Like a mighty pine forest going through harsh weather, Heather asks you to be persistent, careful, and hardworking at this time to accomplish a task or achieve a goal. It involves a conscientious and steady approach to work, characterized by thoroughness, attention to detail, and a commitment to completing tasks to the best of one's ability. Diligence implies a dedication to excellence and a willingness to exert sustained effort despite obstacles or challenges. Practice consistency in your creative projects. Follow up on loose ends. Don't be afraid to take a new opportunity and give yourself space to think things over. Meditate with pinecones when faced with new developments that impact your situation. Pinecones are often associated with renewal and growth because they are a vital part of the reproductive process of conifer trees. As seeds are released from mature pinecones and new trees grow, they symbolize the cycle of life, regeneration, and the promise of new beginnings. But not without due diligence for protection. Consult with a professional. You don't have to approach this alone if it means potential missteps.

Heather's do-it-yourself attitude is commendable. Your ability to figure something out is what we, as a species, deserve. However, Heather could indicate something negative when your socially avoidant attitude obstructs the beauty of teamwork, belongingness, and community. The reluctance and resistance to gatherings and dealing with people is expected. However, people need people. We need each other, and we only have so much time on this planet in our state to make a difference. Just as the plants, animals, and microorganisms in a forest rely on each other for survival, humans depend on one another for various aspects of life. We rely on social connections, relationships, and cooperation to meet our physical, emotional, and psychological needs. In a forest, different species often cooperate and interact for mutual benefit through symbiotic relationships or mutualistic interactions. Heather reminds us that humans thrive in communities where individuals support each other, share resources, and collaborate to achieve common goals. Forest ecosystems thrive because of their biodiversity, with each species contributing uniquely to the overall health and resilience of the ecosystem. Your role in your town matters even if you live in a shack in the middle of the woods. Diverse human communities benefit from the strengths, skills, and perspectives of individuals from various backgrounds and experiences. Just as the health of a forest depends on collective efforts to protect and preserve it, societal well-being relies on shared responsibility and collective action to address challenges such as environmental degradation, social injustice, and economic inequality.

Heather wants you to accept that this is your home. And it's your responsibility to care for it - but it doesn't mean you have to do it alone. You can find solitude if you perform due diligence rooted in your social and community footprint. You bring energy, skills, and experiences that can benefit the greater collective. This often means starting your own business, running for office, taking up an independent study, or booking a retreat. Heather explores the interconnectedness of valuing your individuality and its impact on society so that you can enjoy solitude at home.

Brown - Ground Thyself

Grounding oneself refers to connecting to the present moment, one's body, and the environment to foster a sense of stability, security, and inner peace. Brown anchors oneself to the here and now, especially during times of stress, anxiety, or emotional upheaval. Grounding techniques vary widely and may include mindfulness exercises, sensory activities, physical movements, or creative expression. Change is the only constant in life that we know for sure. Brown is a color that appears in readings before and during periods of crisis, transition, and flux. Brown wants you to engage in grounding exercises connecting the senses and the environment. For example, focus on the sensation of your feet on the ground, the texture of objects around you, or the sounds in your environment. Use grounding objects such as a stress ball, smooth stone, or fabric to focus your attention. Spend time in nature to reconnect with the natural world and find solace in its rhythms and beauty. Take a walk in the park, sit by a body of water, or observe the sky, trees, and wildlife. Nature has a grounding effect that can help soothe the mind and restore balance.

Brown also indicates a need for routine and structure. Establish routines and rituals in your daily life to provide a sense of stability and predictability. Set aside time for self-care, exercise, meals, and relaxation to create a structure during times of change. In your color reading, Brown reminds you that you're looking for stability, efficiency, resolutions, and achievement. Routines and structure provide stability and predictability, which can help reduce feelings of uncertainty and anxiety. Knowing what to expect and having a clear framework for daily activities can promote security and comfort. Your situation could change or is in the middle of changing, so it's essential to focus on the consistent aspects of your life so you're not swept away by being overwhelmed and distracted by shockwaves of new information to destabilize your spirit. A routine can improve efficiency and productivity by streamlining tasks and reducing decision fatigue. When certain activities become habitual, less cognitive effort is required to complete them, allowing individuals to focus their mental energy on more complex or demanding tasks. Structures help individuals manage their time effectively by allocating specific time slots for different activities. This can prevent procrastination, increase accountability, and ensure that essential tasks are prioritized and completed on time. Following a structured routine can create a sense of accomplishment as you meet your goals and fulfill your responsibilities. Achieving small milestones and consistent routines can boost self-esteem and confidence.

When Brown is reversed or in a challenging influence, the situation feels rigid and monotonous, and you could be experiencing burnout from the pressure. Excessive rigidity in routines and structure can lead to inflexibility and resistance to change. Individuals may become overly reliant on familiar routines and need help to adapt to new situations or environments, limiting personal growth and exploration. Repetitive routines can become monotonous and dull, leading to feelings of boredom and dissatisfaction. Lack of variety and spontaneity in daily activities can diminish creativity and zest for life, contributing to stagnation or emptiness. Relying too heavily on external structures and routines may result in a sense of dependency and learned helplessness. In your situation, how are you putting the responsibility on someone else or on an outside entity to handle or resolve? When Brown is revered, you may struggle to initiate or manage tasks independently without the guidance of a structured framework, leading to feelings of incompetence or inadequacy. While routines can help reduce stress by providing organization and predictability, they can also become sources of stress if they become too demanding or overwhelming. Overcommitment to rigid schedules or excessive multitasking can lead to burnout and mental exhaustion.

Practice self-compassion and self-care to nurture yourself with kindness and understanding during transition periods. Treat yourself with patience, gentleness, and acceptance, recognizing that change is a natural part of life. Brown encourages us to strike a balance between structure and flexibility to accommodate changing circumstances and maintain overall wellness and courage to be presently resilient.

Café - Create Sacred Space

Sacred space holds special significance and is imbued with spiritual or religious meaning. It can be a physical location, such as a temple, church, mosque, or shrine, or a natural setting, like a mountain, forest, or river. Sacred spaces are often designated for worship, prayer, meditation, or other rituals, and they are places where individuals can connect with the divine, experience transcendence, or find inner peace and solace. The concept of sacred space is found in various cultures and religions around the world, and it reflects humanity's desire to honor and commune with the holy or the divine - think of the lost library of Alexandria, wonders of the world, and your backyard.

Café is a grounding color that embodies our place of origin and the places we call home when we are away. In a reading, Café inspires us to become more present in our physical space and akasha. Akasha is Sanskrit for sky or ether. It refers to an ethereal or cosmic plane of existence and is commonly mentioned in spiritual practices when talking about the Akashic Records. According to some spiritual and mystical belief systems, the Akashic Records are a compendium of all human events, thoughts, words, emotions, and intent ever to have occurred in the past, present, or future. Café symbolizes this esoteric archive but generally represents recordkeeping and housekeeping.

When the Café color card appears, you're asked to leave the house, clean your space, and build a focal point or tablescape to connect with your desire to feel at home. Café reminds us of the beauty of having our place of sanctuary. Often, this color wants you to go to a coffee shop or library or go out in nature to reconnect to your home and take care of the environment. It may mean it's time to rearrange your rooms, redecorate, or delete your emails, messages, notifications, or files that are collecting dust and taking up digital space. When negatively influenced, it shows how you may feel subconsciously about your place in the world. The overwhelming sensation of clutter, bottlenecks, and pollution negatively impacts the mood. Additionally, creating a sacred space or fragile safe space based on your prejudices and limited beliefs doesn't justify your place in the world at the expense of others. Let the record show that your exclusive echo chamber of race, religion, and region doesn't erase diversity. It doesn't help humanity whatsoever if the sacred space or safe space you're cultivating ostracizes others because of their gender identity, income, religious beliefs, race, or any other profiling attribute misses the mark on your grading rubric. Humans are meant to build bridges, not walls. Be inclusive.

Small businesses, community spaces, and your home are liminal spaces between the physical and the spiritual realms. You occupy and carry resonance as you move through these spaces, so be sure that you own the energy you bring to a space (offline and online) and the energy you take from a space. Are you adding value? Is the energy exchanged smooth and peaceful? Is there a space to meet others that is neutral territory or personifies common goals that enrich the story of humanity? Cafés are a symbol of great ideas and places where people can meet. The magic of gathering with others is timeless and ancient, so acknowledge the reverence of respecting property and commit to living with more spatial awareness.

Typha - Earth Energy

The magic of cattails inspires Typha. They are often found in marshes, ponds, and other wetland areas. Cattails are known for their ecological importance, providing habitat for various wildlife species and helping to stabilize soil in wetland environments. Cattails' ability to grow in challenging habitats can be seen as a metaphor for endurance and adaptability. When Typha appears in a reading, it represents resource management, resilience, and social stratification.

Historically, many indigenous cultures have regarded cattails as a valuable natural resource. They provide food, shelter, and materials for crafting provisions such as baskets and mats. In this context, cattails symbolize sustenance and the interconnectedness between humans and nature. Over time, humans learned to bend the elements of the earth to create an ecosystem of abundance. Typha may suggest you look at your finances and recognize areas of improvement. Do you have multiple revenue streams of income? The ecology of money on Earth is very influential, and Typha wants you to absorb and retain financial literacy—store provisions for a rainy day. And reflect on optimizing your network of people you know to feel sustained and nourished. Your energy, time, and money are resources that others (even corporations) depend on, so it's critical that you identify where you want to channel your reserves, especially during challenging and adverse times. Delineate clear pathways of where your money is coming and going. Typha wants you to be adaptable and open to sourcing new renewable energy that may come from people, places, and things outside the ecosystem you already maintain.

When Typha is in a challenging position or reversed, it's a message of overspending resources and social stratification. Stop spending frivolously. That's a straightforward message to glean from Typha's negative influence. A more demanding challenge influencing your situation could be breaking free from colonization through systems of socioeconomic suppression that promote poverty consciousness, in other words, social stratification. Poverty consciousness focuses on lack, scarcity, and limitations rather than abundance and opportunities. Individuals with poverty consciousness tend to perceive the world through a lens of scarcity, believing that there is not enough to go around and that they are destined to struggle or suffer. The struggles and sacrifices that they've endured are then used to micromanage their experiences and fragment their sense of belonging in the world. In response, this creates a gateway to crime, homelessness, and more fear that the privilege will then be used to keep poor people poor. Segregation doesn't solely happen based on the color of your skin. Social stratification is the structured division of a society's populace into distinct groups determined by various socioeconomic factors such as wealth, income, race, education, ethnicity, gender, occupation, social status, or acquired power. This hierarchical arrangement assigns different privilege levels to each group within the societal framework. It's the elusive

Hunger Games we all are born into but can transform with some immense mental, emotional, spiritual, and physical determination on our part. Corporate Chaos loves this shit when we stay dirt poor, live paycheck to paycheck, accrue debt, and work building billionaires' dreams but not our own until the retirement phase of our lives.

Working hard is admirable, but at what cost? Colonization is when one country or group of people (or corporations) establishes control over another territory, often exploiting its resources, labor, and inhabitants for economic, political, or cultural gain. Colonization historically has been driven by various motives, including economic expansion, the pursuit of individual wealth, religious conversion, and geopolitical dominance. When it comes to natural resources, colonization often involves the extraction, exploitation, and execution of the colonized territory's natural wealth to benefit the colonizing power. Corporations and governing bodies have colonized us en masse. Humans are seen as resources through the eyes of the elite. Colonizers often exploit populations through forced labor systems such as slavery, indentured servitude, or coerced labor in plantations, mines, and other resource extraction industries. You cannot survive in this world without a job. We all are corralled into education systems at an early age and programmed to answer: what do you want to be when you grow up - ad nauseam.

Typha is the raw and unadulterated bluntness you need to create checks and balances in your situation. Excess is only sometimes abundant. It's up to you to decide what's worth keeping and what to pass up. You are a resource of the Universe, but it doesn't mean you have to settle for less, cower from negotiating more money, or feel defined by social stratification as we endure modern colonization under the thumb of Corporate Chaos. Like cattails, you can stand above the muck of being marginalized and consciously choose to flourish in adversity. Allow the light of you to shine stubbornly—your persistence and commitment to drain the swamp pay for itself. There's more than enough in the world to go around and plenty of space to finally figure out what and who you want to be when you grow up.

Canyon - Deep Perspective

Native American cultures have myths and legends explaining the origins of geological features, including canyons. In some cultures of the southwestern United States, there are stories about the Great Spirit or other powerful beings shaping the land. These stories often involve potent forces of nature, such as thunderstorms, floods, or earthquakes, and emphasize the common theme in the color deck.

Interconnectedness between humans and the natural world.

One such story involves a great flood sent by the Great Spirit to cleanse the earth of corruption. As the waters recede, they carve deep channels into the world, creating the intricate network of canyons and gorges that we see today. In this interpretation, canyons are seen as sacred places, imbued with spiritual significance and connected to the earth's natural cycles of renewal and rebirth. Another variation of this legend involves the actions of heroic or mythical figures who shape the landscape through their deeds or struggles. According to Hopi mythology, the creation of the Grand Canyon and the river flowing through it is attributed to two brothers, Pokanghoya and Polongahoya. They are said to have fashioned the canyon by casting lightning bolts and shaping mud. They formed significant landmarks such as Tokonave (Navajo Mountain) and Neuvatikyaovi (San Francisco Peaks) and created salt beds in eastern New Mexico. Over time, the Hopi people established annual pilgrimages to gather clay from the Sipapuni (the cultural origin of the Hopi ancestors) and salt from a cave situated along the Colorado River within the Grand Canyon. These legends serve not only to explain the physical features of the landscape but also to impart cultural teachings and spiritual lessons about the relationship between humans and the natural world. They emphasize the importance of respecting and preserving the land and recognizing the power and wisdom of the natural forces that shape it.

When Canyon appears in a reading, you're asked to experience a shamanic journey, go on a vision quest, and find inspiration and meaning in the geography surrounding you. How does the land reflect your mood and intentions? How does your home personify an extension of the land around you? Canyon's message asks you to think deeper about your situation and how the environment shapes your perspective. Combining deep thinking, self-reflection, and a deep respect for one's home and land can lead to a profound sense of fulfillment and purpose. Deep thinking and self-reflection can help individuals recognize the interconnectedness between themselves, their community, and the land they inhabit. By reflecting on how their actions impact the environment and the well-being of others, individuals can cultivate a deeper sense of responsibility and stewardship toward their home and land. See Jasper. Canyon allows you to explore your values, beliefs, and personal connection to your home and land. By contemplating what the land means to you and why it is important, you can develop a stronger sense of identity and purpose rooted in the relationship with your backyard. Deepening one's understanding of one's cultural heritage and community traditions can foster a greater appreciation for the land and its significance. By participating in rituals, ceremonies, and practices that honor and respect the land, individuals can strengthen their sense of belonging and purpose within their community.

Canyon reversed or negatively influenced indicates a fear of falling into a rut and succumbing to others with shallow intentions to take advantage of you or the land. Leveling a cornerstone of the community for a parking lot or displacing people through gentrified, inflated, and overpriced development plans are some pain points this color has shown over the years. Canyon also may reveal tendencies of self-deprecation to avoid connecting with others on a deeper level. Self-deprecation happens when you undervalue yourself, often through humor or modesty. It involves making disparaging remarks about your abilities, appearance, or character traits in a joking manner to deflect depth. Self-deprecation can serve various purposes, such as diffusing tension, seeking validation, or expressing humility. However, excessive self-deprecation can undermine self-confidence and contribute to feelings of inadequacy or low self-esteem. It's essential to balance acknowledging one's flaws and strengths while maintaining a healthy self-worth. Over time, self-deprecation erodes not only how you see yourself but how others come to see you.

Canyon is a potent reminder in reading to deepen one's appreciation for the unique characteristics and history of one's home and land. You can proactively protect and preserve your home and land by embracing a sense of place and cultivating a connection to the land. Don't be afraid to carve your path.

Shea - Beauty or Beast

Shea is inspired by Ori, the Yoruba word for shea butter, which comes from the seed and bark of the shea tree. In Yoruba culture, Ori refers to the head, but it holds a beautiful significance beyond its physical aspect. It is believed to be the seat of consciousness, destiny, and personal identity. In Yoruba spirituality, one's "Ori" is considered sacred and is often honored through prayers, rituals, and offerings to ensure alignment with one's destiny and spiritual growth. Shea, showing up in your reading brings out your creature comforts and promotes a healthy self-care routine. It inspires you to take care of your head and mental health. You're asked to prioritize things you need to feel comfortable with so that your reputation and identity express themselves peacefully and authentically while working with the spirit of Shea. Be your own beauty guru and makeup artist.

Yoruba culture is characterized by a deep sense of spirituality and reverence for ancestors, with beliefs centered around a pantheon of deities known as Orishas. Traditional Yoruba religion, known as Ifá or Orisha worship, involves rituals, ceremonies, and divination practices to maintain harmony with the spiritual world and ensure the community's well-being. Yoruba culture also encompasses vibrant artistic traditions, including sculpture, textiles, beadwork, and drumming, as well as elaborate ceremonies and festivals celebrating important life events and cultural heritage. In addition to Nigeria, Yoruba communities can be found in other parts of the world, including the Americas, where Yoruba culture and religion have influenced Afro-Caribbean and Afro-American traditions such as Santería, Candomblé, and Voodoo. These practices are not meant for anyone to perform or touch naively. These ancient customs are intended to be taken seriously and held with utmost respect and regard for their origins. Shea isn't a color to whitewash or appropriate cultural significance because it's attractively exotic. Exploiting diversity is disgraceful, and this could be a strong indication when Shea appears reversed or negatively influenced in a reading.

This grounded Shea energy honors your earthen expression while navigating feeling beautiful or beastly. But it's not always easy to feel attractive or see our true nature, so Shea's energy is here to help us take care of ourselves and lean into the folds of our personality like a paper crane in origami. When Shea is negatively influenced or reversed, it can underscore feeling ugly and unkempt about the situation. The "beauty or beast" dichotomy reflects the extreme and dichotomous nature of body dysmorphia, where individuals oscillate between idealizing and demonizing their appearance. This distorted perception can lead to significant distress, impaired social functioning, and difficulty in maintaining healthy relationships. Treatment for body dysmorphia often involves therapy, medication, and support groups to help individuals develop a more realistic and positive self-image. You could be struggling to see yourself realistically and lovingly in this situation, fueling your mental unrest. Body dysmorphia is a mental health disorder characterized by obsessive preoccupation with perceived flaws or defects in one's appearance, which are often unnoticeable or minor to others. In this context, "beauty" represents the idealized or desired image individuals with body dysmorphia may aspire to achieve. They may fixate on specific aspects of their appearance, striving for an unrealistic standard of beauty that they believe will bring them happiness or acceptance. Conversely, "beast" represents the negative self-image and distorted perception individuals with body dysmorphia may have of themselves. They may hyperfocus on perceived flaws or imperfections, viewing themselves unattractive, undesirable, or even monstrous. In a reading, Shea is not a diagnosis and should not be treated as one. If you believe you're struggling with body dysmorphia, please schedule an appointment with your doctor and mental health professional as soon as possible. Your body is a temple, and you deserve to treat it with love.

Shea is a solid synchronicity for checking on the terrain of your mental health and taking the necessary steps to meet with your wellness team so they can help you navigate the ups and downs of your life and work. If you feel you aren't unique or beautiful enough, Shea is a strong inspiration that beauty is in the eye of the beholder. You are enough to someone and deserve to practice rituals of self-care that promote balance between feeling beautiful and beastly. There is strength in activating your beast mode and working out. When you exercise, you become grounded in the source of primal power. Shea is nature's way of shedding your thoughts like a snake to exfoliate your karmic past. Contrast is a normal part of our human experience. I hope the color deck highlights how you see yourself and the world with kinder and more compassionate eyes because you are a mighty and beautiful soul with unlimited strength to tame your inner beast.

Jasper - Steadfast Stewardship

Jasper is the figurehead at the table that hosts difficult family meetings, the color of a toothpick holding last-minute event appetizers together, and the wooden beehives found in an apiary for bee conservation. Jasper is an intuitive buzz in your reading to remind you to lead and be open to being led if it prioritizes sustainable stewardship. Stewardship is responsible for managing financial, environmental, or human resources. It involves making decisions and taking actions that prioritize long-term sustainability and the well-being of others over short-term gains or personal interests. In essence, stewardship consists of acting as a caretaker or guardian, ensuring that resources are used wisely and ethically for the benefit of both present and future generations. Jasper is the project manager and power of attorney of the color deck who wants you to engage in practical short-term tasks that sustain long-term goals through consistent and forthright effort.

Jasper emerges in your situation to pull you out of the mental gymnastics of your dreams and prompt you to take tangible actions that align with your thoughts and words. No shortage of projections and platitudes shows up in conversations and over Zoom meetings. Collect evidence, proof, and testimony. Inquire about quality assurance and potential risks involved. Jasper seeks integrity in your situation and asks you to plan practically and be open to pioneering your work even if no one else seems to listen or take you seriously. When working with Jasper, avoiding trying to match or exceed the lifestyle, budget, resources, and possessions of your neighbors or peers is helpful. A common reason Jasper appears in reading is that you possess this headstrong desire to maintain a similar standard of living as those around you, often leading to materialistic pursuits or financial strain to appear equally successful or affluent.

When Jasper is negatively influenced, it reveals it is rooted in comparisonitis. Comparisonitis is like a bug that sneaks into our minds, making us constantly measure ourselves against others. This habit often leaves us feeling not good enough, envious, or just plain down on ourselves. Whether it's looking at what others have or what they've achieved, we start sizing up our worth and success based on theirs. But here's the thing: this comparison game can seriously mess with our happiness and growth. It's like trying to run a race while constantly looking over your shoulder – you'll never reach the finish line feeling fulfilled.

Your station in life isn't meant to be precisely the same as someone else's. This makes you unique. You possess your own experience that no one else could ever take away. Jasper's self-made persistence and tenacious craftsmanship for collective good allow you to sustain happiness by staying in your lane. In your situation, what you commit to grows. Leadership doesn't have to come through extroverted narcissistic fragile masculinity or how many followers you have on social media. Steadfast stewardship is about recognizing that self-acceptance is the most efficient form of leadership because your hard work eventually pays off. Trust the process. Jasper brings the message that you should lead with love. This means empowering others to take ownership of their roles and contribute to the greater good, fostering a culture of collaboration, accountability, and continuous improvement.

Jasper shares a similar theme in *The Oak and the Reed,* one of Aesop's fables. It's a short story with a moral lesson about an oak tree and a reed that grow near each other. The oak tree boasts of its strength and resilience against the elements, while the reed humbly acknowledges its weakness and flexibility. When a storm arrives, the mighty oak is uprooted and falls, while the flexible reed bends with the wind and survives. The point is that flexibility and humility are often more valuable than strength and pride, especially regarding leadership, sustainability, and stewardship.

Tumbleweed - Native Worldliness

Tumbleweeds are the prickly, dried-up, detached branches or stems of certain plants, typically thistles known as Russian thistle, windwitch, or common saltwort. They break off from their roots and are blown away by the wind, often rolling across the landscape. You can find them in arid regions like deserts, where the dry climate and open landscapes facilitate their formation and movement. When Tumbleweed appears in a reading, it identifies feelings of detachment, wanderlust, and evanescence. It's a color for anyone feeling homesick, experiencing an empty nest, or navigating grief. As the saying goes, those who wander are not always lost. Tumbleweed is a grounding and protective color energy that helps you find balance and reclaim your time within transience.

Life is unhinged, feral, and ever-changing, so we must roll with the punches. Tumbleweed is an excellent reminder to thrive in harsh environments and learn to adapt to your situation, the challenging aspects of inquiry, and bureaucracy. In your life and work, contrast and change contextualize your human experience and deepen the quality of your character and moral compass. If you've been feeling lost and abandoned, Tumbleweed indicates you're craving the divine nature of free-spiritedness. Tumbleweed wants you to embrace new experiences and explore the world beyond your race, religion, and region. It's a sign to expand your sensibility to unfamiliar territory, customs, and philosophical beliefs outside of your purview.

Should Tumbleweed appear reversed or dominantly influenced in a reading, it comes as an omen. Often, in cinematic Western and apocalyptic showdowns, you'll see a desolate tumbleweed cameo briefly before conflict comes to a head, foreshadowing pain, sacrifice, and loss. You're asked to plot how you'll mitigate risk and overcome obstacles in your situation should things worsen, resources dry up, or death occur. It's an excellent time to research and review wills, trusts, and estates. The rugged and untamed nature of the world tends to uproot us from what and who we know and displaces us when we least expect it, so Tumbleweed can be viewed as a predictive frequency, signaling the end of one phase and the beginning of another. It symbolizes endings, closure, and the start of new chapters in life. Tumbleweed is like the Tower and Death cards in traditional tarot.

While Tumbleweed dispels your naivete about the world, it also reinforces having faith when blessings are disguised in unorthodox circumstances. Be open to unexpected arrivals, detours, and acquaintances here to change your life and expand your native worldliness. Native worldliness is a deep understanding and familiarity with one's culture, environment, and way of life. Most access this through family; however, if you're a free-spirit, lone wolf, or an outsider, life gives you an advantage to having an acute awareness of one's emotions and those of others. Tumbleweed helps you attune yourself to subtle nuances in emotions and be able to understand and empathize with the experiences of others beyond the color of your skin, heritage, or familial roots. It involves a nuanced awareness of the customs, traditions, values, and social dynamics within a particular community or society, and you become a first-hand anthropologist assimilating yourself to the diverse terrain of the human spirit. Native worldliness encompasses the knowledge, experiences, and perspectives inherent to individuals who have grown up or lived extensively within a specific cultural or geographical context and invites you to appreciate, not appropriate, the culture.

Cultural appropriation happens when members of another culture adopt or use elements of one culture, typically without permission or understanding and often with disregard for the original cultural significance or context. It involves borrowing or appropriating aspects of a marginalized or minority culture by a dominant culture, which can lead to the exploitation, misrepresentation, or commodification of those cultural elements. Cultural appropriation can perpetuate stereotypes, erode cultural traditions, and contribute to the marginalization of the communities from which the culture originates. Tumbleweed appearing in a reading can indicate working towards supporting a more respectful, inclusive, and equitable approach to cultural exchange and expression.

Overcoming cultural appropriation involves several steps:

Education and Awareness: It's essential to educate oneself about the cultural significance, history, and context of the practices, symbols, or traditions being appropriated. This includes understanding the cultural meanings behind them and recognizing the impact of appropriation on the communities involved.

Respect and Sensitivity: Approach cultural exchange with respect, sensitivity, and humility. Recognize that cultures are not commodities to be borrowed or consumed but living, dynamic systems of knowledge and identity. When appropriate, seek permission, guidance, or collaboration from members of the culture.

Authentic Representation: When engaging with elements of a culture, strive for genuine representation and accurate portrayal. Avoid stereotypes, caricatures, or superficial interpretations that distort or misrepresent the culture.

Acknowledgment and Credit: Acknowledge the origins and contributions of the culture you borrow from. Give credit to the sources and creators while being transparent about the cultural influences behind your work or actions.

Empowerment and Collaboration: Instead of appropriating, seek ways to empower and uplift marginalized voices and communities. Foster genuine collaboration, exchange, and dialogue that respects the autonomy and agency of all parties involved.

Reflection and Accountability: Reflect critically on your actions, biases, and privileges. Hold yourself and others accountable for instances of cultural appropriation and be open to learning from feedback and criticism.

Corporate Chaos loves erasing cultures through propaganda, appropriation, and war. In human history, countless traditions and languages eradicated and merged under the hammer of modernity have taken their toll on our collective spirit. As we continue to evolve together and face more fragmented factions isolated in fear from one another, remember that impermanence is the only constant we know for sure. Change is hard; unfortunately, there will be pain, suffering, and death. Still, suppose there's one element of Tumbleweed to help orient yourself during dystopian rhetoric, disinformation campaigns, and desolate demagogues. In that case, the level of wisdom, adaptability, and resourcefulness of being human is divine. Humanity isn't a wasteland, love; it's a Wonderwall.

Fawn - Ancestry & Family

Fawn, echoing the gentle, earthy hues of deer coats, conjures feelings of warmth, serenity, and familial unity. Within the realm of family and ancestry, Fawn holds symbolic weight by linking us to our generational roots and the lasting impact of our family. Remember where you come from. Fawn is the color of the sand as you walk a beach where your ancestors once strolled. It's the color of your dog's fluff on the floor. It's the back of photographs tucked inside a memory box—the morning coffee you share with your mom. Fawn is a gentle, delicate, and compassionate color energy used to connect with our ancestors through spirit animals and signs in nature. Fawn symbolizes the hourglass of our humanity and the continuity of our lineage. The enduring presence of ancestors within your family tree is highly influential at this time. Just as deer roam through forests with a sense of grace and harmony, the color Fawn signifies the interconnectedness of family members across time and space, spanning generations with an unbroken thread of heritage. You are being asked to invoke the spirits of your ancestors and weave healing threads to reprogram your consciousness in how you identify and relate to family.

You long to embody a sense of nostalgia and reverence for family time, reflecting the wisdom and traditions passed down through generations. Much like the tender embrace of a close-knit family, Fawn offers solace and reassurance, nurturing that sense of belonging and sentient connection we desire naturally. Mirroring the instinctual care and support found within familial relationships, Fawn shows you the unconditional love and guidance passed from parent to child, grandparent to grandchild, forming the cornerstone of familial bonds. Discover a family bond with animal companions, too. It's how we should feel toward our pets and honoring them as an integral part of our family system. Celebrate their birthday. Speak to them with kindness. All sentient life is connected and meaningful. If you're living or coming from a farmhand lifestyle with barbaric practices to abuse or harm pets, it is not the status quo of respecting life, liberty, and the pursuit of happiness. Gaslighting your children into abusive mental, emotional, and physical punishment is also not a flex for life, liberty, and the pursuit of happiness. You do not own your children, and you do not own your pets. They are not property your narcissism wants to control. They are sentient beings and require treating them with the utmost respect and care and strengthening your bond with them through love, not criticism.

Fawn finds you at a crossroads of trust and codependency when reversed or negatively influenced in a reading. Issues regarding trust and codependency within a family can manifest in various ways, often stemming from unresolved conflicts, unmet needs, or dysfunctional relationship dynamics. Trust issues may arise due to past betrayals, broken promises, or a lack of open communication, leading to insecurity and skepticism among family members. Codependency issues typically involve unhealthy patterns of behavior characterized by excessive reliance on others for validation, self-worth, or emotional support, often resulting in enmeshment and boundary violations. If trust and codependency issues persist despite efforts to address them, consider seeking support from a qualified therapist or counselor experienced in family therapy. Professional outside intervention can provide valuable insights, strategies, and support for navigating complex family dynamics and fostering healthier relationships because they can offer an outside perspective and are ultimately detached from the inherited baggage.

Eventually, the young deer leave their mothers and are expected to outrun the world's dangers. Being forced to survive on your own is scary. Humans created systems like schools and developmental work programs to transition our young into adulthood and acclimatize them to societal expectations. Corporate Chaos has, of course, politicized these systems and made it excruciatingly difficult to maintain the bare necessities, and older people (including our ancestors) haven't faced the ever-changing levels of oppression wreaking havoc on adulthood presently. Being forced to navigate the world independently can be a daunting experience, especially for anyone facing adversity. Self-sufficiency requires practical skills, emotional resilience, and a sense of identity. Fawn aims to facilitate this transition and prepare you for adult responsibilities and complexities.

Are you considering returning to school or enrolling in an online education program to sharpen your skills? Schools play a crucial role in this process by providing structured environments where you can learn academic subjects, develop critical thinking skills, and acquire social competencies. Beyond imparting knowledge, schools serve as a means for personal growth and self-discovery, helping you to explore interests, talents, and values that help you redefine your family's worth. You can learn valuable communication, teamwork, and conflict resolution lessons through interactions with peers and teachers, preparing your mind to handle opportunities and challenges. Similarly, developmental work programs and internships offer practical experiences that complement formal education, allowing people to apply classroom learning in real-world settings. These programs expose participants to professional environments, industry practices, and workplace dynamics, helping them develop essential skills such as time management, problem-solving, and adaptability. Some corporations structure their program to require recruiting only those with a higher education degree from a high-ranking post-secondary institution before considering their application. Moreover, internships provide opportunities for mentorship and networking, connecting young adults with seasoned professionals who can offer guidance and support as they navigate their career paths. In addition to educational and vocational opportunities, communities often provide support structures to assist young people in their journey toward independence.

Family, friends, and mentors offer emotional support, encouragement, and advice, serving as anchors during times of uncertainty and transition. Your family may not have been given the same opportunity to advance their education and be born during a time of heightened technological advances, so it's your responsibility to pull yourself up from your bootstraps and take the reins so you can reprogram your family tree. It may also take a village to raise your vibrations and be open to community organizations and social services offering resources such as counseling, job training, or financial assistance to individuals facing challenges or barriers to self-sufficiency. Ultimately, the transition and sustainability of adulthood is a multifaceted process that requires a combination of education, experience, and support.

Although Fawn is a warm color of togetherness, it's an essential message of detachment. Adulthood is not a personal attack on your spirit. Nor is it an indicator of your worth as a human being. It's a complex phase of our human experience that no one truly enjoys or has all the answers to. You may be experiencing a heightened vulnerability around aging and finding it difficult to accept where you are now. Fawn involves setting and maintaining emotional boundaries with family members. This means recognizing where your feelings and experiences end and where those of others begin. It's about understanding that you are not responsible for the emotions or actions of others and that you have the right to prioritize your emotional well-being. You're being asked to accept family members for who they are without judgment or attempts to change them. It's about recognizing everyone has strengths, weaknesses, and life experiences and accepting them with compassion and understanding. It also emphasizes the importance of self-care and self-awareness. This means prioritizing activities and practices that promote your physical, emotional, and mental well-being, even if it means taking a step back from family dynamics or relationships that may be draining or harmful.

You are exactly where you need to be. Although that may feel painful, considering the injustice and inequity in the world, you are not disconnected from spirit because you find yourself in your trajectory. The societal expectation or traditional life path of going to school, getting a job, getting married, and having kids is often called the "life script" or the "traditional life trajectory." It reflects a standard cultural narrative or normative sequence of life events that many people are expected or encouraged to follow. This sequence has been deeply ingrained in many societies and historically seen as a marker of success or fulfillment. However, it's essential to recognize that individual experiences and choices may vary, and only some follow this prescribed path. You are not obligated to follow in your family's footsteps.

UNIVERSAL CHAKRA

Black - Dark

Black is often described as the absence of light or the complete absorption of light. In terms of light, black is the absence of any visible light, meaning that no light is reflected or emitted, giving the perception of darkness. From a scientific standpoint, black is not considered a color like other colors, such as red, blue, or green. Instead, it results from the absence or absorption of light wavelengths. When an object appears black, it absorbs most or all wavelengths of light across the visible spectrum rather than reflecting them. Regarding pigments and dyes, Black is typically created by mixing multiple pigments that absorb various wavelengths of light. The absence of light or the complete absorption of light can manifest in multiple everyday interactions and scenarios.

When you're in a completely dark room or environment, such as a closed closet or a basement with no windows, you experience the absence of light firsthand. In these situations, objects may become indistinguishable or invisible because there's no light to illuminate them. Shadows are formed when an object blocks light, preventing it from reaching the surface. In areas with little or no light, shadows can appear darker, creating the perception of depth and dimension. Objects that are black in color appear dark because they absorb most or all the light that strikes them. For example, a black car parked in direct sunlight may feel much hotter to the touch than a white car because it absorbs more sunlight. When you shine a light on a surface that absorbs most wavelengths of light, such as a black fabric or material, the light is absorbed rather than reflected. This results in the surface appearing dark or black to the observer. In photography and art, lighting and shadows can create dramatic effects by emphasizing areas of light and darkness. Artists often use black pigment or paint to add depth and contrast to their compositions. On electronic displays such as televisions, computer monitors, and smartphones, black pixels are typically achieved by turning off the backlighting or using pixels that absorb light rather than emit it. This creates areas of darkness on the screen. The absence of light or the complete absorption of light plays a significant role in our perception of the world around us, influencing how we see and interact with our environment daily.

Black is often associated with darkness, mystery, power, and elegance. Commercially, it can evoke feelings of authority, sophistication, seriousness, fear, or negativity. Black is commonly used in mystery novels, films, and TV shows to create an atmosphere of suspense and intrigue. Characters dressed in black often signify hidden intentions or secretive personas. It speaks to rebellion and nonconformity in fashion and subcultures like goth, punk, and emo, frequently embraced as a symbol of rebellion against societal norms and expectations. It represents individuality, defiance, and a rejection of mainstream values. Black is a classic color associated with formal attire, such as tuxedos and evening gowns. It conveys a sense of elegance, sophistication, and timeless style, making it a popular choice for formal events and high-end fashion. In contexts like business, politics, and law enforcement, Black is wrapped in the ego of authority and power. People in positions of authority may wear black clothing or use black accessories to project a sense of strength, control, and dominance. Across many cultures, black is the traditional color of mourning, symbolizing sadness, loss, and respect for the deceased. In funerals and memorial services, mourners wear black clothing as a sign of reverence and solemnity. In art and literature, Black can be used symbolically to represent many themes touching on the unknown, death, evil, or the unconscious mind.

When Black appears in your reading, you're asked to focus on what's hidden. Explore behind-the-scenes details for more context and depth regarding your situation. Go over the timeline like a detective to collect evidence of the who, what, where, when, why, and how your current situation came to be. What are you trying to solve? Look at the absolute edges of your inquiry and find the boundaries defining certain beliefs, people, and factors that structure the situation. Put your findings in a Venn diagram. What aspects easily express conformity, and which reflect nonconformity? Is there an overlap? Black wants you to pay attention to the framework and matrix of your life and work. Look at ingredient lists in your food and beauty products, read the fine print on contracts and terms, and follow your intuition and instincts to the source.

Source energy is what Black (and White) personifies in the color deck. Hermetic philosophy is a set of philosophical and esoteric teachings that originated in ancient Egypt and were later developed in Hellenistic Greece. It encompasses various spiritual and philosophical ideas, including alchemy, astrology, and theurgy. One of the central principles of Hermeticism is the concept of "as above, so below," which suggests that there is a correspondence between the macrocosm (the universe) and the microcosm (the individual). Duality is a common theme in Hermetic philosophy, reflecting the belief that reality is composed of opposing forces or principles that are interconnected and interdependent. These dualities often include light and darkness, good and evil, masculine and feminine, and spirit and matter. Concerning the color Black, Hermetic philosophy and duality can be interpreted in several ways: Light and Darkness: In Hermeticism, light is often associated with spiritual enlightenment, while darkness symbolizes ignorance or the material world. Black, representing darkness, can be seen as the absence of light or spiritual understanding. However, it can also represent the hidden or unseen aspects of reality necessary for growth and transformation. Unity of Opposites: Within Hermeticism, duality is not viewed as a strict division between opposing forces but as complementary aspects of a unified whole. Black, associated with darkness, can symbolize the unity of opposites, where light and darkness coexist and are interdependent, as seen in a Yin and Yang symbol. Alchemical Symbolism: In alchemy, another aspect of Hermetic philosophy, the color Black is often associated with the initial stage of the alchemical process, known as the nigredo or blackening. This stage represents the dissolution of the ego and the breaking down of old structures to facilitate spiritual transformation and rebirth. Hermetic philosophy and duality provide a rich framework for understanding the symbolic significance of the color Black, representing both the hidden aspects of reality and the transformative process of spiritual evolution. You may wait to get to the bottom of things, but your investigation will discover details worth surveilling. Black indicates more than meets the eye, so don't be afraid to try and find out why.

Should Black be negatively influenced or challenged, it calls for utmost protection. When Marianne Williamson stood on the Democratic presidential primary debate stage in 2019 and spoke about the "*dark underbelly of American society*" being collectively influenced by a "*dark psychic force*," she was not wrong. Narcissism, apathy, fascism, surveillance capitalism, and disease are not avenues of absolution for Corporate Chaos. Your time and energy are a sacred resource on this planet, and some systemic programs and initiatives are so corrupt that their sole purpose is to absorb your attention, your psyche, and your well-being. Protect yourself. Unplug from the chaos and retreat to a place of peace and love. Perhaps it's time to get off the hamster wheel and realize it's time to throw in the towel. It's okay to walk away. It's OK to take a sabbatical. Stop allowing energy vampires to feed on your aura. Reclaim your time on this planet and cut ties. Estrangement is a joyous decision when executed correctly. But don't allow your ego to use severance as a ploy for conjuring another tale of victimization and antagonistic patterns to avoid the maturation of your soul.

Black is a complicated color energy to work with if you're unaware of the absence or absorption of light in your life and work. Be mindful of how you hide yourself from others and how others may take advantage of your humanity without your permission. Balancing this takes time and years of practicing self-care. There's an ever-changing flux between giving and taking and conforming and nonconforming to society, so be mindful of the absolute edges and lengths you would go to find the source. And remember that those edges will expand and contract the more you live life. So, try not to be too afraid of the unknown because there's a lot out there that we still don't know. Darkness tends to feed the light and give it a reason to shine.

Smoke - Ignorance & Mystery

Smoke refers to deception, illusion, or trickery to create a false impression or disguise the story in half-truths. It often implies using clever tactics or techniques to obscure reality or mislead others. The phrase "smoke and mirrors" originated from the world of magic, where magicians would use smoke and mirrors as devices to create illusions and make things appear different from what they are. In a reading, Smoke reveals things are not as they seem, and there's an attempt to manipulate perception or conceal the truth. It also indicates in your reading you should stay vigilant regarding distractions and crises that take your attention off your priorities. Diversion is a central theme in cultivating ignorance and mystery. Corporate Chaos has become quite pernicious at blowing smoke up their shareholders' asses, often at the expense of our collective humanity and our planet.

Although Smoke may provoke confusion, ignorance, and red flags in a reading, it could also represent echoes of intrigue that beguile the mind. You want to tell a memorable story and enchant an audience with impressionable effects. Smoke reveals that you or someone you know enjoys arousing debate, conflict, and desire. The wonder and mystique of performance and presenting oneself with an air of mystery could create more fascination for you now. What aspects of your situation do you feel seduced, captivated, and enthralled? The alluring influence of Smoke is spellbinding during rituals using incense and smudging tools. In rituals and spiritual practices, sage is often used for its cleansing and purifying properties to remove negative energies and promote healing, clarity, and protection. Smudging is a ritualistic practice that involves burning sage leaves and wafting the smoke around a person, space, or object to cleanse and purify it. This can be done by lighting a bundle of dried sage leaves (often called a "smudge stick") and gently blowing out the flame, allowing the embers to produce smoke. The person performing the smudging then moves the smoke around the body, room, or object, typically using a feather or hand, while setting intentions for purification and protection. Sage is believed to be able to clear away negative or stagnant energy from a space, person, or object. By burning sage and smudging with the smoke, practitioners aim to release negative emotions, thoughts, or energies, creating a more positive and harmonious environment. It's essential to approach the use of sage in rituals with respect and mindfulness, honoring its cultural and spiritual significance. Additionally, some people may be sensitive to smoke or have respiratory issues, so it's advisable to use sage in a well-ventilated area and consider alternative cleansing methods if necessary.

Since Smoke occupies performance, it also indicates that you or someone involved in the situation may be motivated or engrossed by appearances and exploiting public perception. Are you attempting to control the situation to look better than what and who you are now? Smoke pulls the wool over people's eyes and can indicate a superficial belief system polluted by performative marketing, politics, allyship, and activism. Performative marketing is corporate strategies or campaigns prioritizing appearances and public perception over genuine commitment to social or environmental causes. Companies may engage in performative marketing to appear socially responsible or "woke" without significantly changing their practices or policies. Performative politics are political actions or statements more about signaling virtue or ideology than enacting meaningful change. Politicians or public figures might engage in performative politics by making grand gestures, speeches, or symbolic acts without following through with substantive policy changes or addressing systemic issues. Performative allyship refers to actions or expressions of support for marginalized groups that are more about appearing virtuous or avoiding criticism than genuinely advocating for or standing in solidarity with those groups. For example, someone might post on social media about supporting a specific cause but fail to take meaningful action or educate themselves on the issues the marginalized group faces. Performative activism prioritizes optics and symbolism over tangible efforts to bring about real change. Performative activism often is funded programs and efforts by political action committees, foreign organizations, and institutional investors that engage in protests, rallies, or social media campaigns to sway public opinion, gain attention, or demonstrate their commitment to a cause but have zero interest in solving the problem or curing the disease.

Smoke encourages you to become aware of organizations and individuals that inflate appearances and numb perception and reward grandstanding to conjure the illusion of benefits while exploiting their audience's obliviousness and blind spots. Ignorance is not always blissful. We all face real-world problems and consequences as a collective, which go beyond our religion, race, and region in which we reside. Smoke asks leading questions to uncover the truth without bias. Imagine the smoky atmosphere of a jazz club in the 1920s or the smoke-filled rooms of 1940s film noir. You're a detective or journalist investigating crimes against humanity. Look for patterns in your reading that reveal whether actions and words align. Gather evidence and receipts to track and stay organized as you unravel the mystery of your situation. Under a surveilling eye and quest for knowledge, your intuition is a powerful agent to decode rumors and suspicions.

Smoke is the fog you feel between light and dark. This in-between state happens when something is partially revealed, or there's a mix of clarity and obscurity, so information and identity are incognito. It's time to embrace this period of penumbra, a transitional zone where you explore the unseen dissonance affecting your mood. Smoke wants you to practice *revelare ex obscuritate*, which in Latin means "to unveil from obscurity" or "to reveal from darkness," capturing the notion of bringing something hidden or unknown into the light or making it evident. Holding self-evident truths requires constant adjustment as we sort through the gray matter of our conversations, defragment political factions, and transfer wealth and power out of the pockets of Corporate Chaos and back into the hands of everyday people disenfranchised by darkness.

White - Light

White is the combination of all visible wavelengths of light being reflected equally. When light strikes an object, the object absorbs specific wavelengths of light and reflects others. If an object reflects all wavelengths of visible light equally, it appears white. White represents light's complete and total reflection, often connecting to purity, clarity, and enlightenment themes in spirituality and philosophy. White suggests the absence of impurities or negativity because it is associated with the purity and innocence of spirit or soul. In spiritual practices, White may symbolize being free from "sin," ignorance, or negative emotions.

When white light passes through a prism, it undergoes dispersion, separating into its component colors and creating a spectrum. This occurs because different wavelengths of light bend by varying amounts as they pass through the prism, causing them to spread out and form a rainbow-like display of colors. In the context of the meaning of the color White, the prism serves as a metaphor for understanding the composition of white light. When white light passes through a prism and is dispersed, it reveals that white light is composed of a spectrum of colors, including red, orange, yellow, green, blue, indigo, and violet. This dispersion of white light into its constituent colors can symbolize the diversity and complexity within simplicity. Just as white light contains all colors within it, the symbolism of white can represent the integration and unity of diverse elements. However, when passed through the prism of experience or analysis, these elements can be differentiated and understood in their complexities, much like how humanity is experienced on Earth. So, when

White appears in a reading, it invites you to look beyond the simplicity and uniformity of your surface thoughts to reveal the richness and diversity within your situation to see with clarity.

White asks you to lighten up and to stop taking the situation personally. Your unquenchable expectation of perfection is causing you to miss the mark on the situation. Simplify your perspective and approach things from a higher perspective that celebrates feeling lighthearted, free, open, and unified with the source of love. You may be playing the victim and must reconnect with your white-hot truth. White is an envelope of information that reminds us not to be too hasty with giving other ultimatums or making life-changing decisions right now based on self-righteousness. Surrendering to the light does not make you less than or weaker than the opposition. We all are white light. Learn to detach from the demons that try to make you believe in yourself and that the situation isn't perfect.

Like Black, White may be used to cloak oneself to invoke invisibility and protection. The function usually is to appear serious, professional, and elitist. The institutionalized color of White has been culturally indoctrinated to push supremacy, crusades, and barbaric bureaucracy of socioeconomic oppression to sterilize our consciousness and fragment our familial ties of being human. The extreme force of White power detaches us from our democracy. It is erasing what makes us different and unique, often under the guise of religion and politics. White, when negatively influenced, comes through oppressing others because of their opinions and lifestyles as they fall outside of one's cultural paradigm. You or another person related to the situation may be covering up or glossing over flaws, mistakes, or unpleasant truths, often to make something or someone appear more favorable or acceptable than they genuinely are. It might involve downplaying or omitting certain aspects of past events to present a more flattering narrative, telling white lies. It may be found in delivering a product or company in a way that obscures negative aspects or exaggerates positive ones. This act of concealing or distorting information to present a more favorable image is whitewashing, and it creates more harm in the world than good.

White is also a color of silence and removing oneself from the situation to avoid involvement and responsibility. Absenteeism has some benefits, but if it ultimately alienates others, leaving them ill-equipped to defend themselves, is it productive or lighthearted to watch the pain and suffering of others? At the same time, you sit there detached and aloof. Humanity requires active participation, and if you're not going to get involved, the least you can do is let your hands get dirty in other constructive and conscious ways that promote love, not war. White is the color of peace, and it promises hope. So, you're being asked to create more hope when you might struggle to find it in yourself, detach from self-centered worry, and commit to serving hope and peace for others. Volunteer yourself to extend yourself beyond personal or professional limitations. White wants you to express compassion, empathy, and altruism now.

This is a time for grace, not greed.

Watermelon - Mindfulness

In a world often bustling with noise and distractions, finding moments of mindfulness becomes a sacred practice, a refuge amidst the chaos. Amidst the rainbowlicious colors in *The Color Mage Oracle*, one might not immediately think of the magic behind the humble Watermelon. As you delve deeper into its essence, Watermelon reveals itself as a sweet mindfulness guru, offering profound lessons in embracing the present moment. At its core, mindfulness is about awareness and presence, the act of being fully attuned to the here and now. And what better embodiment of this principle than Watermelon, whose seasonal arrival heralds the warmth of summer and social gatherings? As you slice through the verdant rind of your day-to-day errands and responsibilities, you're invited into a sensory experience that demands your full attention. The vibrant hues of its flesh, the subtle aroma that wafts through the air, the juicy sweetness that explodes on our taste buds – each sensation a gentle reminder to be present and savor the moment's richness. Don't be afraid to feel and lean into practicing mindful eating. There is no need for elaborate rituals or complex meditations; instead, you're invited to engage in your senses fully, to relish the simple pleasure of nourishing your body with nature's bounty. With each bite, we become attuned to the rhythm of our breath, the texture of the fruit against our lips, and the coolness that soothes our parched throat. In this communion with the melon, there is no room for worries of the past or anxieties of the future – only the sweetness of the present moment. But the Watermelon's teachings extend beyond the realm of taste and sensation. As a symbol of abundance and fertility, it reminds us of the richness within each moment if only wc have the awareness to see. Like the myriad seeds that populate its core, each containing the potential for new life, every moment holds the promise of growth and transformation. By embracing the Watermelon's wisdom, we learn to cultivate a mindset of abundance and see the beauty that surrounds us, even in the simplest things.

The pink hue of its flesh symbolizes love, compassion, and the nurturing aspects of the heart chakra. It reminds us to approach the world with an open heart and to cultivate empathy and kindness towards ourselves and others. As we indulge in the pink sweetness of the Watermelon, we are reminded to connect with our emotions, to honor our feelings without judgment, and to embrace the healing power of love. On the outside, the vibrant green swirl of the Watermelon's rind represents growth, renewal, and the vitality of nature. It speaks to the energy of the heart chakra, encouraging us to recognize the hand we've been dealt and focus on the mindful sensations of our efforts paying off. The ease you feel as you take another juicy bite out of life. It calls attention to reaping what you sow. Just as the Watermelon vine stretches toward the sun, reaching new heights, you, too, are invited to expand your awareness and embrace change and transformation as integral parts of our journey toward wholeness. And so, let us raise a slice of Watermelon to our lips, letting its juices dribble down our chins as we immerse ourselves fully in the experience. In its sweet flesh, we find a mirror reflecting the essence of mindfulness – a reminder to slow down, savor the sweetness of life, and rejoice in the infinite abundance of the present moment.

Alchemy - Transformation

In the ancient art of alchemy, practitioners sought to transmute base metals into gold, a metaphor for spiritual enlightenment and attaining perfection. Central to this mystical pursuit was the concept of transformation, a process mirrored in the butterfly's metamorphosis. Through the Alchemy color card, we can explore the profound relationship of the butterfly as a catalyst for personal evolution and spiritual awakening, and at the heart of the alchemical process lies the principle of transmutation—the idea that through inner work and spiritual purification, one can undergo a profound metamorphosis.

The butterfly is a potent symbol of transformation, embodying the alchemical journey from lumbering existence to effervescent enlightenment. Like the alchemist's crucible, the cocoon represents a sacred vessel of transformation—a place of incubation and inner refinement where the raw material of the soul undergoes a profound alchemical process. Within the chrysalis, the caterpillar dissolves into formless chaos, shedding its old identity and embracing the liminal space of the unknown. In this state of dissolution, the alchemical *prima materia*—the raw material of the soul—is broken down and purified, paving the way for its eventual reintegration into a higher form. As the butterfly emerges from its cocoon, it symbolizes the culmination of the alchemical process—the transformation of the base self into the enlightened self. With wings unfurled, it soars into the heavens, liberated from the constraints of its former existence and infused with the radiant light of spiritual illumination. In its graceful flight, the butterfly embodies the alchemical axiom "*solve et coagula*"—to dissolve and coagulate—breaking down the old to make way for the new.

Alchemy's combination of colors carries its significance in the transformation journey. Purple, the color of royalty and spiritual insight, represents the awakening of the third eye chakra—the seat of intuition and higher consciousness. As the butterfly spreads its wings, it invites us to open our minds to new possibilities, transcend the limitations of the material world, and embrace the infinite wisdom of the cosmos. Gold, the goal of the alchemical process, symbolizes spiritual enlightenment and the attainment of divine perfection. Like the Philosopher's Stone, it represents the integration of opposites—the union of heaven and earth, spirit and matter, light and dark. In the golden glow of the butterfly's wings, we glimpse the radiant splendor of our true divine nature, a reminder of the inherent potential for transformation within each of us. Silver, the color of the moon, and the feminine principle represent the receptive and intuitive aspects of the soul. As the butterfly dances in the moonlight, it beckons us to embrace the mysteries of the unconscious mind, to honor our intuition and inner knowing, and to trust in the guidance of the divine feminine. Finally, Black, the color of the *prima materia*, represents the darkness of the unknown—the fertile void from which all creation emerges. In the shadowy depths of the cocoon, we confront our deepest fears and insecurities, surrendering to the transformative power of the alchemical process. By embracing the darkness, we find the light, the hidden treasures of the soul waiting to be unearthed.

In your reading, Alchemy is a powerful reminder of the inherent potential for transformation within each of us. Through inner work, spiritual practice, and self-knowledge, you can embark on your alchemical journey, shedding the lifeless weight of your egoic self and ascending to the vivacious heights of spiritual enlightenment. As we embrace the transformative power of Alchemy's colors, we unlock the secrets of our butterfly effect and alchemist's art, unlocking the hidden treasures of the soul and realizing our true divine nature as mystics on this planet.

New Age - Evolution

In the tapestry of human history, the emergence of the New Age movement represents a vibrant thread woven with the aspirations of spiritual seekers, visionaries, and truth-seekers alike. At its core, the New Age movement embodies a profound sense of evolution—a journey of consciousness unfolding across time and space. Through its eclectic blend of spiritual beliefs, practices, and philosophies, the New Age movement catalyzes the evolution of human consciousness, inviting individuals to explore new horizons of possibility and potential. Central to the ethos of the New Age is the idea of spiritual awakening and transformation. It recognizes that humanity stands at a crossroads—a pivotal moment in our collective evolution where we're called to transcend the limitations of the past and embrace a higher vision of reality.

Drawing inspiration from diverse spiritual traditions, ancient wisdom teachings, and modern metaphysical insights, New Age in your reading invites you to embark on a journey of self-discovery and self-realization. This journey will lead you closer to realizing your true divine nature. At the heart of the New Age lies a profound sense of interconnectedness—recognizing the unity of all life and the world wide web of existence. New Age is a firework display of our momentary existence on the planet and the importance of technology, medical advances, and new scientific discoveries, inviting us to expand our awareness beyond the confines of the egoic mind and embrace the inherent oneness of the universe. Permit yourself to light up the sky with your radiance. Burst through the blockages and recognize that your evolution is inseparable from the evolution of the cosmos—a cosmic dance of consciousness unfolding in infinite layers of complexity and beauty.

New Age's combination of colors is significant in the journey of evolution and spiritual growth, displaying a cacophony of colors. With its soft concrete texture and ashy hue, Champagne gray connects you to the grounding energies of agriculture, architecture, and abundance on Earth. New Age provides stability and support as you navigate your life's and work's ever-changing currents. Chartreuse yellow on the card highlights your power, confidence, and self-esteem. As you awaken to the evolutionary impulse within yourself, the solar plexus chakra serves as a beacon of inner strength, empowering you to step into your full potential and embrace the challenges and opportunities that come your way with courage and conviction. Milky white, the color of an illuminated galaxy, represents the crown chakra—the gateway to higher consciousness and divine wisdom. As we ascend to higher levels of awareness, the crown chakra opens us to the infinite possibilities of the cosmos, guiding us on our journey toward enlightenment and spiritual liberation. Dark Violet purple, the third eye chakra color, symbolizes intuition, insight, and inner vision. As we awaken the third eye chakra, we gain access to higher realms of perception and understanding, allowing us to see beyond the physical world's limitations and tap into the boundless wisdom of the unseen universe. In the New Age, evolution is not merely a linear progression towards a predetermined stagnant endpoint but a dynamic and ever-unfolding process of becoming.

It is a journey of self-discovery and self-empowerment that invites you to embrace the full spectrum of your human potential and co-create a world rooted in love, compassion, and unity. As we awaken to the evolutionary impulse within us, we become active participants in the evolution of consciousness, each contributing our unique gifts and insights to the tapestry of human experience. In your reading, the New Age card serves as a beacon of hope and inspiration—a testament to the boundless possibilities that await you on the evolutionary journey of life. You have an opportunity to choose utopia over dystopian narratives. Do your actions and vision expand or contract the evolution of our humanity? Allow magic to evolve your lifestyle.

Kiss - Goddess Freya

In the rich tapestry of mythology, few figures embody the essence of raw love and desire as profoundly as Freya, the Norse goddess of beauty, fertility, and war. As the radiant embodiment of feminine power, Freya weaves her magic through the realms of love and connection, inspiring mortals and deities alike to embrace the transformative power of intimacy and passion. Her association with the heart chakra is central to Freya's mythology—the energetic center of love and connection within the body. Just as Freya's essence radiates with the warmth of unconditional love, so too does the act of kissing serve as a potent symbol of heart-centered connection, uniting consciousness with body positivity and intimate connection. In the ancient tales of Norse mythology, Freya's allure and charm captivate the hearts of gods and mortals, drawing them into her embrace with the promise of boundless love and passion. Like the flower's delicate petals unfolding under the sun's gaze, Freya's presence ignites you to inquire about desire. When Kiss appears in a reading, your guides awaken dormant longings within your soul, and you're asked to surrender to the physical and spiritual ecstasy.

As the goddess of love and fertility, Freya presides over matters of the heart, guiding souls on emotional growth and transformation. In the sacred color of Kiss, Freya's essence infuses the exchange with the energy of divine love, weaving together threads of pink and slate gray to reveal passion and tenderness locked away under mental duress. Pink, with its soft and gentle hue, symbolizes the unconditional love and compassion that flow freely from the heart chakra—the energetic center of love and connection within the body. In the tender embrace of pink, Kiss is a way to get closer to your body, illuminating the path to deeper intimacy and emotional fulfillment with yourself. How do you see yourself in the mirror?

Slate gray, with its muted and understated tone, represents hard times and the stonewall complexity of human emotion

— can you recall a time when you saw yourself as a hopeless romantic with dampened desires hitting rock bottom? This is where love and longing intertwine. You are asked to kiss the lips of your Divine nature to free yourself from purgatory. Pining for admiration, validation, and love is a fool's errand. Have you been disassociating your divinity based on skewed thoughts? False beauty standards, gender conformity, and lack of money can make us feel ugly and unworthy. In the Kiss color card, a twinge of slate gray serves as a mirror, reflecting the nuances of human emotion and the profound longing to connect with people regardless of race, religion, or region.

Kiss forms an interlocking pink and slate gray chainmail in your auric field to protect yourself in everyday struggles. This color acts as a suit of armor of light and shadow, passion and restraint, vulnerability and strength. Upon the tender lips of Freya's words, these colors stretch across space-time, weaving together the threads of love and connection into a timeless expression of beauty. For Freya, kissing becomes more than a physical act—it becomes a sacred ritual, a gateway to the depths of the soul where love resides in its purest form. As we open our hearts to the beauty and wonder of our multisensory experience as a living being, we embrace the infinite possibilities of our human spirit. Just as Freya embodies the eternal dance of love and desire, so too does Kiss in your reading serve as a timeless expression of the human heart's longing for connection, intimacy, and self-acceptance.

Kiss your hand and place it on your heart.

Paradise - Heaven on Earth

Paradise stands as a shimmering oasis through a heart-centered mindset of hope and aspiration that beckons us to transcend the mundane world's limitations and embrace the human spirit's boundless possibilities. In your color reading, Paradise represents the ultimate expression of tranquility — a utopian vision of bliss, harmony, and perfection that holds the promise of eternal fulfillment. At its essence, Paradise embodies the concept of heaven on earth—a celestial realm of transcendent beauty and spiritual abundance that exists not in some distant future or afterlife but here and now within the depths of the human heart. It's showing up in your reading as a state of being where the external and internal worlds merge, where the boundaries between self and other dissolve, and where every moment is infused with the radiant light of divine presence.

In the religious and spiritual traditions of the world, Paradise takes on various forms and manifestations. In Christianity, it is symbolized by the Garden of Eden—a paradisiacal haven of innocence and purity. Humanity is believed to have originated in perfect harmony with the natural world and the divine. In Islam, Paradise (known as Jannah) is depicted as a celestial realm of eternal bliss and reward for the righteous—a place where the faithful are reunited with their loved ones and bask in the presence of Allah. Beyond its religious connotations, Paradise represents a state of inner peace and harmony that transcends the limitations of external circumstances. It is a place where individuals are free from suffering, conflict, and turmoil and can experience a profound sense of unity with themselves, others, and the universe. It is a realm of natural beauty and abundance, where lush landscapes, crystal-clear waters, and exotic flora abound—a testament to the inherent majesty and splendor of the natural world. Paradise is the hope and aspiration you desire despite the challenges and adversities of life. A better world is possible. Fear and Corporate Chaos prefer us to be lazy and apathetic. Our jaded society would instead create illusions of grandeur and the mirage of misery instead of actualizing real love, compassion, and empathy in our daily lives, then strive for a more harmonious and fulfilling existence for ourselves and future generations. In embracing the concept of Paradise as heaven on earth, you're invited to awaken to your inherent divinity and recognize the sacredness of all life beyond race, religion, and region.

In the quest to manifest heaven on earth, the vibrancy of color paints the canvas of our reality, infusing each moment with the hues of divinity and grace. Within the ethereal realm of the crown chakra—the energetic center of spiritual connection and transcendence—we find the convergence of Auroral Pink, Aged Lavender, Indigo, and Primrose Purple, each carrying profound symbolism and meaning that expands upon the principles of heaven on earth.

Auroral Pink shocks the darkened sky of a dystopian worldview with an elevated display of laser-focused love. As we awaken to the radiance of heaven on earth, this pink serves as a beacon of light, illuminating the path to intimacy and emotional fulfillment. It represents the cauterization of love in all its forms—love for oneself, love for others, and love for the divine—a sacred reminder that we are all interconnected in the web of existence, and we let go of the hell that imprisons us so we may break free from our obsession with what makes us miserable.

Aged Lavender is a kind of gray in Paradise, representing the veil of illusion that separates us from the divine. In pursuing heaven on earth, Aged Lavender serves as a reminder of the ephemeral nature of reality—the transient nature of material wealth, status, and power. It calls us to look beyond the surface of things, penetrate the veil of illusion, and seek the eternal truths at the heart of existence. Do you feel progress is stagnant, and you struggle to accept aging? Your inherited trauma may be fostering arrogance, hindering genuine progress, as you lack the same privileges, comforts, and achievements seemingly available to younger generations.

Indigo represents the gateway to higher consciousness and spiritual insight with its deep and mysterious hue. As we ascend to heaven on earth, Indigo bridges the finite and the infinite, guiding us on a journey of inner exploration and self-discovery. It invites us to open the doors of perception, expand our awareness beyond the confines of the egoic mind, and tap into the boundless wisdom of the cosmos.

With its regal and majestic tone, Primrose Purple represents the culmination of spiritual evolution and divine grace. In the radiance of heaven on earth, purple serves as a symbol of spiritual awakening and enlightenment, inviting us to transcend the limitations of the egoic self and to bask in the light of divine presence. It reminds us that we are co-creators of our reality, capable of manifesting heaven on earth through acts of love, compassion, and service to others. As we align our hearts and minds to the radiance of humanity's diversity, we awaken to the eternal truth that heaven is not a distant destination to be reached solely through your race, religion, or region but a state of being to be cultivated and nurtured in every moment of our human experience.

Iris - Eternal Spring

In the vast interplay of nature's beauty, Iris emerges as a revolutionary symbol of eternal spring—a timeless harbinger of renewal, hope, and transformation that transcends the boundaries of time and season. With its delicate petals unfurling in a kaleidoscope of vibrant hues, the Iris beckons us to embrace the perpetual cycle of rebirth and growth that unfolds within the heart of the cosmos. Rooted in ancient mythology, the Iris carries the legacy of goddesses and deities who personified the essence of renewal and fertility. In Greek mythology, the Iris was linked to the goddess Iris, whose rainbow-hued path bridges the mortal realm and the divine. As a messenger of the gods, Iris embodied the spirit of renewal and hope, carrying messages of guidance and inspiration to humanity. In ancient Egypt, the Iris was associated with the goddess Isis for wisdom, magic, and fertility. The Iris's intricate petals and vibrant colors were believed to mirror the layers of knowledge and understanding that one must navigate to attain enlightenment. Thus, Iris became a beacon of spiritual awakening, guiding seekers on inner transformation and self-discovery.

Iris contains colors of purple and blueberry intermingling together to weave a narrative of inner vision and spiritual awakening that resonates with the rhythm of the human experience. In your reading, Iris embodies the essence of spiritual enlightenment and divine wisdom. As the color of the third eye chakra, its purple smudging effect invites us to gaze inward, to explore the vast expanse of our inner landscape, and to unlock the hidden mysteries of the cosmos. Within the embrace of Iris's petals, purple serves as a beacon of inner vision. This guiding light redirects our attention to how our path to self-discovery and higher consciousness upcycles itself as the world around us ebbs and flows. The splashes of blueberry, with its rich and succulent tone, add depth and complexity to the palette of the Iris, infusing it with the energy of psychic protection. Like the deep, dark depths of the night sky, blueberry evokes a sense of mystery and wonder, prompting us to delve into the hidden recesses of our subconscious mind and embrace the infinite possibilities that lie beyond the realm of ordinary perception.

Iris echoes the eternal spring of spiritual enlightenment and humanity's inner vision awakening. Just as the natural world undergoes a process of regeneration during springtime, so does the human spirit, which has the potential to awaken to higher truths and expanded consciousness. Iris enriches the mind and body to restore wisdom, intuition, and spiritual insight; when it appears in a reading, it reminds of the transformative power of inner growth and self-discovery. As you gaze upon Iris, be open-minded to the boundless potential within yourself — the infinite capacity for growth, transformation, and renewal that awaits you on the journey of self-discovery. In the language of flowers, Iris speaks of protection and strength as a guardian of the eternal spring that flows ceaselessly within the depths of the soul. As its delicate petals open in the gentle breeze, the Iris whispers of the eternal cycle of birth, growth, decay, and renewal that weaves its way through the fabric of existence. With each petal that unfurls, we step closer to realizing our highest potential, guided by the radiant light of divine presence that shines forth from within. In a reading, it evokes a sense of timeless beauty and grace—a reminder that even amidst life's trials and tribulations, the spirit of renewal and hope endures. Iris wards off evil spirits and brings good fortune to those who cultivate its presence. Its sword-like leaves are guardians of the eternal spring, shielding the tender blossoms from harm and nurturing their growth amidst the changing tides of time. You are protected currently. As you immerse yourself in the vibrant hues of the Iris, embrace the eternal spring of your being—to awaken to the inner vision and intuitive wisdom that lies at the heart of your true nature. Yet, perhaps most profoundly, the Iris sends a message for you to access your reservoir of resilience, courage, and hope that flows ceaselessly within the depths of your soul. In its vibrant colors and graceful form, the Iris invites you to embrace the ever-renewing cycle of life and to trust in the inherent beauty and wisdom that lie at the heart of existence, even through grief and radical times. As we gaze upon the Iris's iridescent bloom, we are reminded that no matter how dark the night may seem, the dawn of a new day is always on the horizon. Unfurl your soul unapologetically. There's no shame in starting over, rebranding, and repurposing something old to feel new again. Rejuvenate your energy field, social media feed, and calendar.

Blush - Cheerful Love

In the delicate dance of human emotion, Blush emerges in your color reading as a radiant symbol of cheerful love—a fluttering expression of affection that resonates with the heart's deepest desires. Whether as a soft, rosy hue or a gentle flush of the cheeks, Blush embodies the essence of warmth, tenderness, and emotional vulnerability, inviting us to embrace the beauty of love in all its forms. At its core, Blush symbolizes the innocence and sincerity of romantic feelings—a gentle flutter of the heart that accompanies moments of attraction, admiration, and affection. It speaks to the vulnerability of the human spirit, the courage to open oneself to the possibility of love, and the joy of connecting with another soul on a deeper level. When challenged or negatively influenced, Blush can evoke embarrassment and self-consciousness—a fear of vulnerability that arises when our true feelings are laid bare for the world to see. In moments of Blush-induced discomfort, overcoming the fear of judgment or rejection and embracing our emotions' authenticity without reservation can be challenging. However, overcoming embarrassment is not about suppressing or denying our natural responses but embracing them with self-compassion and acceptance. By reframing Blush as a symbol of emotional transparency and honesty, we can learn to celebrate our vulnerability as a testament to the depth of our feelings and the sincerity of our intentions. Your spirit guides and intuition want you to see the world with more inner confidence and self-assurance so that you can help alleviate feelings of embarrassment and self-consciousness.

Suppose you've felt guilty about recognizing your inherent worth and value. In that case, you can approach this situation with grace and poise, knowing that your feelings are valid and worthy of respect. Practicing mindfulness and self-awareness can also be instrumental in overcoming feelings of embarrassment. By tuning into the physical sensations and emotions that arise when we Blush, we can gain insight into the underlying thoughts and beliefs that may contribute to our discomfort and cultivate a greater sense of ease and acceptance in moments of vulnerability. Many find this color energy popping up when they feel insecure about their identity in the world. Arguments brew out of displaced fears about whom we believe and whom others think we concern their unique perspective, which causes more harm in family dynamics and social interactions. Miscommunication is a byproduct of not listening to each other. You may not see your situation holistically because you've been overcommitting to defend your viewpoint while never intending to leave your pedestal for fear of losing power and taking feedback personally to the point of self-inflicting mental and emotional wounds. You want to feel in control and reach a point of perfection. Still, in the process, you're frantically stumbling over your counterpoints in discussion or failing to provide apparent alternatives, leaving you flustered and ultimately feeling inferior to others involved. You may have reached a point where you have not said anything, and this silence will only allow resentment to fester.

Blush indicates tension between individuals in a color reading, but it also invites you to embrace yourself and others, prioritize love, and approach situations with light-hearted cheerfulness. This attitude avoids shame and fosters personal growth. Confrontation facilitates self-discovery. Embracing vulnerability with courage and compassion transcends embarrassment, fostering authentic connection and heartfelt expression. It's time you accept yourself and others, choose to prioritize love in the conversation over everything else, and approach the situation with contentment that doesn't shame yourself or another into a corner of isolation and fear. Don't steal someone else's opportunity to grow because you've built your identity around the animosity between fear's gravity and love's levity.

Spirit - The Hero's Journey

Hero is gender-neutral. In the hero's journey, the concept of Spirit plays a profound role, embodying the essence of the protagonist's quest for self-discovery, transformation, and ultimate triumph. Throughout this narrative arc, the hero encounters various challenges, confronts inner and outer obstacles, and embarks on a transformative journey that transcends the ordinary realm of existence. Spirit, in your color reading, symbolizes the inner drive, resilience, and transcendental force that propels you forward on your quest. At the beginning of the situation, you may find yourself in a state of ordinariness, feeling disconnected from your true potential and purpose. This sense of being ordinary catalyzes the hero's quest, prompting you to embark on an adventure of self-discovery and growth. In embracing their ordinary nature, the hero acknowledges their vulnerabilities, limitations, and fears and recognizes their untapped potential. Leveraging the feeling of ordinariness, you can begin the journey with humility, openness, and a willingness to learn and grow. As you look at your situation and decide, you must accept that participating in life comes with trials, tribulations, and encounters with mentors, allies, and adversaries. Along the way, you learn to become a hero of your means. You can harness the power of Spirit, tapping into your inner resilience, courage, and determination to overcome challenges and obstacles. As you progress on your journey, you'll undergo a transformation process fueled by the awakening of your Spirit. These trials and tribulations of being human inspire you to confront fears, doubts, and insecurities, gradually transcending the limitations and embracing authentic potential.

Spirit becomes the guiding force in the color oracle that empowers the hero in all of us to persevere in the face of adversity, stay true to our values and beliefs, and ultimately emerge victorious. It's your zero-to-hero era. To feel extraordinary within the context of the hero's journey, one must embrace the transformative power of the Spirit and embark on a journey of self-discovery and growth. This involves cultivating a deep self-awareness, authenticity, and purpose and tapping into inherent resilience, courage, and creativity.

The color card shows a spectrum of heroic transformation from feverish pinks to an almost healed flesh tone. The striations of colors reflect the scars we endure as heroes on our journey. As you work with Spirit, know it can represent the wounded warrior archetype or Chiron in your astrological birth chart. It's a common motif found in myths, legends, and storytelling across cultures. It typically represents a character who has suffered significant physical, emotional, or psychological wounds, often because of past trauma, battles, or hardships. Despite their injuries, the wounded warrior displays courage, resilience, and a sense of duty or honor. This archetype embodies resilience, redemption, and the capacity to overcome adversity. The wounded warrior may struggle with their visible and invisible injuries, yet they persevere in their quest for healing, redemption, or justice. It's a colorful tribute to our disabled and veterans. When Spirit appears in your reading, you're being called by the Divine to tap into your inner strength, determination, and the triumph of the human spirit over adversity. The wounded warrior may transform throughout their journey, confronting their past wounds, facing inner demons, and ultimately finding healing, redemption, or a sense of purpose. They may draw upon their experiences of suffering to empathize with others, inspire hope, or fight for a more significant cause. Examples of the wounded warrior archetype can be found in various mythological and literary works, such as Achilles in Greek mythology, who is both physically and emotionally wounded by the Trojan War but continues to fight bravely or Frodo Baggins in J.R.R. Tolkien's "*The Lord of the Rings*," who carries the psychological burden of the One Ring and the scars of his journey to Mount Doom.

Chiron is often called the "Wounded Healer" asteroid or comet in astrology. Its significance lies in representing the deepest wounds and vulnerabilities in an individual's psyche and the potential for healing and transcendence. Chiron's placement in a natal chart indicates areas of profound pain or insecurities that the individual may grapple with throughout their lifetime. These wounds are often related to feelings of inadequacy, rejection, or abandonment, and they can manifest in various aspects of the individual's life, including relationships, career, and self-image. However, despite its association with pain and vulnerability, Chiron symbolizes the potential for growth, transformation, and spiritual awakening. The placement of Chiron in a natal chart can signify areas where the individual can heal themselves and others, often through acts of compassion, empathy, and self-awareness. In a color reading, the presence of Chiron is seen through Spirit as an invitation to confront and integrate one's deepest wounds rather than avoiding or suppressing them. By acknowledging and working through these wounds, individuals can experience profound healing and transformation, leading to greater self-acceptance, wholeness, and spiritual fulfillment. Life always seems to throw us curve balls and may even wound us verbally, mentally, emotionally, and physically, so when Spirit shows up in your reading, you asked to complete soulful reconnaissance to find the origin of your wounds and the resilience of your human spirit in the face of adversity, the openness toward redemption, and the capacity for personal growth and transformation even if it means committing to see yourself not as a puppet of Corporate Chaos, but an instrument of divine intelligence invading the monotonous 9 to 5 grind.

A drawback to Spirit happens when we compulsively obsess over celebrities and influencers. Hero worshiping is the excessive admiration or idolization of someone, often a public figure or celebrity, to the extent that their flaws, mistakes, or problematic behaviors are overlooked or excused. This phenomenon can lead to an unrealistic perception of the individual as flawless or infallible, and it may contribute to a skewed power dynamic in which the person being idolized is placed on a pedestal above criticism or accountability. To avoid hero worship, remember that everyone, including those we admire, is human and imperfect. It's essential to acknowledge and accept the flaws and limitations of the individuals we admire rather than idealizing them. Encourage critical thinking and skepticism, even towards those we admire. It's essential to objectively evaluate their actions, beliefs, and behaviors rather than blindly accepting or justifying them. Instead of fixating on one individual as the epitome of success or virtue, seek inspiration from a diverse range of people and perspectives. This can help prevent the tendency to over-idolize any single person. Focus on principles, not personalities. Rather than idolizing specific individuals, please focus on the values, principles, and ideals they represent. This allows for admiration of the positive qualities they embody while acknowledging that no one person is perfect. Hold yourself and the individuals you admire accountable for their actions and behaviors. Recognize that holding someone accountable does not diminish their accomplishments or positive attributes; instead, it reinforces the importance of integrity and ethical behavior. By being mindful of these strategies, you can avoid the trap of hero worship and create a healthier, more balanced approach to admiration and inspiration.

By embracing one's ordinariness and harnessing the power of Spirit, one can transcend limitations, overcome obstacles, and achieve extraordinary feats. Spirit is a powerful symbol in the hero's journey, representing the inner drive, resilience, and transformative power that propels us on our quest for self-discovery and growth. By leveraging the feeling of ordinariness and embracing the power of the Spirit card, you can embark on a life-changing journey of self-transformation and emerge as an extraordinary hero in your own right.

Memory - History & Impressions

Do you remember who you are? You are a living time capsule of the almighty, all-expansive universe. You came here with a special mission and purpose that pulls you toward the people, places, and things that give you a unique human experience. Beyond religion, race, and region, you were born to remember. The fondness you feel when you reflect on everything that brought you to this moment and taking responsibility for how you used your time isn't for the faint of heart. You are the architect of your world. You are curating energy and weaving together elements to make meaning out of your human experience. Memory is a lazy, hazy day of color that speaks of history and impressions that leave a mark on our minds. In this current version of yourself, your soul stamps the world with your energetic signature every damn day with the many choices you make or choose not to make until the very last breath you take when you leave the physical world all behind, so how do you want to be remembered? Our brain and heart connection is like an algorithm coded by design to interact with the world around us, so all the information, chemicals, and thoughts you consume matter. How you think about yourself and others influences your memories and perception of reality. This power is not for the weak but for the bold and the beautiful brave enough to make good with their unique imprint in the space-time continuum. In your color reading, memory symbolizes personal and collective identity continuity. It connects the past with the present, allowing individuals and societies to maintain a sense of continuity over time. Your past does not define who you are—making mistakes happen. Memory represents accumulated knowledge and experience. It is often associated with wisdom, allowing individuals to learn from past experiences and apply that knowledge to present and future situations. You are being asked to pioneer, trailblaze, and embrace feeling memorable. Memory acknowledges history and nostalgia, but it also celebrates imagination and creativity. Your memories provide the raw material for storytelling, artistic expression, and innovation, allowing people to reframe and reinterpret past experiences in new ways.

In many cultures, Memory symbolizes the legacy of ancestors and the heritage of a community or family. It preserves traditions, customs, and histories, ensuring they are passed down through generations. It plays a crucial role in honoring and paying tribute to people, events, and experiences that have shaped individual lives and collective histories. Periods in our human experience are memorable milestones that display the diversity of what it means to be human in a specific place of consciousness. Heritage sites and memorials commemorate the catharsis of change and loss. Memory's blue-gray sky, faint purple mountains, and smoky strands of straw billowing on the color card is an indication that you have the emotional landscape to not shape the narrative, values, and conversations through your craft and life's purpose but also the liberty to tell your own story while honoring the stories of those that came before and give inspiration to those yet to come. Memory can serve as a repository of moral and ethical lessons. By recalling past events, individuals and societies can learn from mistakes and successes, guiding future decisions to benefit everyone, not just a select few.

When Memory is reversed or challenged, it's a sign of forgetfulness and arrested development. Forgetting who you are is very common. Life throws you into situations that allow you to re-discover yourself over and over until the light of who you are breaks through. After years of commitment, therapy, and cultivating a spiritual practice, we all can fall into a rut of old routines and bad habits. Your past baggage may be circling back in your head to remind you of where you come from and why you no longer carry that shit in the first place. Memory wants you to permit yourself to be someone worth remembering in all the good ways, but don't get caught up in the need to freeze time. Suppose you've been feeling reluctant to change and growing up and out of your comfort zone. In that case, Memory catalyzes to help you deal with where your growth is stunted and recognize how you continue to exhibit behaviors, attitudes, and social dynamics typical of your adolescent years despite aging physically. Being stuck in the past and stubbornly refusing to live beyond your history keeps you small and limited. There is always new information and new opportunities to assimilate as we collectively evolve as a society.

The expression "forgive but not forget" means letting go of resentment and anger toward someone who has wronged them. However, one should remember the event to avoid repeating the same situation or allowing the same harm to occur again. It emphasizes the importance of emotional healing through forgiveness while advocating for caution and awareness to prevent future hurt. While forgiveness can alleviate some negative emotions, not forgetting can mean continuously revisiting the trauma. This retention of painful memories can prevent full emotional recovery, as the hurt remains a persistent part of the person's consciousness. Remembering past wrongs can create barriers to trusting others, as individuals may become overly cautious or suspicious. This can hinder the formation of new, healthy relationships and perpetuate feelings of isolation or mistrust. Continuously recalling negative experiences can reinforce a victim mentality, where the individual may struggle to see themselves as anything other than someone wronged. This can limit their ability to see their growth and potential beyond the trauma. Holding on to memories of being wronged can affect self-esteem and self-worth, as individuals may internalize the negative experiences and believe they are defined by them. Proper closure often requires forgiveness and letting go of the past. Not forgetting can keep the wound open, preventing the individual from entirely moving on and embracing a future free from the shadows of their past.

Memory wants you to move on from your trauma and loss. To balance the idea of "forgive but not forget" in a healthy way, you can work through your emotions and experiences with the help of therapy or support groups, integrating the lessons learned without allowing the memories to dominate your life. Use the memories as a guide to set healthy boundaries rather than as a reason to hold onto resentment or fear. Emphasize personal growth and resilience gained from experiences, shifting the focus from the past hurt to present and future possibilities. Give yourself a chance to feel hope. Imagine a new outcome. Tell a different perspective about your story that embraces triumph, honor, and progress. Dwelling excessively on past traumas is debilitating and can keep the most joyful person stagnant, invisible, and insignificant. However, in those moments of anger, fear, and confusion, remember that being human is about becoming better and leaving the world better than when you arrived. So, I ask again, do you remember who you are?

Focus - Guidance & Direction

Focus is the color of details highlighting how you want to scale your presence and influence worldwide. One takes small steps to achieve a more significant production or project. Breaking your progress into manageable pieces has a benefit over the long term. Still, you need to be clear on the vision of what you want and who you are so that you're not overly invested and hyper-fixated on vanity numbers on social media, how much money you do and do not have, and the bottomless addictions we use to quench an insatiable thirst for validation and coping. Perhaps you need to review if the means justify the ends. Whatever you give your attention and energy to will expand and become more prominent in your life and work. Consistent incremental wins outshine the one-hit wonders. Focus brings guidance and direction to your situation to remind you that you are uncovering information like an archeologist unwrapping papyrus in an abandoned tomb or a forensic specialist looking under the microscope to find the tiniest evidence of life on a new planet. Focus is confirmation that you can use tools, research, and software in your situation to discover and explore the terrain of your human experience. This could also mean it's time to look in a new direction outside your comfort zone to gain a renewed sense of confidence. Be curious. You can learn more about yourself and the willpower to prioritize quality over quantity.

The obstinacy one shows toward Focus comes from a fear of not having a choice and the lack of detail for context that takes the attention and intention off the nuances of the situation. Disassociating themself from their fault or involvement shifts the blame and spotlight on another person or topic. Avoiding the truth and denying facts over fiction creates faulty infrastructure and unnecessary risk. When negatively influenced and challenged, Focus reveals where passive-aggressive attempts to pigeonhole a different person, place, or thing in a limited and defined worldview. This compartmentalization takes power, mood, and conversation away from the contrarian. It moves it to the hands of the conformist whose rigid micromanagement of the world is rewarded, celebrated, and indoctrinated through religion, government mandates, and other means of Corporate Chaos propaganda to have the public consciousness focus on fear rather than love.

In a color reading, you must ask yourself: is what I'm focusing on coming from a place of love? Am I assuming things because of fear? If the worst thing to happen about this situation existed, then what or who would it look like? Ultimately, you know that love has no gender or religion. Love does not care about money, rank, or what clothes you wear. This truth is inherent to every human being, but we get caught under the net of other people's narratives. Corporate Chaos has, for millennia, focused on micromanaging our human experiences and devaluing love in the world so that fear can profit from war, famine, and poverty. This vicious machine of lies and disinformation is used to fragment our humanity, dissolve our democracy as a species, and obscure what we see and know so that it maintains a constant state of chaos.

Focus invites you to assess the scope of your place in the situation. You are not here to be omniscient. Predicting and controlling human behavior can be presumptuous when assumptions are made without considering the complexity and individuality of people. Overgeneralizing and glossing over the details of your situation is the biggest obstacle stopping you from progressing in your life and work. If you feel like you're talking to the wall, putting your head down in the sand, or being treated as just another number, remember to redirect the attention and intention of your conformity and build a platform that celebrates your diversity. Your oddity can be your commodity. Come out. The light of love reaches the deepest and darkest spaces of our minds, so allow the color of Focus to guide you in a new direction.

Rain - Water Energy

Water is essential for all life, making it a powerful symbol of fertility, renewal, and life. Rain is often associated with renewal and cleansing. It washes away dirt and dust, providing a sense of purification. This cleansing effect extends metaphorically to human experience, symbolizing the washing away of troubles, grief, and negativity. After a period of rain, the air feels fresher, and the landscape appears revitalized, highlighting Rain's role in rejuvenation. Rain can symbolize various emotions and states of being in literature and art. It frequently represents sorrow and melancholy, mirroring the tears of sadness or heartbreak. Scenes with rain often convey a mood of introspection and contemplation by staying indoors, suggesting an inward journey or emotional catharsis. Hillary Duff's song, *Come Clean*, personifies the essence and magic of Rain. Kissing or singing in the rain can represent emotional authenticity and a sign of growth. Farmers welcome rain as it nourishes crops and sustains agricultural life. This association extends to the idea of rain bringing new beginnings and opportunities as it prepares the ground for new seeds to sprout. Rain's unpredictability and sometimes destructive power also symbolize the uncontrollable forces of nature and life's uncertainties. Storms and heavy rains can be metaphors for life's challenges and turbulent times, underscoring the resilience required to endure and overcome adversity.

In a color reading, Rain celebrates the fluidity of your human experience. People, places, and things are like containers for our emotions. Catching every droplet of who we are in that moment. For numerous reasons, water is considered holy and mighty in magical arts and spiritual practices, spanning cultures and traditions. Its symbolic and practical uses reflect its essential nature and profound influence on life and spirituality. Since water is universally associated with purification and cleansing, it's commonly used in spiritual practice to wash away impurities and negative energies. Wudu in Islam is the ritual washing before prayers that cleanses the body and prepares the soul for worship. For Hindu rituals, Ganges water is considered sacred and purifying, often used in ceremonies to wash the body and spirit. For Baptism in Christianity, water symbolizes the washing away "sins" and the individual's rebirth into a new, purified life. Holy wells, natural springs, and fountains in various places worldwide are often believed to have healing properties and are revered sites of pilgrimage and veneration. In magical arts, water is a conduit for spiritual energy, enhancing the flow of mystical power. Water is used in scrying. A practice of looking at something, in this case, water (or other reflective surfaces), to gain insight or predict the future. People often practice scrying by gazing at the color cards to connect with their intuition. A favorite way to work with water energy is to charge water. Practitioners usually charge water with intentions or magical energy by placing it under the moonlight or speaking incantations over it, believing it can store and transmit these energies.

Masaru Emoto, a Japanese researcher, conducted experiments in 1994 suggesting that water can respond to human emotions and intentions. He claimed that water exposed to positive words, music, and thoughts would form aesthetically pleasing, well-organized ice crystals when frozen. In contrast, water exposed to negative influences would form disfigured, chaotic crystals. Emoto documented these findings with photographs of the ice crystals, proposing that water can reflect the consciousness of its environment. A similar effect has been done with apples and words!

Water is embedded in many cultures' mythologies and religious stories, often associated with gods and goddesses. In Japanese mythology, Suijin is the Shinto god of water, revered as the deity who governs all forms of water, including rivers, lakes, and rain. Often depicted as a dragon or a serpent, Suijin is believed to protect fishermen, provide bountiful harvests, and ensure the purity of water sources. Shrines dedicated to Suijin are commonly found near bodies of water, where offerings and rituals are performed to appease the god and secure his blessings. The lore surrounding Suijin underscores water's essential and revered nature in Japanese culture, highlighting its vital role in agriculture, daily life, and spiritual practices.

Yemaya and Oya are potent deities in the Yoruba religion, each embodying distinct aspects of water and natural forces. Yemaya, the mother goddess of the ocean, symbolizes nurturing, fertility, and creation, often depicted as a mermaid or a beautiful woman surrounded by seashells. She is revered for her protective and life-giving qualities, offering solace and abundance. Oya, on the other hand, is the goddess of storms, winds, and transformation associated with the Niger River. She represents change, destruction, and rebirth, reflecting nature's tumultuous yet necessary forces. Together, Yemaya and Oya teach the balance of life's nurturing and transformative powers, illustrating water's dual role in creation and change.

Rain's role in the color deck is profound and multifaceted. It is a powerful symbol of purification, life, and spiritual energy, deeply embedded in diverse cultures' rituals, mythology, and religious practices worldwide. Its universal significance highlights its essential nature, connecting the physical and spiritual realms in a tangible and profoundly symbolic way. Water is sacred, and you're invited to use it to anoint, bless, restore, cleanse, and reflect the flow of your human experience.

Poison Ivy - Reactions & Deadly Sins

Poison Ivy, known for its irritating and toxic properties as a plant, brings a color-coded message when reading about the nature of morality and how one reacts to the world around them. Traditionally, its symbolism revolves around danger, caution, transformation, and the hidden threats beneath the surface. Still, we'll take the leafy underbelly of our collective consciousness further by looking at the forest of your thoughts and feelings as a whole ecosystem instead of an isolated echo chamber. When Poison Ivy appears in a reading, you're asked to reflect on what aspects of your situation make your skin crawl and cause you to break out in hives. How is your body viscerally reacting to your dreams, goals, and conflicts? Your body is an essential tool for the spirit to guide you, and it naturally responds to people, places, and things with an innate response. Survival. Your brain releases chemicals, causing reactions to see and experience the world in a specific way. Corporate Chaos hijacked our minds with religion, game theory, and human design, wreaking havoc on impulse control, incentivizing addiction, and controlling the masses through subliminal visualizations and clickbait. The digital spaces of social media are littered with angry face reactions and bot farms. Being human is an acid trip for the soul. Food and drug administrations are alongside the Centers for Disease Control and World Health Organizations, attempting to sustain order in the sea of research and development and regulating pharmaceutical power. Poison Ivy wants you to run diagnostics to assess toxicity levels that may appear socially and environmentally. Your body is your business. Trust this. Allow your spidey senses to tingle on the web. What are your non-negotiables when collaborating with others and committing your body and mind to a cause or project? Boundaries are vital for keeping order, but are you reacting or seeing the situation as an endangerment to your worldview out of spite or negligence? Poison Ivy is a wickedly inspiring color revealing how we regulate our behavior and suppress self-expression for fear of upsetting others or inciting adverse reactions to what comes naturally to us.

Sin is fake news. It's an unnatural sociopolitical construct designed to use the fundamentals of religion as a platform to maintain superiority complexes and groom narcissists. You were not born with sin. Neither are you punished or struggling because of sin. You do not sin. Jesus did not die on the cross to forgive sins. Jesus was murdered by an organized sociopolitical movement designed to control the narrative and influence the population. Take sin and throw it in a bin. Any platform that denounces love is morally corrupt. The interplay between social media reactions, the concept of the Seven Deadly Sins, and the origins of sin presents a compelling narrative about the nature of morality and control in contemporary society. Poison Ivy's Electric Green explores how social media amplifies behaviors traditionally labeled as sinful, the historical and religious origins of these sins, and the argument that sin is a socially constructed concept used to regulate behavior and ultimately suppresses our human rights to self-expression through life, liberty and the pursuit of happiness - sans prescribed mommy and daddy approved religion.

Social media platforms have become integral to modern life, profoundly influencing how we interact, perceive ourselves, and judge others. These platforms often magnify behaviors associated with the Seven Deadly Sins, turning personal vices into public spectacles: pride, greed, wrath, envy, lust, gluttony, and sloth. Social media is a breeding ground for pride, where users curate idealized versions of their lives to gain validation through likes and followers. This digital vanity fosters a culture of narcissism and self-obsession, leading individuals to seek constant external validation. The pursuit of wealth and material success is prominently displayed on social media, where influencers showcase luxury lifestyles. This perpetuates a culture of consumerism and greed, driving people to covet what they see online and measure their self-worth by their material possessions. Digital platforms become arenas for wrath, where users engage in aggressive debates, cancel culture, and online harassment in the comments section. The anonymity of the internet emboldens individuals to express anger and hostility without facing immediate repercussions. Social media's highlight reels and posts can incite envy as people compare their lives to the seemingly perfect lives of others. This can lead to feelings of inadequacy and resentment, harming mental health and personal relationships. The internet is rife with content that exploits lust, from provocative images to explicit material. The easy accessibility of such content can distort perceptions of body image and foster unhealthy attitudes toward intimacy. Gluttonous behaviors are often glorified on social media, where indulgence in food, drink, and excess is celebrated. This can normalize unhealthy habits and contribute to issues like obesity and addiction. The addictive nature of social media can promote sloth, encourage procrastination, and reduce productivity. Endless scrolling and binge-watching distract individuals from more meaningful and productive activities. Have you been sitting in a room with another living being glued to your phone? It is human to enjoy a good thirst trap and decompress with an endless scroll of animal videos, but you must be mindful of how you consume and react to social media. The animosity behind our technology can be one of the most viral and toxic forms of self-expression, creating a barrier to being human.

The concept of the Seven Deadly Sins originates from early Christian teachings, particularly those of Evagrius Ponticus, and was later formalized by Pope Gregory I. These sins were identified as fundamental human vices that led to spiritual decay and separation from God. The idea of sin itself is deeply rooted in religious narratives, such as the story of Adam and Eve in the Garden of Eden, where disobedience to divine command resulted in the original sin and humanity's fall from grace. These religious teachings framed sin as actions or states of being that deviate from God's will, inherently evil and deserving of punishment. The notion of sin instills moral order, guiding individuals towards virtuous behavior by defining and condemning specific actions and desires. While sin has traditionally been viewed through a religious lens, a critical perspective suggests that the concept of sin is a socially constructed tool used to regulate behavior and maintain social order. This view of sin, rather than an inherent moral failing, is a program of thought designed to suppress self-expression and micromanage life, liberty, and the pursuit of happiness. By labeling certain behaviors sinful, societies can control and restrict actions deviating from accepted norms. This regulation often extends to personal identity and expression, such as sexuality, ambition, and individualism. For example, labeling non-heteronormative sexual orientations as sinful has been used to justify discrimination and suppress LGBTQ+ rights. The condemnation of pride, envy, and lust can be seen as efforts to suppress natural human desires and emotions. These restrictions can stifle creativity and self-expression, forcing individuals to conform to restrictive moral codes that limit their potential and happiness. Historically, religious and political authorities have used the concept of sin to maintain power and control over populations. These authorities can manipulate social norms and values to serve their interests by defining and enforcing what constitutes sinful behavior. This has included using sin to justify oppressive practices such as witch hunts, censorship, and the persecution of dissenters. The sin of greed, while morally condemned, is paradoxically promoted in capitalist societies where wealth accumulation is a sign of success. This contradiction highlights how the concept of sin can be manipulated to maintain economic hierarchies and class divisions, punishing the poor while excusing the excesses of the wealthy.

The relationship between social media reactions, the Seven Deadly Sins, and the origins of sin reveals a complexity between individual behavior, societal norms, and control mechanisms. Social media rewards and programs behaviors traditionally labeled as sinful, creating new public scrutiny and judgment forms and exacerbating toxicity, viewing sin as a sociopolitical construct made to oppress and control others who don't ascribe to your viewpoints or perceived lifestyle challenges traditional notions of narcissistic morality clauses. It suggests that sin is more a tool for maintaining order and power than an inherent moral failing. When Poison Ivy appears in your reading, remember not to fixate on flaws but strive to detox deadly sins to restore a natural sense of balance and beauty. Again, sin is not natural; it's the opinion of some asshole on a power trip. This perspective calls for a critical reevaluation of how we define and respond to so-called "sinful" behaviors, advocating for a more inclusive and liberating approach that respects individual autonomy and promotes genuine well-being and happiness.

Ghostland - Afterlife & Forgetfulness

Do you feel the empty, cold space of abandonment? Ghostland is the purgatory one feels when they forget who they are and why they're in the situation in the first place.

The afterlife is a concept in many religions, philosophies, and cultures, referring to a realm or state of existence that follows physical death. Some philosophies, like existentialism or materialism, may deny an afterlife, viewing death as the end of individual existence. When Ghostland appears in a reading, it affirms an end, closure, and an opportunity to move on from past experiences. There's a lingering and haunting quality when Ghostland appears, and it tends to tell readers that they've ghosted their identity, desire, and goals. Where do you see yourself procrastinating in your situation? Is the money flow stalling and preventing you from feeling happy and safe? Does the end feel too finite and leave you unmotivated to pursue a goal or task because it no longer feels challenging or scarce? It can also be related to the concept of "hedonic adaptation," where the initial excitement and drive wane as one becomes accustomed to the progress or success achieved, reducing the perceived value or urgency of continuing.

Hedonic adaptation, also known as the "hedonic treadmill," is a psychological phenomenon where individuals return to a relatively stable level of happiness despite major positive or negative events or life changes. Essentially, people quickly get used to changes in their life circumstances, whether good or bad and revert to their baseline level of happiness over time. Everyone has a baseline level of happiness that they tend to return to after the impact of new experiences or changes fades. It applies to positive events (like getting a promotion or winning the lottery) and negative events (like losing a job or experiencing a loss). The boost or dip in happiness from these events is typically temporary. People tend to adjust automatically, and their happiness levels stabilize back to their baseline. This concept explains why people often continually seek new goals and achievements to increase their happiness, as the satisfaction from previous accomplishments diminishes over time. Understanding hedonic adaptation can help make more sustainable choices for well-being, focusing on experiences and practices that foster long-term satisfaction rather than temporary boosts. Ghostland appears in a reading and illustrates the human tendency to take for granted and forget what you have achieved or acquired, leading to a perpetual chase for new goals to regain the sense of novelty and excitement. This way of walking through life but never allowing anything to shift your baseline substantially can be a blessing and a curse.

Ghosts, even friendly ones, are bound to a specific place and can serve as a metaphor for how people might feel trapped by their circumstances or past experiences, particularly when they hit rock bottom. In many cultures, ghosts are often depicted as spirits tied to a particular location, usually due to unresolved issues or unfinished business. This symbolizes being stuck in a situation or emotional state, unable to move forward or find peace. After hitting rock bottom, a person might experience temporary despair. Over time, due to hedonic adaptation, they can adjust back to a more stable emotional state. However, as ghosts are bound by unresolved issues, individuals might feel anchored to their low points by lingering problems or a negative mindset. To overcome the feeling of being stuck and to rise from rock bottom, consider these steps, drawing parallels to freeing oneself from the metaphorical "haunted" state: Recognize and accept where you are without denial. Just as a ghost must come to terms with its past, acknowledging your current state is crucial. Determine what is keeping you tethered to this low point. These could be unresolved emotions, unaddressed problems, or unhealthy thought patterns. Work on resolving these issues. This might involve forgiveness (of yourself or others), addressing unfinished business, or seeking professional help. Establish new, meaningful goals to create a sense of purpose. As a ghost might find peace by completing unfinished business, setting and working toward new goals can provide direction and motivation. Develop strategies to cope with future challenges, such as practicing mindfulness, building a support network, and maintaining a healthy lifestyle. Cultivate a mindset of gratitude and focus on positive experiences to counterbalance negative ones. This can help shift your baseline happiness upwards over time. Embrace the idea of continuous self-improvement and growth. Just as hedonic adaptation suggests that people return to a baseline, you can keep raising that baseline by constantly evolving. By understanding Ghostland and seeing it show up in your reading, you can better appreciate the importance of resolving past issues and striving for continuous growth and resilience, ultimately helping to overcome obstacles and move beyond what's haunting you.

Disease - Stress & Negativity

This is the scariest color card in *The Color Mage Oracle.* Very simply, it just means you're stressed to bits. Everything about your situation is under immense pressure, causing anxiety, depression, and apathy. Seeking professional help is the most robust way to help you return to a state of ease and positivity. The original sense of "disease" as "lack of ease" directly relates to stress. Stress disrupts a person's comfort and well-being, creating physical and mental discomfort. Chronic stress can lead to various illnesses, making the person literally "dis-eased." Negativity and stress are closely linked. Negative emotions and thoughts can contribute to stress, affecting physical health. This connection between mind and body underscores how a "dis-ease" can result from psychological factors as much as physical causes.

When Disease appears in a reading, it wants you to see stress and negativity from an objective point of view. Seeing stress from an objective point of view involves detaching oneself from the immediate emotional reactions and assessing the situation logically and factually. Regular meditation can help create a mental space between you and your stressors, allowing for a more detached perspective. Learn to recognize common cognitive distortions (e.g., catastrophizing, overgeneralizing) that amplify stress. By identifying these, you can challenge and reframe your thoughts more rationally. It would help if you looked at your situation from a third-person perspective. When thinking about the problem, try to view it as if you are an observer or as if it is happening to someone else. This can help reduce emotional intensity and provide clarity. If you keep a journal, you can change the narrative and write about your stressors in the third person. For example, instead of "I am stressed about this deadline," write "Bernard is feeling stressed about this deadline." Always consult a therapist or counselor. A mental health professional can provide an unbiased perspective and help you understand and manage stress more effectively. Acknowledge that experiencing stress is a normal human response. Treat yourself with the compassion you would offer a friend in a similar situation. Accept your stress and commit to actions that align with your values rather than trying to eliminate stress.

Negativity is a bitch. When someone is constantly negative and tends to self-prophecy their stress, it is often referred to as having a negative cognitive bias or negative thinking patterns. If this negativity is persistent and pervasive, it may also be related to Pessimism, a general tendency to expect the worst. Pessimists often focus on the negative aspects and outcomes, which can lead to self-fulfilling prophecies of stress and failure. This occurs when a person's expectations about a situation or themselves lead them to behave in ways that cause those expectations to come true. In this context, consistently negative expectations can increase stress and create a cycle of stress reinforcement. Making a mountain out of a molehill is a cognitive distortion where an individual anticipates disaster, sees minor issues as significant problems, and blows a nuanced comment out of proportion, causing more havoc and chaos in the conversation. This catastrophizing leads to heightened stress and anxiety, resulting in more disease and discomfort. This state where a person feels they have no control over their situation and thus stop trying to change or improve it is learned helplessness. This can stem from repeated negative experiences and contribute to ongoing stress and negativity. They excessively focus on negative thoughts and feelings, repeatedly thinking about past distressing events. This can exacerbate stress and contribute to a negative outlook, *see Ghostland*.

When Disease appears, you want to look at your situation and acknowledge any ways you may be contributing to self-induced stress. It would help if you reframed your attention to solutions instead of problems. This color card may also indicate that you're fixating on symptoms and byproducts instead of the discomfort's core cause. The human experience is multifaceted, so you need to approach your situation holistically and look at it from all angles to have a clearer picture of how each individual, concept, and area influences one another.

Chronic stress is a type of stress that occurs over a prolonged period, resulting from ongoing pressures and demands. It is characterized by the continuous activation of the body's stress response system, leading to persistent physical and emotional strain due to work-related pressures, such as high workloads, job insecurity, and conflicts with colleagues or supervisors. Ongoing financial instability or debt, marital conflicts, caregiving responsibilities, social isolation, dealing with chronic illness or long-term health conditions, and living in unsafe or unstable environments all contribute to feelings of disease and are examples of chronic stress daily.

On the other hand, when disease is reversed or challenged, it could be an invitation to self-efficacy and eustress. Self-efficacy is a concept introduced by psychologist Albert Bandura. It refers to an individual's belief in their ability to execute the behaviors required to produce specific outcomes successfully. In other words, it is the confidence a person has in their capability to control their functioning and events that affect their lives. Eustress is a type of stress that is positive, beneficial, and motivating. Self-efficacy and stress encourage you to start with small, manageable tasks and gradually increase difficulty. Learn from others who have dealt with this situation or similarly adjacent so that you can have an estimation instead of a rigid, definite expectation. Review and celebrate your achievements as you make progress. Not enough people learn to practice healthy self-recognition for fear of looking selfish. Any bit of success matters.

Disease wants you to focus on and dedicate yourself to daily activities that promote a positive use of your resources, time, and energy. What small action can you achieve right now to feel excitement, satisfaction, and fulfillment or meaning out of the situation? "If all you can do is crawl, then start crawling." – Rumi

Chamuel - Ask for Help

You are not alone in the Universe. What you're experiencing is not unique to you. Others are facing the same beasts that plague our world. The vast majority of ordinary people are not in direct decision-making positions of power and authority, so when Chamuel appears, it's beckoning you to recognize that you need not rely on your strength at this time. Hopefully, doctors, therapists, friends, relatives, and spouses should offer this to your situation. Don't be afraid to get a second opinion. Ask for help - despite looking like a fool, regardless of money, and certainly if you've been expected to live as a lone wolf. Chamuel is often invoked to help heal relationships, whether they are romantic, familial, or platonic. The archangel's energy promotes understanding, forgiveness, and emotional healing, which can mend broken bonds and enhance existing connections. Chamuel is associated with fostering compassion and unconditional love. This archangel helps individuals open their hearts to others, increasing empathy and kindness in their interactions. By promoting these qualities, Chamuel aids in building more robust, more supportive relationships.

When Chamuel appears in a reading, you can ask the Universe for help. Your guides are all around you at the ready. Chamuel helps individuals find inner peace and self-love. People can better form healthy relationships and attract supportive individuals at peace. Chamuel's energy is said to assist in letting go of negative emotions and past hurts that may hinder personal growth and relational harmony. Chamuel can be called upon to guide individuals in their social connections, helping them to find the right friends, partners, and social networks. This guidance can lead to more meaningful and supportive relationships where individuals feel valued and understood. By invoking Chamuel, people believe they can bring positive energy into their lives and surroundings. This positive energy can attract like-minded individuals who offer support, encouragement, and love, enhancing one's social and relational experiences.

Systemic oppression does not solely affect singular marginalized groups of people. Marginalization happens in layers, and it's challenging to manage discrimination if you attempt to compartmentalize your identity, culture, and mindset. The system can discriminate against anyone for anything at any time. This is the abuse of power that Corporate Chaos wields, and Chamuel's message acts as a force to protect you in these times of change, chaos, and crisis. Peace is the answer. Chamuel's message invites you to look at your situation and see the cause and effect of your involvement or lack of action contributing to peace. Your task right now is to commit to walking a heart-centered path. Heart-centered actions and goals are those driven by compassion, empathy, kindness, and a genuine desire to contribute positively to the well-being of others through community building. Heart-centered actions and goals create a sense of unity, belonging, and mutual support among community members.

Heart-centered community building starts with empathy and understanding. It involves actively listening to community members' needs, concerns, and aspirations. By fostering an environment where people feel heard and valued, communities can address issues more effectively and create solutions reflecting collective will. A heart-centered approach emphasizes inclusivity and celebrates diversity. It ensures that all community members are included in decision-making processes and activities regardless of their background, culture, or status. This creates a sense of belonging and strengthens the community's social fabric. Heart-centered community building prioritizes collaboration over competition. It encourages working together towards common goals, sharing resources, and supporting one another. This collaborative spirit helps pool talents and skills, leading to more innovative and sustainable outcomes. Engaging in acts of kindness and service is a hallmark of heart-centered community building. Whether volunteering, helping neighbors, or organizing community service projects, these actions foster a supportive and caring environment where members feel connected and valued. Trust and transparency are fundamental to heart-centered community building. Community leaders and members can build trust by being honest, open, and consistent in actions and communication, which is crucial for long-term unity and cooperation.

Heart-centered goals include creating safe and welcoming spaces for all community members. This involves addressing and mitigating discrimination, violence, or harassment, ensuring everyone feels secure and respected. Encouraging personal growth and development within the community is another heart-centered goal. This can be achieved through educational programs, workshops, and support groups that help individuals develop skills, confidence, and a sense of purpose. Heart-centered community building also considers the impact on future generations. It involves adopting sustainable practices that protect the environment and ensure the community's longevity and health. This forward-thinking approach demonstrates care and responsibility for the planet and its inhabitants. Regular community events and gatherings that celebrate togetherness and shared successes are vital. These activities help to strengthen bonds, create lasting memories, and reinforce the community's identity and values. Finally, heart-centered community building encourages positive change and continuous improvement. It involves proactively addressing issues and seeking ways to enhance the quality of life for all community members. By prioritizing empathy, kindness, trust, and sustainability, communities can create strong, supportive networks where all members feel valued and empowered to contribute to the collective well-being.

Sekhmet - Fire Energy & Warrior Spirit

Sekhmet, an ancient Egyptian goddess, is one of the most powerful deities in the Egyptian pantheon. Her name translates to "The Powerful One," and she is depicted as a lioness or a woman with the head of a lioness. Sekhmet is known as the goddess of war, destruction, and healing. She embodies the duality of fierce protection and nurturing care, central to her mythology and worship. Sekhmet's lioness form symbolizes her role as a fierce warrior. She was believed to protect the pharaoh in battle, annihilating enemies with her breath of fire and searing gaze. Her destructive power was feared and revered, as it was essential for maintaining Ma'at (cosmic order). Paradoxically, in a reading, you can interpret Sekhmet as also associated with healing. Light burning away the darkness. Her destructive energy was believed to have the power to cleanse and purify. As a healer, she was invoked during plagues and epidemics. Priests of Sekhmet were skilled in medicine, and she was worshiped in many temples dedicated to health and well-being. You are what you consume. Sekhmet is often linked to the sun, particularly the destructive heat of the midday sun. She is considered an aspect of the Eye of Ra, a powerful solar deity. This connection reinforces her dual nature, as the sun can sustain life and cause harm. As a protective deity, Sekhmet was seen as a guardian of the pharaoh and the nation. Her wrath was directed against those who threatened the stability and security of Egypt, embodying the idea that destruction can be a form of protection.

Orange, a standard flame color, symbolizes warmth, energy, and transformation. It represents the creative and sustaining aspects of fire. Sekhmet, in your reading, reveals a burning intensity for change. Invoke the heat and the heart of the flame. It symbolizes power, passion, and the potential for both creation and destruction inherent in fire. In many traditions, fire rituals involve red, oranges, and gold to invoke energy, strength, and purification.

Through Hinduism, Agni, the fire god, is a vital deity representing the fire of the sun, lightning, and domestic hearths. Fire rituals (Yajna) are central to Hindu worship, symbolizing purification and the divine witness to offerings. For Native Americans, fire is seen as a sacred element that provides warmth, light, and the means to cook food. It plays a crucial role in various ceremonies and is considered a living entity with its spirit. Fire is a living element. You are asked to seek the elemental realm for divine intervention, protection, and a spark to blaze a new trail to overcome any oversaturation in your life and work at this time. The concept of "Hi" (fire) in Japanese tradition is one of the five elements (Godai) and is associated with spirit, passion, and energy. It is essential in physical and metaphysical practices, including martial arts and Shinto rituals. Sekhmet embodies fire's fierce and nurturing aspects, and orange and red colors are deeply interwoven with fire's symbolism across cultures. These colors evoke energy, transformation, and intense emotions, reflecting the dual nature of fire as both a creator and a destroyer.

Archangel - Air Energy & Guardianship

An archangel is a high-ranking angel in various religious traditions, particularly Christianity, Judaism, and Islam. The term "archangel" comes from the Greek "archangelos," which combines "arch," meaning chief or principal, and "angelos," meaning messenger. Archangels are considered leaders among angels, often tasked with significant roles in the divine order, such as delivering messages from God, overseeing other angels, and protecting humanity. Angels, including archangels, are believed to be spiritual beings created by God. In Judeo-Christian traditions, they are often depicted as messengers and servants of God, existing to carry out His will. The concept of angels is also present in Islam, where they are seen as beings created from light who serve Allah by delivering revelations to prophets, among other duties. Archangels are primarily seen as divine messengers, bridging the gap between the holy and the mortal. This role is exemplified by Gabriel, who delivered significant messages in both the Old and New Testaments of the Bible. Archangels like Michael are depicted as warriors, protecting humanity from evil and leading the heavenly armies against the forces of darkness. This warrior aspect emphasizes their role in maintaining cosmic order and justice. Archangels such as Raphael are associated with healing and guidance, offering comfort and aid to humans. This reflects their role as benevolent protectors and nurturers.

When Archangel appears in your color reading, look for messages and indications for clarity, purity, and preciousness of trusting the strength of your wings. At this time, you may be stuck in fear. Too afraid to leap of faith and trust the process in the present moment. Archangel is a welcome color reaffirming that the Universe has your back - in perfect love and trust. The shimmering quality of gold from the card can also evoke the idea of lightness and connect with your ethereal connection to the celestial realm. The air symbolizes intellect, communication, and the breath of life in various cultural traditions.

Air (aether) was one of the four classical elements. It was considered the purest and most essential element, embodying the breath of life and the soul. In Greek mythology, Hermes, the messenger god, shares similarities with archangels and is associated with the air element. Hermes's role in delivering messages and guiding souls mirrors the functions of archangels. In Hindu tradition, air (Vayu) is one of the five significant elements (Pancha Mahabhuta). Vayu is the deity of wind and breath, symbolizing life force (prana) and movement. In the Wu Xing system of Chinese philosophy, air is associated with the element of wood, which governs growth, vitality, and the spring season. It emphasizes the dynamic and expansive qualities of air. For Native Americans, the air is often seen as a life-giving force, carrying prayers and thoughts to the divine. It is associated with the directions of the East, symbolizing new beginnings and enlightenment.

Thinking about your situation, how well are you communicating details and ideas, and can you visually display your reality to gather a higher perspective on what's currently taking place? Do you feel responsible for your situation or another person by acting as the wind beneath their wings?

It might be helpful to approach your situation through a Socratic method of thought and communication. The Socratic Method, named after the classical Greek philosopher Socrates, is a form of cooperative argumentative dialogue between individuals based on asking and answering questions to stimulate critical thinking and illuminate ideas. It involves a dialectical process that explores complex concepts by breaking them down into their parts through rigorous questioning. This method encourages deep understanding and self-awareness. This is where you're engaging in systematic questioning to explore beliefs and underlying assumptions through critical questioning, recognizing the limits of one's knowledge, and being open to new perspectives so that you can face this situation with intellectual humility. Using the Socratic Method in personal development, you engage in a continuous process of self-examination, learning, and growth, leading to a deeper understanding of yourself and more effective strategies for achieving your personal and professional goals.

The concept of guardianship is central to both archangels and the air element. Archangels protect, guide, heal, and enlighten humanity, embodying the essence of guardianship. The air element, essential for life, intellectual clarity, and spiritual connection, is a guardian of well-being and knowledge. The colors gold and purple in your reading further enhance this connection by symbolizing the divine wisdom and purity inherent in the roles of archangels and the air element of your philosophical constructs and beliefs.

Prometheus - Gifts of Humanity

Ever wonder why a candle flame has a teardrop shape? The heat from the flame warms the nearby air, causing it to rise. Cooler air and oxygen then rush in at the base of the flame and increase as they heat up. This continuous convection current stretches the flame into the familiar teardrop shape. However, this process relies on gravity. Without gravity, the heated air around the candle flame doesn't rise, eliminating convection currents. As a result, the flame becomes spherical.

Prometheus, a titan from Greek mythology, is renowned for his act of stealing fire from the gods and giving it to humanity. His name means "forethought," highlighting his role as a thinker and a benefactor of mankind. This myth encapsulates themes of knowledge, rebellion, and the quest for enlightenment. When Prometheus appears in a color reading, you're guided to the pursuit of knowledge, enlightenment, and technological advancement. Prometheus empowered humans to progress, innovate, and develop civilizations by giving fire to humanity. There's a quality of rebellion and sacrifice that surrounds your situation. Prometheus's defiance against Zeus represents the spirit of rebellion against tyranny and the willingness to endure suffering for the greater good. His punishment (being bound to a rock with an eagle eating his liver) symbolizes the cost of challenging divine authority and the enduring struggle for freedom. The macro-narrative ultimately influencing your situation is embodying and identifying yourself as a protector of humanity. Prometheus is seen as a guardian and protector, advocating for human development and welfare. His actions reflect a deep compassion and commitment to human progress.

The colors of Prometheus reveal auburn, a rich reddish-brown color that symbolizes warmth, stability, and maturity. It is often associated with the earth and nature, reflecting a deep connection to the natural world. It also represents the gifts of the earth—agriculture, sustenance, and the stability necessary for human societies to flourish. The twinge of Sky Blue and the striation of movement of the card's color speak to tranquility, inspiration, and limitless possibilities. It is associated with the sky and the heavens, evoking calmness and creativity. You are on the horizon of inspiration and intellectual pursuit, encouraging humans to reach for the sky in their quest for knowledge and understanding. Orange is a vibrant color, symbolizing energy, enthusiasm, and creativity. Approach this situation with warmth, invigorate your senses with innovative practices and look to new frontiers. Fire's vitality drives your willpower for human innovation and artistic expression.

Prometheus is also a powerful invocation and tribute to Hypatia of Alexandria. She was a prominent philosopher, mathematician, and astronomer in the Hellenistic era. She is often seen as a symbol of knowledge, intellectual freedom, and the tragic consequences of fanaticism (which can be the message should the color be challenged or negatively influenced). Like Prometheus, Hypatia devoted her life to pursuing knowledge and enlightenment. Her teachings and scholarly work were pivotal in preserving and advancing scientific and philosophical thought. Hypatia's brutal murder by a mob reflects the dangers faced by those who challenge prevailing beliefs and authority, paralleling Prometheus's suffering for his defiance.

Prometheus's myth resonates deeply with the human pursuit of enlightenment and progress with its rich symbolism of fire, knowledge, and sacrifice. Auburn, sky blue, and orange represent different facets of the gifts Prometheus brought to humanity—nature's stability, intellectual inspiration, and creative energy. The stories of Prometheus and Hypatia highlight the timeless struggle for knowledge against oppressive forces, a theme celebrated in various cultural and spiritual traditions, including Gnosticism, which emphasizes the divine spark and the pursuit of inner wisdom.

Gnostic Societies celebrate divinity through the pursuit of esoteric knowledge and inner enlightenment. Your pursuit of gnosis is the belief in a divine spark within each individual, reminiscent of the fire Prometheus gave to humanity, symbolizing inner wisdom and the potential for divine knowledge. Color is an applicable way to experience our divine spark. The quest for direct, personal understanding of the sacred, often through introspection and mystical experiences, aligning with Hypatia's and Prometheus's emphasis on intellectual and spiritual enlightenment, is why you are here. You are here to emphasize your inner journey towards enlightenment, valuing personal experience and inner revelation as paths to understanding the divine nature of humanity.

Be what you seek. Become the answer. Believe you are the gift.

La Luna - Inner Flow & Cycle

La Luna, the moon, has been a powerful symbol across various cultures and societies throughout history. Its phases and presence in the night sky have inspired myths, legends, and interpretations, representing the rhythm of time, the inner flow of emotions, and the cyclical nature of life. The moon's phases, from the new moon to the full moon and back, symbolize the perpetual cycle of change and renewal. This cycle mirrors the natural rhythms of life, from birth to growth, decay, and rebirth. Often associated with femininity, La Luna represents the divine feminine, embodying qualities such as intuition, nurturing, and emotional depth. Many cultures view the moon as a goddess, influencing tides and human emotions. Since we see the moon because of the sun's light reflecting off its surface, the moon symbolizes illusions, mystery, and the subconscious. Its light in the darkness is seen as a guide through the unknown, illuminating hidden truths and deeper understanding.

In Greco-Roman mythology, the moon is personified by goddesses such as Selene/Luna and Artemis/Diana, representing beauty, hunting, and the protection of women. In modern Western culture, the moon is often a symbol of romance, dreams, and inspiration, playing a significant role in literature and art that explores stories about werewolves and lunacy. In Chinese mythology, Chang'e, the Moon Goddess, lives on the moon, symbolizing immortality and the elixir of life. The Mid-Autumn Festival celebrates the harvest and the full moon, symbolizing unity and family reunion. The moon is often associated with animals like rabbits and natural phenomena, emphasizing a harmonious relationship with nature.

In your color reading, La Luna under a full moon represents completion, fulfillment, and the peak of energy. Its influence extends to the inner flow of emotions and personal cycles. The moon's phases reflect the ebb and flow of human experiences, mirroring the emotional highs and lows that shape personal growth. The moon's waxing and waning phases symbolize the ebb and flow of emotions. Waxing phases are associated with building energy and setting intentions while waning phases signify release and introspection. Many spiritual practices align with the moon's phases. For instance, moon rituals often involve meditations, affirmations, and activities that resonate with the current phase, such as manifesting desires during the new moon and releasing negativity during the full moon. The new moon signifies new beginnings, potential, and the planting of seeds for future growth. It is a time for setting intentions, making plans, and introspection. The new moon is often a period of reflection and planning. In some Indigenous traditions, it marks the start of new cycles and the time for personal and communal renewal.

You want to reflect on how you're allowing your emotions to make decisions in your life and work. Are you projecting an outdated narrative even though your circumstances have changed? Could you rely on outside forces to dictate how you feel because you want to keep your emotions at bay instead of openly in play? La Luna is a trickster energy and connects you to the whimsical world of the fae. When you leave the system or outside influence unchecked, you risk disassociating yourself from your cadence and rhythm. Be wary of exclusivity when this color is negatively influenced.

With its profound symbolism, La Luna serves as a universal emblem of change, mystery, and inner wisdom. Its cyclical nature connects deeply with the rhythms of life and the human experience. The full moon and new moon each carry distinct meanings, representing the culmination of efforts and the commencement of new journeys. Across various cultures, the moon remains a powerful symbol, reflecting the interconnectedness of the natural world and the continuous flow of time and emotions.

Retrograde - Reflect & Review

Retrograde refers to the apparent backward motion of a planet as observed from Earth. This optical illusion occurs because of Earth's relative positions and motions and other planets' orbits around the Sun. In astrology, retrograde periods are significant for introspection, review, and reevaluation. When Retrograde appears in a reading, you're asked to look inward, revisit past issues, and reassess current situations. These periods often highlight areas that require change or adjustment. They allow for correcting mistakes, revisiting unresolved issues, and refining plans. This introspective time allows for deeper understanding and growth. Each planet in retrograde brings unique influences and challenges, prompting individuals to reflect on different aspects of their lives.

Mercury retrograde has become a household astrological influence associated with misunderstandings, delays, and technical glitches. It's a time to review communications, double-check plans, and reconnect with people from the past. Ganesha, the Hindu god revered as the remover of obstacles and the deity of intellect and wisdom, is closely associated with themes relevant to Mercury retrogrades. During Mercury retrograde periods, infamous for causing disruptions in all communication, travel, and technology formats, Ganesha is a welcome deity to petition for assistance. His role as the lord of beginnings and remover of obstacles makes him an ideal deity to invoke for smooth communication and to resolve misunderstandings and delays that typically characterize Mercury retrogrades. Ganesha's elephant head, symbolizing his immense wisdom and understanding, coupled with his vehicle, the mouse (representing overcoming even the smallest of obstacles), reinforces his ability to navigate and rectify the challenges posed during these retrograde phases, ensuring clarity and successful endeavors.

Venus retrograde is a period of influence to reassess relationships, self-worth, and personal values. It encourages reflection on past relationships and redefinition of what brings joy and beauty. Hathor, the ancient Egyptian goddess of love, beauty, music, and happiness, is intricately linked to the themes highlighted during Venus retrogrades. Venus retrogrades are periods of introspection and reevaluation of love, relationships, and personal values, often prompting a reassessment of what brings joy and beauty into our lives. Embodying these very aspects, Hathor serves as a guiding figure during such times. Her association with fertility, maternal care, and the arts underscores the importance of nurturing relationships and appreciating beauty in the world and within us. By channeling Hathor's energy, individuals can navigate the reflective nature of Venus retrogrades, finding balance and harmony in their connections and reevaluating their core values to align more closely with their true desires and needs.

Mars retrograde would be a time to reflect on war strategies and seek peace, symbolizing the need for balanced aggression. Under this influence, you look to transform your anger and frustrations and create what you desire. Mars retrograde prompts a review of how we assert ourselves, our ambitions, and how we handle anger and conflict. It's time to redirect your energy constructively. Ares, the Greek god of war, embodies Mars retrogrades' assertive, bold, and sometimes tumultuous energy. Mars retrogrades are periods when the usual direct and aggressive forces are turned inward, leading to introspection about how we handle conflict, assert our desires, and take action. Ares, known for his fierce and unapologetic nature in battle, symbolizes the raw, unfiltered power and courage needed to confront and resolve internal and external conflicts. During Mars retrograde, invoking the spirit of Ares can help individuals reassess their approach to conflict and aggression, encouraging them to channel this energy more constructively and strategically. Reflecting on Ares' traits, one can find the strength to face challenges head-on, make bold decisions, and assert oneself with clarity and purpose, transforming the chaos of retrograde into a period of significant personal growth and empowerment.

Jupiter retrograde inspires introspection on personal beliefs, spiritual growth, and long-term goals. It encourages reassessing philosophies and life paths that expand justice, morality, and personal prosperity. Saraswati, the Hindu goddess of knowledge, music, art, wisdom, and learning, perfectly embodies growth, expansion, faith, higher education, and luck. Saraswati is revered as the goddess who bestows the knowledge essential for personal and spiritual growth. She symbolizes the flow of wisdom and consciousness, crucial for expanding one's intellectual and artistic capabilities. Saraswati's association with higher learning makes her an ideal figure for those seeking to broaden their understanding and engage in deep study and reflection. Her blessings are believed to bring good fortune and luck, particularly in educational and artistic endeavors. Through her attributes, Saraswati inspires faith in the pursuit of knowledge and the transformative power of education, aligning closely with the expansive and enlightening qualities associated with optimizing Jupiter retrograde.

Saturn retrograde is a severe time to review responsibilities, commitments, and life structures in your daily routine and schedule. It highlights the need for patience and perseverance. Shani, also known as Saturn in Hindu mythology, is the god closely associated with daily discipline, responsibility, structure, and karma. Shani is revered as the deity who governs hard work, perseverance, and adherence to duty, embodying the principles of discipline and responsibility. His influence is believed to bring about lessons that reinforce the importance of structure and the consequences of one's actions, both positive and negative, reflecting the concept of karma. Shani's role in enforcing justice and ensuring that individuals face the results of their actions aligns perfectly with the themes of karma, making him a powerful symbol for those striving to lead disciplined, responsible lives within a structured framework. By understanding and respecting Shani's teachings, individuals can cultivate a life of integrity, accountability, and balanced karma. Now is a time for you to face karma and reflect on past actions, urging and prioritizing integrity.

Uranus retrograde is a carnival act of unorthodoxy and nonconformity. From Norse mythology, Loki is a god often associated with innovation, rebellion, change, and individuality that works well with a Uranus retrograde. Known as a trickster and shape-shifter, Loki embodies the spirit of unpredictability and transformation. His actions often challenge the gods' established order, leading to chaos and renewal. Loki's cunning nature and ability to think outside conventional norms symbolize innovation and unconventional thinking. While sometimes disruptive, his rebellious acts also foster change and adaptation within the Norse pantheon. Loki's complex personality reflects the tension between individuality and social norms, highlighting the importance of embracing one's unique identity and questioning authority. As a figure of mischief and creativity, Loki continues to resonate as a symbol of rebellion and innovation in mythological and cultural contexts. This period encourages rethinking personal freedom, societal norms, and innovative ideas. It's a time to embrace change from within.

Neptune retrograde wanders into inspiration. It's a period of reflecting, reviewing your dreams, and exploring the mystical paradox of creativity. Morpheus, the Greek god of dreams, is closely associated with dreams, intuition, spirituality, and illusions. In Greek mythology, Morpheus is responsible for shaping and delivering dreams to mortals while residing in the dream realm. He embodies dreams' mystical and ethereal nature, which serve as gateways to deeper subconscious realms and spiritual insights. Morpheus' domain includes not only the realm of dreams but also the realm of illusions and the fluidity between reality and fantasy. As a symbol of intuition, Morpheus inspires individuals to explore the inner realms of their psyche, interpret symbolic messages from dreams, and connect with spiritual dimensions beyond ordinary consciousness. His presence in mythology underscores the profound influence of dreams and intuition on human understanding and spiritual growth, making Morpheus a fitting deity associated with these themes. Neptune retrograde is a time to dispel illusions, enhance spiritual practices, and confront hidden fears and fantasies. It calls for clarity in the subconscious.

Pluto retrograde will push you out of your comfort zone like most retrogrades, but this one strips you of your prejudices and assumptions so that a new version can take shape. In Aztec culture, Pluto retrograde would resonate with the deity Mictlantecuhtli, the god of the underworld, symbolizing a period of profound transformation and renewal. Mictlantecuhtli is deeply associated with Pluto retrogrades and their themes of transformation, power, rebirth, and the unconscious. As the ruler of Mictlan, the realm of the dead, Mictlantecuhtli governs the cycles of death and rebirth, symbolizing the transformative process during Pluto retrogrades. Like Pluto, who rules over the depths and unseen forces of the unconscious mind, Mictlantecuhtli oversees the journey of souls through the underworld, where profound inner transformation occurs. During Pluto retrograde's intense introspection and release, invoking Mictlantecuhtli can aid in confronting deep-seated fears, shedding old patterns, embracing personal regeneration, and activating a will for shadow work and cord-cutting ceremonies. His association with power underscores the transformative potential inherent in facing the shadow self and integrating unconscious aspects into conscious awareness, leading to profound spiritual rebirth and renewal. Mictlantecuhtli's role as a guide through the underworld mirrors Pluto's transformative influence, highlighting the cyclical nature of life, death, and regeneration in mythological and astrological contexts. Pluto retrograde is about allowing yourself time and space for deep introspection, confronting hidden power dynamics in your situation, and embracing transformation. It's a time to let go of what no longer serves and embrace rebirth.

Retrograde's brassy copper color swirling in a vast dark navy expanse represents your reality in the womb of consciousness. Understanding astrology helps put some aspects of our existence into a language we can understand and allows consciousness to feel more tangible simultaneously. Especially when making decisions and orienting ourselves as we voyage the deeper reaches of the mood and mayhem of the Universe, it appears in a reading to emphasize your need for reflection and review of cultural influences and introspection into the fluctuations and patterns of the psyche. Each planet's retrograde offers unique lessons and opportunities for growth, encouraging us to revisit, reassess, and realign our lives. Through this process, we can gain deeper insights and foster a more profound understanding of ourselves and our place in the universe.

Ego - Shadow & Void

Ego's dark matter is a message to embrace self-preservation, shadows, and the void. Punk, emo, and goth movements are typical aesthetics for Ego because it's through these styles that many took being ignored and repressed by mainstream society and created an identity, culture, and a way of being out of emptiness. Ego is an anthem to let your freak flag fly. Take your power back from those who bullied you. Ego appears in a reading to acknowledge what makes you different from what already exists. This edge keeps society transforming, encourages you to push the boundaries of consciousness, and keeps your instincts sharp. The ego is a fundamental concept in psychology and philosophy, representing the self conscious part of an individual's personality. It encompasses one's sense of identity, self-esteem, and perception of oneself to others and the world. Understanding the ego involves exploring its symbolism and contextualizing concepts like the shadow and void across diverse cultural perspectives. The ego is symbolized as the conscious mind, where thoughts, perceptions, and memories reside. It acts as a mediator between the id's primal instincts and the superego's moralistic demands, as Sigmund Freud proposed. Carl Jung expanded this concept by introducing the idea of the shadow—the unconscious aspects of the ego that are repressed or ignored. What have you been sweeping under the rug recently? The ego strives to maintain a cohesive sense of self-image, often through defense mechanisms that protect against threats to self-esteem or identity. Fundamentalist religions and political parties have used defense mechanisms of people to hijack identities to serve corporate ego and corporate reform. This is what fuels Corporate Chaos.

The shadow represents the darker, hidden aspects of the psyche that are often rejected or suppressed. This concept is prevalent in various spiritual and psychological traditions. For example, in Jungian psychology, integrating the shadow through shadow work involves acknowledging and accepting these aspects to achieve psychological balance and wholeness. In Buddhism, the void (sunyata) signifies the concept of emptiness, not as nothingness but as the potential for limitless transformation and realization of one's true nature. Ego wants you to live according to your true nature. Come out of the closet. Rebel the labels. Define life on your terms. Confront conflict. Be bold and make some noise for silence, especially under the duress of Corporate Chaos, which means death.

Pandora's Box, from Greek mythology, serves as a profound allegory for the human ego and its intricate relationship with shadow work and the void. When Pandora opened the forbidden box, she unwittingly unleashed all troubles and afflictions. This act symbolizes the ego's curiosity and tendency to explore hidden aspects of the self—the shadow. Amidst the chaos, hope remained within the box, representing the potential for transformation and redemption through introspection and self-awareness. Shadow work involves confronting these hidden aspects—fears, insecurities, and repressed emotions—acknowledging their existence and integrating them consciously into one's psyche. The void within Pandora's box mirrors the depths of the unconscious, where profound insights and personal growth emerge from embracing darkness. Thus, Pandora's box is a poignant metaphor for the ego's journey toward self-discovery and the transformative power of navigating the shadow to find meaning and resilience in life's challenges.

The darkness represents the unknown, the unconscious, and the unexplored aspects of the self. Embracing darkness through shadow work fosters resilience, creativity, and deeper self-understanding. Ego showing up does not mean you were born wrong or evil according to religion, political dogma, or social stigma. If anything, the ego is an invitation for a midnight rendezvous with darkness to gather introspection and wisdom and to nurture your intuition for spiritual insight. Many indigenous cultures view darkness as a sacred space for healing and connecting with ancestral wisdom. Shadowwork is a transformative process that involves delving into the unconscious to confront and integrate suppressed emotions, desires, and traits. When Ego appears, your situation requires a hellhound companion to explore and navigate rock bottom, deep-seated fears, and traumas imposed by race, religion, and region. By embracing the shadow, individuals can achieve greater authenticity, emotional resilience, and self-acceptance. Practices such as meditation, journaling, and psychotherapy facilitate this journey, promoting personal growth and spiritual development.

You are on a riverboat, rowing through conscious identity and self-perception, navigating between internal drives and societal expectations. Understanding and integrating the shadow and void in multicultural ways enriches this exploration, offering pathways to profound personal transformation, spiritual growth, and mystical experiences. Embracing darkness through shadow work is not about succumbing to negativity or criticism but rather about harnessing its transformative potential for achieving authenticity, resilience, and a deeper connection with oneself and the world. Open your box.

Minos - Inner Saboteur

Rusted iron bars are strewn across a wasteland. Minos is a color of personal fallout and our apocalyptic predisposition toward the world and ourselves. Where Paradise flounces utopia, Minos is a color of dystopian domestication. Where in your life do you feel lost, trapped, and abandoned? This confirms both internal and external suffering. Do you think your mind is entangled by a crown of thorns? What aspects of your situation do you feel or have felt crucified, gutted, and exiled by others while their mockery viciously echoes throughout the labyrinth of your thoughts?

Minos, a name deeply rooted in Greek mythology, is often associated with self-sabotage and sacrifice, reflecting universal themes in various cultural narratives. King Minos of Crete, a central figure in ancient myth, symbolizes power corrupted by personal flaws and the ensuing consequences, which can be interpreted through the inner saboteur archetype. In Greek mythology, Minos is the son of Zeus and Europa, who ascended to the throne of Crete. His rule, while marked by prosperity and cultural advancement, is also tainted by his actions that lead to his downfall. The most prominent example is the story of the Minotaur, a monstrous offspring born out of Minos' defiance and neglect of divine will. To conceal this abomination, Minos commissioned the construction of the Labyrinth, an intricate maze from which escape seemed impossible. This act of hiding away his problems instead of confronting them is a classic manifestation of self-sabotage.

The symbolism of Minos extends beyond Greek borders, finding parallels to other cultural stories that echo the themes of inner conflict and sacrifice. Loki, the trickster god, embodies similar traits in the Norse tradition. His actions, driven by mischief and deceit, ultimately lead to catastrophic outcomes for himself and the gods, mirroring Minos' journey of self-inflicted turmoil. In Hindu mythology, Ravana, the demon king of Lanka, reflects the self-destructive path of excessive pride and ambition. Despite his immense power and wisdom, Ravana's refusal to heed wise counsel and his ego-driven decisions lead to his eventual downfall, akin to Minos' tragic narrative. These mythological figures illustrate the concept of the inner saboteur, an archetype representing the part of ourselves that, often subconsciously, undermines our success and well-being. In your reading, this archetype can manifest in various forms, such as self-doubt, procrastination, or destructive habits.

Recognizing and working through this inner saboteur is crucial for personal growth and self-improvement. Addressing the inner saboteur involves self-awareness and introspection. One must identify the negative patterns and behaviors that hinder progress. For Minos, his refusal to confront the Minotaur symbolizes avoidance of personal issues. In modern psychological terms, this could be seen as denial or repression, where an individual refuses to acknowledge the aspects of their personality or past that cause them pain or fear. To overcome the inner saboteur, one must be willing to face these hidden aspects, much like Theseus confronting the Minotaur in the labyrinth. This confrontation involves embracing vulnerability and seeking help through therapy, support groups, or personal reflection.

This is your journey of transforming self-sabotage into self-empowerment, converting the labyrinth of confusion and despair into a path of clarity and resilience. The color of Minos represents a profound narrative of self-sabotage and sacrifice but also a warning not to give up. Suffering and the friction of discourse are natural. Often, when Minos appears in a reading, there's this hidden tendency to be nihilistic about our circumstances because we feel we don't have enough. Corporate Chaos wants us to feel this way. It destabilizes us and numbs us with the intent of distracting us. Nihilism is a philosophical doctrine that suggests life is without objective meaning, purpose, or intrinsic value. It posits that all values are baseless and nothing can be known or communicated. Nihilism often leads to the belief that existence is senseless and that traditional beliefs and institutions are unfounded. This worldview can profoundly influence an individual's behavior, particularly concerning self-sabotage. Nihilism emerged prominently in the 19th century, influenced by thinkers like Friedrich Nietzsche, who proclaimed "God is dead" to express the collapse of traditional values and the rise of a disenchanted worldview.

Nihilism's central tenet is that life lacks intrinsic meaning, which can lead to a profound sense of purposelessness. Without a guiding purpose or belief in the value of your actions, you may feel unmotivated to pursue goals or engage in meaningful activities. This lack of motivation can manifest as self-sabotage, where people undermine their efforts and achievements because they see no point in striving. I'm tormented by this daily, and every day, I make it a point to allow myself to be enchanted by life and bewitched by simple things like walking and giving myself time to feel the world around me.

Corporate Chaos denies climate change and other progressive platforms because it threatens the systemic oppression and polluted propaganda fostered by nihilism. If nothing matters, the distinction between constructive and destructive behavior blurs. Individuals may engage in harmful actions, neglect responsibilities, or fail to care for themselves, viewing these actions as inconsequential. This self-destructive behavior is a form of self-sabotage, driven by the nihilistic belief that such actions bear no significant impact.

The color of Minos reflects starvation, food insecurities, and poor hygiene. There's a reason why it's the color of urine, and it feels dirty. This is a color of poverty and destitution. It's a color energy that the bureaucratic elite billionaires and shady shareholders behind the beast of Corporate Chaos actively neglect and ignore because their vanity, pride, and greed prevent them from actualizing altruism, compassion, and humility. And for what? To flex their god-complex. Nihilism can lead to feelings of alienation from society and other individuals. The belief that social norms and values are meaningless can result in a detachment from communal and relational bonds. This isolation can exacerbate self-sabotaging tendencies, as the support systems that might mitigate self-destructive behaviors are weakened or absent. The poor and often marginalized have a hard time accepting achievements and success because they don't feel inherently worthy within the nihilistic framework imposed by Corporate Chaos. This can lead individuals to undermine their accomplishments or avoid pursuing success altogether. The internal dialogue of "Why bother?" and "What's the point?" becomes a central theme in their thought process, fostering self-sabotaging attitudes and behaviors.

There's hope. Even within a nihilistic framework, individuals can construct their meaning and purpose. Existentialist philosophers like Jean-Paul Sartre and Albert Camus argued for the creation of personal significance despite the inherent meaninglessness of life. Embracing personal projects, relationships, and values can counteract nihilistic despair and reduce self-sabotage. Authenticity involves living per one's true self and values, even in the face of meaninglessness. By acknowledging the absurdity of life and choosing to live authentically, you can combat the negative impacts of nihilism on your behavior. This authenticity helps mitigate self-sabotage by making your way through a sense of integrity and self-respect. Developing psychological resilience can help you cope with the existential challenges posed by nihilism. Practices such as mindfulness, self-compassion, and cognitive-behavioral strategies can strengthen mental resilience, enabling you to navigate feelings of meaninglessness without resorting to self-destructive behaviors. When Minos appears, you are motioned to engage with others who share similar struggles and can provide support and a sense of belonging. While nihilism may suggest the futility of social bonds, many find solace and strength in collective experiences and mutual understanding. This community support can be crucial in overcoming self-sabotaging tendencies.

Minos is a powerful allegory for the inner saboteur archetype, emphasizing the importance of self-awareness and the courage to confront and transform our inner demons. Understanding and working through the inner saboteur can transcend the destructive patterns that hold us back and pave the way for a more fulfilling and authentic life. Every rose has its thorn.

Sepia - Old Thought

Sepia, a reddish-brown pigment derived from the ink of the cuttlefish, is renowned for its use in art and photography. Historically, sepia tones were widely employed in 19th and early 20th-century photography, lending images a warm, nostalgic quality. Sepia is often associated with memory, nostalgia, and the passage of time. This evocative hue can represent the persistence of old thoughts and the interplay between antiquated and modern ways of thinking. You are asked to recall and record your human experiences at this time. This can be through scrapbooking, content creation, writing, or other mediums to encapsulate your thoughts and experiences.

When Sepia emerges in a reading, it evokes a sense of nostalgia, summoning memories of bygone eras and the sentimental value of the past. As you ponder your circumstances, do you yearn to capture the essence of a time when life seemed simpler, evoking a longing for the past and the solace it brings? This connection to memory is universal, resonating across cultures as a reminder of our shared histories and experiences. In Western societies, Sepia is often associated with the Victorian era and early photography, conjuring images of ancestral portraits, historical events, and the early stages of modern civilization. This nostalgia underscores a reverence for tradition while acknowledging the inevitability of change. In Eastern cultures, Sepia tones can evoke the rich traditions of ancient art and literature. For instance, traditional Chinese ink paintings, though typically black and white, can be seen as precursors to the sepia aesthetic, highlighting the beauty of simplicity and the depth of historical legacy.

Recognizing the value of old thoughts and traditional wisdom is crucial. Sepia reminds us to honor and learn from the past, acknowledging the lessons and experiences that have shaped our present. This involves a respectful engagement with cultural heritage and an appreciation of historical context. While Sepia symbolizes the past, it also highlights the need to integrate old wisdom with contemporary insights. This integration involves adapting and evolving traditional ideas to fit modern contexts, creating a harmonious blend of past and present. Sepia's connection to antiquity can encourage us to scrutinize and challenge outdated beliefs. By examining old thoughts through a critical lens, we can identify and discard those that no longer serve us, paving the way for progressive thinking. The transition from Sepia to color in photography symbolizes the potential for innovation and new perspectives. Embracing this evolution in thought encourages creativity and the exploration of novel ideas, fostering growth and development.

Mythology plays a role in culturally preserving the mood of the times.
Mnemosyne is the goddess associated with memory. Mnemosyne is a figure from ancient Greek mythology, embodying the concept of memory and remembrance. Mnemosyne is one of the Titans, the daughter of Uranus (Sky) and Gaia (Earth). She is the personification of memory and is revered as a deity who preserves humankind's collective memories and histories. Mnemosyne's most notable contribution to mythology is her role as the mother of the nine Muses, whom she bore with Zeus. The Muses are the goddesses of the arts, inspiration, and creative endeavor, each presiding over a different domain, such as epic poetry, history, music, and dance. Their existence highlights the deep connection between memory and the arts, suggesting that memory is the foundation for creativity and cultural expression. As a goddess, Mnemosyne represents the importance of memory in preserving knowledge, culture, and history. She underscores the idea that remembering the past is crucial for understanding the present and guiding the future. In a

broader sense, Mnemosyne symbolizes the power of recollection and the impact of collective memory on human civilization.

In ancient Egyptian mythology, Seshat is a goddess associated with writing, knowledge, and memory. She is often depicted with a stylus and papyrus scroll, recording important events and decrees. Seshat's role emphasizes the importance of documentation and the preservation of knowledge through written records. Seshat is intrinsically linked to memory as the divine record-keeper inscribed significant events, decrees, and knowledge on her papyrus scrolls. Her role emphasizes the preservation of memory and the continuity of knowledge across generations, bridging old thoughts and innovation. By documenting the past meticulously, Seshat ensures that accumulated wisdom informs future advancements, facilitating a dynamic interplay between tradition and progress. Her association with memory and innovation highlights the importance of understanding and preserving historical context to inspire and guide contemporary thought and creativity.

In Mesopotamian mythology, the deity associated with writing, knowledge, and memory is Nisaba (also known as Nissaba or Nidaba). Nisaba is a Sumerian goddess who also embodies the essence of memory through her role as the divine scribe responsible for documenting and preserving knowledge. As the patroness of scribes and scholars, she ensured that ancient Mesopotamia's cultural, legal, and historical records were meticulously maintained, allowing the wisdom of the past to inform and guide future generations. This preservation of old thoughts provided a foundation upon which innovation could flourish, as access to accumulated knowledge enabled new ideas and advancements to be developed in a well-informed context. Nisaba's influence underscores the critical interplay between memory and progress, highlighting how meticulous information recording fosters continuous growth and intellectual evolution.

When Sepia appears in a reading, excavate your situation like an archeologist, find the anthropological power of records and data, and look at your life's history to discover the lore and legend of who you are. Sepia represents the transition between the old and the new. It embodies the shift from black-and-white assumptions to colorful enlightenment, mirroring the evolution of thought and perception. This transition catalogs growth and the continuous adaptation of ideas over time. Recording evidence of your situation and annotating your experiences, for nothing, is sweeter than the scent of a good book next to a cup of tea during the dawn of a new era.

Capture the moment.

Lighthouse - Saving Grace

The fog blankets the horizon, and beyond the mysterious mists, there's a tower pulsating light. Lighthouse is inspired by the torch song "Candle on the Water," originally recorded by Helen Reddy for Disney's live-action/animated film Pete's Dragon. It's my favorite Disney movie. Lighthouse appears in a reading because the situation contains edges, boundaries, and jagged projections that impose danger and is a sign for safe passage and refuge.

A lighthouse, a beacon of light amidst tumultuous seas, holds profound symbolism across cultures, embodying themes of guidance, protection, and salvation. Universally, it serves as a literal and metaphorical savior, navigating ships to safety and offering hope in the face of danger. For maritime stories, lighthouses are revered for their ability to prevent shipwrecks and guide sailors home. This role metaphorically extends to individuals or communities needing direction and salvation. The primary function of a lighthouse is to guide ships safely through treacherous waters. Its towering presence and luminous beacon symbolize clarity and direction in times of uncertainty. In a reading, this guidance represents the quest for moral clarity and the search for a path to safety or salvation in life's challenges.

The concept of saviorism, or the act of saving others, is intricately woven into the symbolism of the lighthouse. It raises ethical dilemmas about prioritizing the needs of the individual versus the collective. This dilemma occurs in multicultural contexts, from personal moral choices to societal decisions impacting communities. The lighthouse's beam of light can be seen as a metaphor for the struggle to balance individual salvation with the greater good. Should Lighthouse be negatively influenced or challenged, it might indicate the paradox of saving one versus many.

Grace is often associated with divine favor or forgiveness, intersecting between offering second chances and redemption. Just as a lighthouse provides a beacon of hope and a chance for safe passage, grace gives individuals and communities opportunities for renewal and healing. It embodies the belief in the possibility of transformation and the capacity to overcome adversity.

Conversely, it can mean you are giving someone too many chances or expecting others to give you more than your fair share. Grace can sometimes be misinterpreted or misused within religious and charitable contexts.

Instead of fostering accountability and ethical responsibility, grace may be exploited as a justification to evade socio-economic duties that challenge religious teachings or political ideologies. Traditionally seen as a source of divine mercy and compassion, Grace can be manipulated to excuse misconduct or negligence. Individuals or institutions may invoke grace to avoid facing consequences for actions that harm others or violate ethical standards. Misusing grace allows individuals or organizations to sidestep accountability for their socio-economic obligations. This could include neglecting duties such as caring for the marginalized, promoting justice, or addressing systemic inequalities. Grace may be used as a scapegoat to deflect criticism or scrutiny regarding decisions that prioritize religious doctrine or political dogma over societal well-being. Individuals or institutions may absolve themselves of responsibilities that contradict their ideological beliefs by invoking grace. Within religious institutions, grace is central to teachings on forgiveness and redemption. However, its misapplication can lead to complacency or inaction towards addressing social injustices or economic disparities. Ethically, the misuse of grace raises concerns about integrity and moral accountability. It challenges the genuine application of religious teachings or charitable principles to promote societal equity and justice. While grace offers a pathway to reconciliation and spiritual growth, its misuse highlights the importance of maintaining ethical rigor and accountability. It calls for a balanced approach where grace is not used to evade responsibilities but as a catalyst for compassion, social responsibility, and ethical action.

Lighthouse's symbolism of guidance, protection, and saviorism encapsulates the paradoxical challenges of saving individuals versus collective salvation. It embodies the concept of grace through its role in offering hope, redemption, and a guiding light amidst adversity. In your situation, does resilience, ethical decision-making, and the pursuit of spiritual and moral clarity feel apparent and accessible? Ultimately, Lighthouse inspires us to navigate life's storms with compassion, wisdom, and a steadfast commitment to individual and collective well-being. But be wary of any religion or political faction misusing grace to bypass socio-economic responsibilities only to capitalize on the symptoms of their systemic oppression and pseudo-altruism. This underscores the need for a nuanced understanding and interpretation within your situation's religious, charitable, and political contexts. Who or what requires saving now, and is salvation for personal or communal gains? Who earns the most from the situation's outcome? What do you want right now? By upholding accountability alongside compassion, grace can authentically contribute to positive societal change, uphold moral integrity, and shine a light on how to save yourself at this time.

Tincture - Find the Cure

An apothecary of herbs, incense, lotions, and potions comes to mind when Tincture appears. Amber glass bottles with sturdy corks sit waiting for you to mix inside a bubbling cauldron—a mortar and pestle on guard to grind the following mint for your mocktail. Tincture symbolizes longevity, remedy, and the secret societies of medicine and modern pharmacy. Historically, an apothecary refers to a person who prepared and sold drugs, herbs, and other substances used for healing. It originates from the Latin "apotheca," a storehouse or repository. Apothecaries were prominent figures in early medicine and pharmacy, playing a crucial role in healthcare systems before the development of modern pharmaceutical practices and insurance companies. Historically, a tincture refers to a concentrated solution of a medicinal substance, often alcohol-based, used for its therapeutic properties. In alchemy and herbalism, tinctures are created by extracting active ingredients from plants or minerals, embodying the pursuit of health and vitality through natural remedies. As a medicinal preparation, tinctures symbolize healing and the pursuit of a cure. Across cultures, the quest for remedies that restore health and vitality is universal. Tinctures encapsulate the belief in nature's ability to solve ailments, offering hope for wellness and longevity.

Tincture has been culturally associated with the pursuit of youthfulness and vitality. In various cultures, herbal elixirs and alchemical potions were believed to possess rejuvenating properties, promising to reverse the effects of aging and restore vigor. Our beauty industry invests much cash into research, development, and marketing to promote and sell anti-aging products to mass markets. This symbolism reflects humanity's enduring desire to defy the passage of time and preserve youthful vitality. Metaphorically, tinctures evoke themes of time travel and aging. They represent the intersection of past knowledge with present aspirations, where ancient remedies are rediscovered and repurposed in modern contexts. This connection to time underscores the cyclical nature of human pursuits—seeking wisdom from the past while navigating the challenges of aging and change. Today, tinctures are used in alternative and complementary medicine, emphasizing natural remedies and holistic health practices. They symbolize a shift towards integrative approaches to wellness, blending ancient wisdom with contemporary scientific understanding. In a color reading, my love (I say this *gingerly*), Tincture is a reminder that you have an expiration date.

Mortality is a tough pill to swallow. I'm bereft that the party of the human experience must end. Through blue zones of centenarians and as we continue to make new medical advancements despite snake-like insurance companies that constrict our accounts and well-being, the lifespan of a human being appears to be lengthening in society. Still, we must face the reality that our physical bodies will enter an everlasting sleep mode.

108 is a powerful number frequency revered for many reasons. Tincture is the 108th color card because it acknowledges mortality, spiritual awakening, and cycles of life and death. In Hinduism, Buddhism, and Jainism, 108 is considered a sacred number with deep spiritual significance. It is believed to represent the universe's wholeness, as it reflects the various aspects of existence—1 (the self or consciousness), 0 (emptiness or completeness), and 8 (infinity or eternity). The number 108 is also linked to celestial bodies and cosmic rhythms. In Hindu astrology and astronomy, there are said to be 108 pithas, or sacred sites, throughout India, representing the cosmic alignment and sacred geography. Traditionally, Hindu and Buddhist malas (prayer beads) consist of 108

beads, which practitioners use for reciting mantras or prayers. Each bead signifies a mantra or a cycle of contemplation, reflecting the journey toward spiritual enlightenment and awareness.

Mathematically, 108 is significant as the hyperfactorial of 3, adding to its mystical and profound nature in numerical symbolism. It affects the distance and diameter between the sun, moon, and Earth. The average distance between the Earth and the Sun is approximately 108 times the Sun's diameter. This astronomical relationship underscores the cosmic scale and interconnectedness within our solar system. Similarly, the average distance between the Earth and the Moon is approximately 108 times the Moon's diameter. This ratio highlights the geometric relationships in celestial mechanics and the precision of cosmic scales. The power of three will set you free. The symbolism 108 relates to mortality through its association with cycles and completeness. It signifies the cyclical nature of life, death, and rebirth—where every end is a new beginning. This perspective aligns with Eastern philosophies that view life and death as interconnected phases of existence. The number 108 integrates dualities such as life and death, light and darkness, and finite and infinite. It invites contemplation on the impermanence of life and the eternal essence beyond physical existence, fostering a deeper understanding of mortality as part of the cosmic order. The symbolic meaning 108 encapsulates profound insights into mortality by highlighting the interconnectedness of life's cycles, the pursuit of spiritual awakening, and the quest for transcendence. When Tincture appears in your reading, it invites you to contemplate mortality not as an end but as an integral part of the cosmic dance, where each moment and cycle contributes to the greater harmony of existence. Through its rich symbolism, 108 offers a framework for embracing mortality with grace, understanding, and a sense of interconnectedness with the universe.

When Tincture appears, you can work with Panacea. They are revered as the goddess of universal remedy, embodying the concept of healing and rejuvenation on a divine level. As the daughter of Asclepius, the god of medicine, Panacea symbolizes the holistic approach to healing and the pursuit of remedies to cure all ailments and diseases. Her name, "Panacea," literally translates to "all-healing," emphasizing her role as a provider of solutions for various health challenges. Panacea's association with medicine intersects with mortality through the promise of alleviating suffering and prolonging life, offering hope in the face of illness and the inevitability of death. Her mythological presence encourages the exploration of remedies and treatments, emphasizing the ongoing quest for healing and the transformative power of medicine in addressing human vulnerabilities and mortality. Her sister is Hygeia, the goddess of health, cleanliness, and hygiene. In Hindu mythology, Dhanvantari is the god of medicine and the physician of the gods (devas). He emerged during the churning of the cosmic ocean (Samudra Manthan), holding a pot of amrita (nectar of immortality), and is revered as the father of Ayurveda, the traditional system of medicine in India. Knowing your Ayurvedic profile is another layer to understanding your holistic self.

Tincture wants you to contemplate your role in promoting health and well-being while navigating the realities of mortality. You must respect the natural order of life and death with awareness and compassion. Take time to look at your situation, life, and work and decide what you will bottle up and carry with you in the next chapter or lifetime. What do you want to do before you die? Who do you want to be? How would you live if you could read your obituary today? Up until this point in time, what do you regret not doing or not saying?

Your body is like a tincture bottle in this reality, containing the distillation of consciousness while it interacts with the effervescence of your soul. Your spirit is naturally generative and capable of producing vitality in all forms, generous beyond comprehension, and genuinely unadulterated by the flux of life. You are the curator of your multisensory and multicolor human experience. Tincture wants you to find the cure. The cure is to be human. And you are the cure.

Made in the USA
Las Vegas, NV
14 January 2025

16364399R10167